Experience, Identity & Epistemic Injustice within Ireland's Magdalene Laundries

Bloomsbury Studies in Religion, Gender, and Sexuality

Series Editors: Dawn Llewellyn, Sonya Sharma and Sîan Hawthorne

This interdisciplinary series explores the intersections of religions, genders, and sexualities. It promotes the dynamic connections between gender and sexuality across a diverse range of religious and spiritual lives, cultures, histories, and geographical locations, as well as contemporary discourses around secularism and non-religion. The series publishes cutting-edge research that considers religious experiences, communities, institutions, and discourses in global and transnational contexts, and examines the fluid and intersecting features of identity and social positioning.

Using theoretical and methodological approaches from inter/transdisciplinary perspectives, *Bloomsbury Studies in Religion, Gender, and Sexuality* addresses the neglect of religious studies perspectives in gender, queer, and feminist studies. It offers a space where gender can critically engage with religion, and for exploring questions of intersectionality, particularly with respect to critical race, disability, post-colonial and decolonial theories.

Becoming Queer and Religious in Malaysia and Singapore, Sharon A. Bong
Beyond Religion in India and Pakistan, Navtej K. Purewal and Virinder S. Kalra
Narrative, Identity and Ethics in Postcolonial Kenya, Eleanor Tiplady Higgs

Experience, Identity & Epistemic Injustice within Ireland's Magdalene Laundries

Chloë K. Gott

BLOOMSBURY ACADEMIC
LONDON • NEW YORK • OXFORD • NEW DELHI • SYDNEY

BLOOMSBURY ACADEMIC
Bloomsbury Publishing Plc
50 Bedford Square, London, WC1B 3DP, UK
1385 Broadway, New York, NY 10018, USA
29 Earlsfort Terrace, Dublin 2, Ireland

BLOOMSBURY, BLOOMSBURY ACADEMIC and the Diana logo are trademarks of Bloomsbury Publishing Plc

First published in Great Britain 2022
This paperback edition published 2023

Copyright © Chloë K. Gott, 2022, 2023

Chloë K. Gott has asserted her right under the Copyright, Designs and Patents Act, 1988, to be identified as Author of this work.

For legal purposes the Acknowledgements on p. viii constitute an extension of this copyright page.

Cover design: Tjasa Krivec
Cover image: Flowers left at the gate entrance to the former site of Sisters of Charity Magdalene Laundry in Donnybrook, Dublin. © Getty Images.

All rights reserved. No part of this publication may be reproduced or transmitted in any form or by any means, electronic or mechanical, including photocopying, recording, or any information storage or retrieval system, without prior permission in writing from the publishers.

Bloomsbury Publishing Plc does not have any control over, or responsibility for, any third-party websites referred to or in this book. All internet addresses given in this book were correct at the time of going to press. The author and publisher regret any inconvenience caused if addresses have changed or sites have ceased to exist, but can accept no responsibility for any such changes.

A catalogue record for this book is available from the British Library.

Library of Congress Control Number: 2021949410

ISBN: HB: 978-1-3502-5442-8
PB: 978-1-3502-5446-6
ePDF: 978-1-3502-5443-5
eBook: 978-1-3502-5444-2

Series: Bloomsbury Studies in Religion, Gender, and Sexuality

Typeset by Deanta Global Publishing Services, Chennai, India

To find out more about our authors and books visit www.bloomsbury.com and sign up for our newsletters

This book is dedicated to every woman who spent time in a Magdalene institution, particularly those whose stories we will never hear.

Contents

Acknowledgements viii

1	Introduction: Survivor narratives and unfinished histories	1
2	Epistemic injustice and credible subjects	19
3	Silence, voice and the ethics of communication	37
4	Inside the institution: Discipline and penance	65
5	Fractured endings and new meanings: Religion and respectability	107
6	Public silence and official voice: Inquiry, apology and redress	147
7	Conclusion: Challenging a lingering silence	185

Appendix A: List of Magdalene institutions 203
Appendix B: List of interviews 204
Notes 207
Bibliography 210
Index 222

Acknowledgements

I wish to begin by extending my thanks and gratitude to all those who shared their narratives in the 'Magdalene Institutions: Recording an Archival and Oral History' project, particularly those who spent time in an institution. Thank you for allowing me to read your words and hear your voices. This was a Government of Ireland Collaborative Research Project, funded by the Irish Research Council; I am particularly grateful to Dr Katherine O'Donnell and the whole research team for allowing me to use the archive for my own work.

Additionally, the research on which this book is based was generously funded and made possible by a three-year Arts and Humanities Research Council grant. I also received funding from the University of Kent School for European Culture and Languages.

My significant thanks go to Gordon Lynch, who has consistently provided support and enthusiasm for my work, as well as encouraging me to think more carefully and expansively. Thank you to Katherine O'Donnell, who has shared her unique experiences and knowledge of the work with me on so many occasions, and in doing so shaped my thinking on the subject in a myriad of ways. I would also like to thank Dawn Llewellyn for a significant amount of support and encouragement in the creation of this work.

To all the members of *Justice for Magdalenes Research*, who shared their passion, dedication and knowledge with me so freely and generously, thank you. This book would not exist without your work.

I am so grateful to all my friends for supporting me in this process. Your love and endless belief in my abilities have kept me going. Particular thanks must go to Toni for working with me over what seemed like an endless summer of crying in the library; and, with Molly, for writing a book which was so energizing and inspiring for my own work. To Tash – your gentle yet insightful critique and your boundless enthusiasm for my ideas were so valuable. To June, for the many discussions which profoundly shaped the way I approach my work; and to Matt, who encouraged me to begin this project, many years ago. I would like to thank the Bent Bars Collective for providing much-needed support. Wayne, Nadia, Chryssy, Agatha and Lamble – thank you for allowing me so much space to talk, or not talk, about my work, as well as modelling ways of thinking and structures of care which were vital throughout the last five years. I am hugely grateful for the love and support I received from all four of my parents and my brother, Felix.

Finally, Sam – without you I would never have finished. I cannot thank you enough.

1

Introduction: Survivor narratives and unfinished histories

In August 2018, Pope Francis visited Ireland as part of the World Meeting of Families. This was the first visit by a reigning pontiff to the country since 1979; during this trip, he met with eight victims of clerical abuse, to whom he spoke about his ignorance of religious institutional abuse in the country. He was apparently 'taken aback' and 'shocked' as to what went on at Mother and Baby homes and professed to have 'no idea' (Brennan 2018) what a Magdalene[1] laundry was. While it seems unfathomable that none of the Pope's advisers gave him even a cursory briefing of this issue before his official visit, Francis' alleged ignorance of the Magdalene institutions in Ireland is far from the primary concern of this book. However, this lack of knowledge speaks to a wider epistemology of ignorance which surrounds the Magdalene institutions, in which knowledge about and acknowledgement of survivor voices is not prioritized. While public interest and academic research on the laundries has increased significantly over the past twenty years, there exists an enduring failure to recognize survivors as producers of knowledge. This silence has thrived in political, social and religious systems of meaning which work together to create contexts in which survivors are prevented from communicating their experiences. This book aims to question this silence, asking how it has been produced and maintained, and disrupting it through an analysis of survivor voices. O'Mahoney (2018) suggests we consider the silence of Magdalene survivors as a form of what Connerton (2008) terms 'humiliated silence', that is, 'broad-scale silence around an event associated with humiliation [which] is covert and unacknowledged, resulting in collusive silence (as a desire to forget the events) and a collective shame' (O'Mahoney 2018: 462). In order to better understand the nature of these silences, on both the individual and collective level, I wish to give a brief history of these institutions in Ireland, before turning to the events by which the Magdalene institutions were made visible in the public consciousness.

Magdalene institutions within the Irish historical context

The last Magdalene laundry in Ireland closed its doors in 1996, but institutions of this nature have existed in some form since the late eighteenth century. Developing out of the eighteenth-century rescue movement designed to control the perceived threat of increased prostitution, by the twentieth century they formed part of a broader institutional response to 'problem women' – women who in some way transgressed social boundaries of post-Independence Ireland and often were guilty of 'being in the way' (Smith 2007: xiii). However, they were not unique to Ireland. Institutional homes for 'fallen women', often known as Magdalene asylums, have existed in societies across the world. By 1900 there were over 300 institutions of this nature in England; and Good Shepherd institutions in particular could be found in Scotland, France, America, Australia and beyond (Thor 2019, Smith 2007, Finnegan 2001). Most of the written history of the laundries in Ireland is focused on the nineteenth century, in part because the religious orders who ran the institutions have, to date, kept their archival records from the twentieth century closed to researchers and survivors. They were made available to the Irish State in 2013, but since then have remained inaccessible to those seeking to learn more about the lives of the women who were incarcerated there.

In the nineteenth century, the laundries primarily operated as a way of controlling prostitution and venereal disease, which were regarded as rapidly growing social problems (O'Mahoney 2018: 456). Although we know less about how the laundries functioned in the twentieth century, most writers on the subject (O'Mahoney 2018; Smith 2007; Luddy 1995) agree that there was a significant shift in the nature of these institutions in post-Independence Ireland, towards a more carceral and punitive model. They also came under the exclusive control of the Catholic Church, while previously there had been both Catholic and Protestant institutions. The institutions became a place to send women who transgressed socially constructed gender norms, those who threatened the 'moral fabric' of the newly formed Irish State (Fischer 2017). This included women who had children outside of marriage, women who committed petty crime and women who had grown up in the industrial school system and were deemed 'at risk' of falling into sin. Typically, women could be sent to a laundry by their family, by a priest or via social services. They spent anything from a few months to their whole lives in these institutions. Conditions were frequently very harsh – washing and sorting laundry without receiving wages, almost always with no information about how long they were to spend there. However, in much of the literature on twentieth-century Irish history, the Magdalene laundries are conspicuous by their absence. For example, they are not mentioned in Terence Brown's text *Ireland: A Social and Cultural History 1922-2002* (2004), or in Roy Foster's *Modern Ireland, 1600-1972* (1989). They are referenced briefly in *The Irish Women's History Reader* (Hayes and Urquhart 2001: 87, 90–2, 93, 128, 143), primarily in Maria Luddy's chapter on prostitution in nineteenth-century Ireland.

By 1922, there were four congregations running ten Magdalene laundries in Ireland.[2] The last institution, on Sean McDermott Street in Dublin, closed its doors in 1996. Throughout this book, I refer to these ten institutions as Magdalene institutions and Magdalene laundries interchangeably. However, it is important to note that they were not part of a formal network of linked institutions and have come to be known as 'Magdalene laundries' only fairly recently. While it is valuable from a research perspective to use this collective term, it is important not to flatten out the differences between the various institutions, run by different religious orders.

The High Park Graves: A history of disturbance

In 1993, the Sisters of Our Lady of Charity of Refuge sold a portion of their land at High Park, Drumcondra, to housing developers.[3] Part of this land included the graveyard for women who had worked in the Magdalene laundry, which had once operated at High Park, closing only two years previously. In order to sell the land, the bodies of the women buried there had to be exhumed and reinterred in Glasnevin cemetery, and the Sisters were therefore required to obtain an exhumation licence. The Department of the Environment granted this licence for 133 bodies, despite the fact that on the exhumation licence, 23 of the women are listed under the heading 'quasi-religious name', and when asked, the nuns admitted that they did not know their real names. They called them 'Magdalen of St Cecilia, Magdalen of Lourdes, Magdalen of St Teresa' and so on. One woman was listed only with a first name. The nuns told the Department that since they had no names, they could not produce death certificates for these twenty-four women. The Department raised no objection to this, apparently unconcerned by the fact that some of the women had died as recently as the late 1960s. The nuns also reported that there were no death certificates for a further thirty-four women. While the names of these women are listed, the cause and date of death for most of them are listed as 'not known'. Failure to register a death occurring on your property constitutes a criminal offence in Ireland. In the case of these women, it would have been the legal duty of the nuns to do this. It seems that for at least fifty-eight women, they neglected to do so (Raftery 2003).

The undertakers engaged in the exhumation process then discovered another twenty-two bodies, which were not covered by the original exhumation licence. Rather than halting the exhumation process and considering the implications of this discovery, the Department of the Environment put through an additional licence allowing the nuns to remove all bodies from the graveyard for the purpose of cremation, which made later identification impossible. The ashes from the High Park graves were then interred in a plot in Glasnevin. A headstone with a list of names now marks the grave. However, if one compares the names and dates on that headstone and the list supplied by the nuns to the Department of the Environment, only twenty-seven match up.[4] This is not the only inconsistency with regard to names on gravestones – for example, at the site in Sundays Well in Cork, names are duplicated between gravesites, making it unclear which grave some women are buried in. In one case the same (relatively unusual) name is on the grave with two different dates.[5]

Action to activism: From the *Magdalen Memorial Committee* to *Justice for Magdalenes Research*

The media reports regarding the 133 graves at High Park in 1993 sparked a wave of action regarding the Magdalene institutions, with a particular focus on working to bring about commemoration and redress for survivors. Specifically, it prompted a group of women to form the *Magdalen Memorial Committee* (MMC). Originally founded by Patricia McDonald, Bláthnaid Ní Chinnéide and Margo Kelly, their goal was to establish a memorial to the 133 women. They succeeded, and in 1996 a park bench was installed in St Stephen's Green. Later, when the remains exhumed from High Park Convent were reinterred at Glasnevin cemetery, memorial gravestones were installed. Once the MMC's goals were met, the group disbanded. However, it was later restarted in the form of *Justice for Magdalenes* (JFM), a volunteer-run survivor advocacy group. Established in 2003 by Mari Steed, Angela Murphy and Claire McGettrick, three adoption rights activists, the group had two main objectives – firstly, to bring about an official apology from the Irish State; and secondly, to establish a compensation scheme for all Magdalene survivors.

In June 2010, JFM submitted an inquiry application to the Irish Human Rights Commission (IHRC), focusing on the State's obligation to protect the women's constitutional and human rights. The IHRC's response, an *'Assessment of the Human Rights Issues Arising in relation to the "Magdalen Laundries"'* was published on 9 November 2010, which concluded that there was significant evidence that the State failed to protect women and young girls from 'arbitrary detention', 'forced and compulsory labour', and 'servitude' (Irish Human Rights Commission 2010). The Assessment made a formal recommendation 'that a statutory mechanism be established to investigate the matters advanced by *Justice for Magdalenes* and in appropriate cases to grant redress where warranted' (Irish Human Rights Commission 2010: 29). The IHRC's Assessment highlighted numerous human rights obligations, which it believed mandated a statutory investigation into the issues and evidence presented by JFM.

In April 2011, JFM made a submission to the United Nations Committee Against Torture (UNCAT), and in June, Maeve O'Rourke made a statement before UNCAT in Geneva, representing the group. On 5 June 2011, the Committee published its concluding observations, expressing 'grave concern at the failure by the State party to institute prompt, independent and thorough investigation into the allegations of ill-treatment perpetrated on girls and women in the Magdalene Laundries' (UNCAT 2011: 6). The Panel recommended:

> The State party should institute prompt, independent, and thorough investigations into all allegations of torture, and other cruel, inhuman or degrading treatment or punishment that were allegedly committed in the Magdalene Laundries, and, in appropriate cases, prosecute and punish the perpetrators with penalties commensurate with the gravity of the offences committed, and ensure that all victims obtain redress and have an enforceable right to compensation including the means for as full rehabilitation as possible. (UNCAT 2011:6)

As a result of this, in June 2011 the Irish government announced the creation of 'The Inter-Departmental Committee to establish the facts of State involvement with the Magdalen Laundries'. JFM submitted its principal submission to the Inter-Departmental Committee (IDC) in August 2012, consisting of a 145-page document collating evidence of State complicity, supported by 796 pages of survivor testimony. After an eighteen-month inquiry, the IDC published a report in February 2013, commonly known as the McAleese report, concluding that there had been significant state involvement in the Magdalene institutions. As a result of this, on 19 February 2013, Taoiseach Enda Kenny issued an official

State apology to the Magdalene women. On the night of the apology, Kenny announced that he had asked Mr Justice John Quirke to make recommendations to the government on a redress scheme for survivors.

Following this, JFM ended their political campaign, having achieved their goal, and *Justice for Magdalenes Research* (JFMR) was established.[6] The main aim of JFMR is to provide for the advancement of education of the general public by researching the Magdalene laundries and similar institutions, as well as providing information and support to the women who spent time in the institutions and their families. Several members of JFMR were previously involved in the project, 'Magdalene Institutions: Recording an Archival and Oral History'. This was a Government of Ireland Collaborative Research Project funded by the Irish Research Council, led by Dr Katherine O'Donnell at University College Dublin, which aimed to interview Magdalene survivors and their family members, as well as visitors to those institutions and other key informants. It represents the first large-scale collection of survivor narratives from women who spent time in Magdalene institutions, and forms the basis of this book.

Survivor voices in the public consciousness

In giving this brief history of the Magdalene institutions in Ireland, particularly the events from 1993 onwards, I wish to highlight the current position of Magdalene survivors in the Irish public consciousness, and the ways in which their experiences are presented in contemporary Irish society, by the religious orders and the Irish State. The treatment of women who died in Magdalene institutions – the lack of care taken around registering their deaths and procuring certificates, the absence of accurate records and the refusal to answer questions regarding this – demonstrates how Magdalene survivors were not constructed as valuable subjects, by either the State or the religious orders. As Katherine O'Donnell writes:

> The disregard with which the four religious orders have treated the remains of Magdalene women speaks volumes to the Irish public, who understand that the careless way the nuns have treated the burial of Magdalene women highlights the treatment the women endured while alive. (2018a: 85)

These women, in a very real sense, have had their identities erased. They were denied their names in both life and death, denied dignity in commemoration. Smith posits the 1993 exhumation and cremation, along with the unveiling of the St Stephen's green monument and the closure of the last laundry in 1996 as three events which

> Speak to the challenges posed by Ireland's architecture of containment as it is remembered, retold, and memorialised in the present. A culturally progressive, economically vibrant, and increasingly Eurocentric Ireland was confronted on these separate occasions within a short three-year span with what Fintan O'Toole has called 'a haunting image of a history that remains largely unwritten, a history that in being disturbed still has the power to disturb (1993)'. (2007: 167)

This disturbing history has recently been made more visible in the public consciousness, through the work of groups such as the MMC and JFM, as well as writers, journalists and documentary filmmakers who focused their attention increasingly on institutional abuse.

Before moving on to further discussion of the existing literature on the Magdalene institutions, and the central focus of this book, I turn to the various ways in which the voices of the women have been brought into the public domain, acknowledging the ways in which Magdalene survivors have and have not been able to have their experiences heard, as well as the structures which have hindered this. One of the earliest examples of this is *Eclipsed* (1988), a play written by Patricia Burke Brogan, preceding public attention raised by the 1993 High Park exhumations. It was first read in Galway in 1988, and first performed by Punchbag Theatre in Galway, and continues to be staged globally. Smith describes the work as one which 'rescues Ireland's Magdalen women from the amnesia at the centre of the nation's nativist history' (2007: 91), highlighting the deep significance of this play in the history of the institutions, particularly for how survivors were thought of by wider Irish society. Burke Brogan based the play on her own experiences as a young novitiate – after joining the Congregation of the Sisters of Mercy, she spent one week overseeing women in a laundry before leaving, horrified at the experience.

While *Eclipsed* undoubtedly was and still is a deeply significant piece of work on the institutions, particularly because of the personal experience Burke Brogan had with the religious orders, Smith makes the case that 'documentary film, more than any other genre of cultural representation, facilitated the historical retrieval of Ireland's Magdalen laundries' (2007:115). He highlights four television documentaries, produced in the 1990s, which prior to the 2002 release of *The Magdalene Sisters* 'cumulatively established the corpus of what many in contemporary society knew about Ireland's Magdalen institutions' (Smith 2007: 117). These were *Washing Away the Stain* (1993), a BBC Scotland production, created in response to the success of *Eclipsed* in Edinburgh; *Sex in a Cold Climate* (1998), a documentary produced and directed by Steve Humphries for Channel 4, which used interviews with four women – three of whom had been incarcerated in a laundry, and one who had grown up in an adjoining orphanage in Limerick; *Les Blanchisseuses de Magdalen* (1998), a French-language documentary; and a segment on the CBS news programme *60 Minutes* in 1999, called *The Magdalen Laundries*, in part as a response to the public outcry caused by *Sex in a Cold Climate*. All four of these were produced by non-Irish media groups, and none of them aired on Irish television. Writing in 2007, Smith makes the point that no Irish media organization had at that time produced a documentary film focusing on the laundries, and as of 2021, this remains the case. RTÉ Television, the State-sponsored national broadcasting organization, finally made the decision to broadcast *Sex in a Cold Climate* in April 2013, fifteen years after it was first shown in the UK.

Sex in a Cold Climate was a source for the 2002 film *The Magdalene Sisters*, an Irish-British drama, written and directed by Peter Mullan. Premiering at the Venice Film Festival, the film tells the story of four girls sent to a Magdalene institution, portraying their living conditions as harsh and basic and the actions of the nuns as cruel and humiliating. In doing so it shone 'the international spotlight on the plight of Ireland's Magdalen women' (Smith 2007: 140). By presenting the survivor narratives through the highly accessible medium of film, Mullan 'offsets the long historical silence that allowed these institutions to maintain their secrecy and invisibility' (Smith 2007: 140). Despite being a fictional account, the film draws heavily on survivor testimony presented in *Sex in a Cold Climate*; if one watches both in succession it is evident how much of this Mullan incorporated into the screenplay. In presenting this testimony, along with other pre-existing cultural artefacts, in a coherent and accessible medium, 'the film confronts viewers with evidence that already existed', insisting that viewers 'acknowledge what heretofore they had chosen to ignore but, invariably, already knew' (Smith 2007: 140).

The 1990s represented a period of significant cultural, social and economic change in Ireland. The emergence of these new forms of representation of the institutions speak to the ways in which this change allowed for the emergence of a new narrative on the Magdalene institutions. In giving survivors a platform and a legitimate context in which to exist, they made space for new forms of knowledge on the laundries, complicating previously accepted narratives and forcing the public to confront the nation's architecture of containment, and their complicity within its structure.

Survivor narratives and oral history

There have also been other oral history projects which have collected the narratives of Magdalene survivors. In 2011, Evelyn Glynn, a postgraduate student at the Limerick School of Art and Design (LSAD), collected sixteen oral histories while researching her MA. These are part of a wider project entitled 'Breaking the Rule of Silence', described by Glynn as a

> Collation of oral histories, from a range of perspectives and experiences including: women who were incarcerated in the institution; workers employed by the Good Shepherds; relatives of women incarcerated; users of the laundry service people who had opportunity to visit the institution. (Glynn 2011)

This project existed as an exhibition at LSAD and can now be seen on the website www.magdalenelaundrylimerick.com/. Glynn was motivated towards this research by her surroundings – the building which houses the LSAD used to be St Mary's on Pennywell Road, a Magdalene laundry run by the Good Shepherd nuns. In 2011, when Glynn was conducting her research, there was no indication on the building that it had once served this purpose. The LSAD website makes brief mention of this fact, stating that the nuns 'ran a Magdalen laundry at the site until it was sold to the regional technical college in 1994' (About Clare St, lit.ie). Glynn's work was an attempt to recover the lost history of the building, to document this deliberate epistemology of ignorance which characterizes the history of the Magdalene institutions.

The College Street campus of the Waterford Institute of Technology (WIT) also sits on the site of a former Good Shepherd laundry. The WIT website states, 'It is located on the site of a former convent complex which was purchased from the Good Shepherd order of nuns in 1994' (Campus Development, wit.ie). Arguably, WIT has made considerably more effort to engage with this chapter in the building's history than LSAD, for example through the ongoing Waterford Memories Project (WMP), led by Dr O'Mahoney. Described as 'an oral history-driven project in digital humanities', the project aims to 'capture and examine the oral histories of those who lived and worked within the Magdalene Laundries and Industrial Schools located in the South-East of Ireland' (*Our Projects*, 2015). To date, there are six interviews with survivors available on the WMP website.

As well as the oral history project, WIT has engaged in public education work around the laundries.

Both of these projects make valuable contributions to the wider body of resources which have helped to bring survivor voices into the public consciousness. However, the small scale of both projects means there has been limited potential to develop a substantial analysis of women's experiences within and after incarceration in Magdalene institutions from them.

Literature on the Magdalene laundries

Despite the limitations in primary resources on the Magdalene institutions as a result of the decision to keep congregational archives closed to researchers, there now exists a significant body of literature addressing the laundries, in particular their place in twentieth-century Irish social history. For example, Frances Finnegan's extensive work, *Do Penance or Perish* (2001), the first book to be published on the subject of the Magdalene laundries in Ireland, provides a comprehensive history of the Good Shepherd laundries in the nineteenth century. Maria Luddy has also written about the institutions in her work *Prostitution and Irish Society* (2007), in particular the link between the growth of Magdalene institutions in Ireland and the nineteenth-century rescue movement. The early history of the Magdalene institutions as sites for 'fallen women' undoubtedly contributed to the popular conception that most of the women sent there had been in some way involved in transactional sex, even in the twentieth century. It is beyond the scope of this book to say whether this conceptualization of women sent to these institutions was correct or not, although analysis of the oral history interviews, considered alongside anecdotal evidence from speaking to survivors, suggests that in the twentieth century this was rarely the case. However, the associations between Magdalene institutions and 'deviant' female sexuality endure. Luddy (2007: 241) highlights the ways in which the women her work focuses upon were 'very rarely treated as individuals, both women and men used them in a symbolic way to argue for political and legal rights. Rights which they, as prostitutes, as women and as citizens, were often denied', and to an extent, the same can be said for women incarcerated in the Magdalene institutions. They were not treated as individuals but, rather, as manifestations of a social problem, guilty of being in the way. An understanding of the links between a conceptualization of women as 'bad' due to their perceived sexual immorality, and a denial of their rights, is crucial for an analysis of women's experiences in twentieth-century Magdalene institutions. Later in this book I will explore the links between gender and national identity in more depth, thinking through how ideas of 'good' women and citizens are produced, and the moral codes associated with this. However, this is also deeply bound up in the specific interactions between gender and religion. Miryam Clough's work, *Shame, the Church and the Regulation of Female Sexuality* (2017) uses the Magdalene laundries as a case study to explore how the church as an institution has so frequently colluded in the shaming of women, and why they are so consistently and overtly shamed for sexual behaviour. Clara Fischer (2016, 2017) also draws on the case of the Magdalene institutions for an exploration of shame, in particular the role played by shame in the State apology and the desire to recover national pride.

Arguably the most influential text on Magdalene institutions in the Irish context is James Smith's book *Ireland's Magdalen Laundries and the Nation's Architecture of Containment* (2007). Smith's work connects what is known about the laundries to what he terms Ireland's 'architecture of containment', namely a system of institutional responses to 'undesirable' subjects. In this way, illegitimate children, single mothers and anyone who threatened the moral fabric of the newly created Irish State were contained in various forms of institutions – industrial schools, Mother and Baby homes, Magdalene institutions – thereby rendering them literally invisible. In doing this, Smith places the Magdalene institutions within a broader framework of social containment in Ireland, thinking through the ways in which the Church and State worked to enact the nation state's nativist politics in the post-independence era.

As mentioned previously, any work on the Magdalene laundries, and, indeed, wider Catholic Church abuse scandals, owes a great debt to the journalist Mary Raftery, whose tireless work ensured that the High Park graves were brought to wider public attention. Raftery also produced and directed *States of Fear* (1999), a three-part documentary series broadcast by RTÉ detailing the systematic abuse suffered by generations of Irish children in the State institutions and religious-run schools. Following this, Raftery, along with Eoin O'Sullivan (1999), the consultant on *States of Fear*, published *Suffer the Little Children* (1999), further exploring the history of Ireland's industrial schools. The book expanded on many of the issues raised by the documentary series, as well as presenting a wealth of new material, including 'startling research showing a level of awareness of child sexual abuse going back over sixty years, particularly within the Christian Brothers' (Raftery and O'Sullivan 1999: 9). The industrial school system forms part of what Smith (2007) described as the nation's architecture of containment, and Raftery and O'Sullivan clearly demonstrate the Magdalene institutions' position within this larger system of control for women and children.

An unfinished literature

Research on Magdalene institutions in Ireland appears across disciplines, from historical and sociological analysis to human rights and legal perspectives. There has been significant work produced which positions the laundries in their social and historical context, as institutions which grew out of the nineteenth-century rescue movement, reflecting a fear of the perceived increasing level of prostitution. There is also an increasing literature on the contemporary position of the institutions in twentieth-century Ireland, as part of a system of social control designed to maintain the moral purity and stability of the newly formed Irish State. The current literature provides as thorough a history as is possible with the available resources, although Smith (2007: xvi) takes care to stress that a comprehensive history of the Magdalene institutions in Ireland cannot exist until religious congregations allow researchers access to archival records. Current writing on the subject is further limited in what it can tell us about the *nature* of women's experiences in these institutions, due to the lack of available resources which would allow for work of this type. While there have been projects and media representations which draw attention to the voices of survivors, until recently there has been no large body of survivor narratives with which to make claims about the nature of survivor experiences.

As demonstrated by recent work from Seal and O'Neill (2019), the creation of the oral history archive is beginning to make this work possible. Their book puts forward an approach to criminology exploring how spaces of transgression are lived, portrayed and imagined. Drawing on an extensive range of source material, examples and methodologies, they ask how questions of gender, sexuality, age, ethnicity, mobility and nationality intersect with lived and imagined space. They include a chapter on the Magdalene institutions as a case study in historical spaces of confinement, drawing on cultural representations and the Magdalene oral history archive to examine the imagination of Magdalene laundries in post-Independence Ireland (Seal and O'Neill 2019: 37). However, their study is limited to an analysis of seven interviews, out of over eighty taken. Their work also focuses primarily on the experiences of the women while in the institutions. In broadening out my analysis, I approach the oral histories as life stories, focusing on the narratives which detail time in the institution as well as those which discuss how survivors negotiated their lives and identities after leaving.

This book not only presents the voices of survivors as having value in and of themselves, but also positions those voices as producers of knowledge on their own experiences.[7] In this way my analysis works towards a better understanding of the nature of their experiences within the laundries, but I also wish to present these narratives as a way in which to analyse the position of the Magdalene institutions in contemporary culture, drawing on the experiences of women after leaving the laundries to explore how the State has both addressed and maintained the systems which allowed the laundries to flourish in the twentieth century. In doing so, my work is indebted to the work done by those who have so comprehensively situated the Magdalene institutions within the specific context of post-Independence Ireland, demonstrating the nuanced and complex interactions between Church, State and society in creating and maintaining these systems of control.

Lingering silences and the production of credible subjects

The decade following the publication of Smith's seminal work on the laundries has seen the production of a diverse body of literature on the laundries, as well as artistic creations and media reports. However, despite this proliferation of interest in and research on these institutions, there exists a very specific silence in discussions on the laundries – namely the voices and narratives of the survivors themselves. Both academic research and broader social work on the laundries have been hindered by lack of access to religious archives, and without a large body of survivor testimony upon which to draw, any reflections on the nature of women's experiences in these institutions, or the impact this had on their later lives, has necessarily been lacking. While much important and valuable work has been done on the subject, there remains an absence in the form of both the voices of the women themselves, and detailed analysis drawing on their narratives. Until recently, they have frequently been denied the space or contexts in which to be recognized as credible knowledge producers. This book aims to engage with and question this silence, asking how it was produced and maintained while the women were in the laundries, as well as in their lives after leaving the institutions, drawing primarily on the Magdalene oral history archive. The creation of this archive signifies a significant increase in the resources available when doing work on the Magdalene institutions, bringing together a large body of survivor voices, as well as those of their family members, activists and others whose lives interacted with the institutions in some way. This book represents the first large-scale analysis of this body of resources. Focusing principally on the interviews taken with survivors of the institutions, I wish to contribute to a better understanding of how women experienced their time in the institutions and the impact this had on their sense of self, rather than attempting to piece together a detailed timeline or history of the laundries in Ireland.

Throughout the book, I consider the value of a theory of epistemic injustice (Fricker 2007) as a way of understanding why this has been the case, engaging with the ways in which survivors of the Magdalene institutions were denied value in their capacity as producers of knowledge due to their particular social identities. I explore the processes by which women who spent time in these institutions were coercively formed into particular religious, gendered subjectivities, asking how disciplinary power in a carceral religious context works to control bodies and selves. I also address how Magdalene survivors have resisted this coercive shaping, through processes of resistance and survival. By placing these processes within a framework of epistemic injustice, I think about how these inscribed identities resulted in instances of what Fricker terms both testimonial and hermeneutical injustice, which continued in the lives of the women after they had left the laundries.

Fricker writes that the overarching aim of her work on epistemic injustice is 'to bring light to certain ethical aspects of our most basic everyday epistemic practices: conveying knowledge to others by telling them, and making sense of our own social experiences' (2007:1). This book is strongly orientated around these everyday epistemic practices. It will explore how women both communicated and were communicated to while they were in the laundries; it will consider the extent to which they were then (un)able to communicate and make sense of those experiences to others after they had left the institutions. Finally, I address how survivors have had their experiences mediated through instances of public voice, and how this both provided them with new contexts in which to be heard, as well as maintaining structures which limited the ways in which they could express their voices. The book demonstrates how the experience of being in the institutions shaped the structures and meanings they drew upon in order to make sense of their lives and their identities. Through this, I aim to work towards a better understanding of the nature of their experiences, situating them within a wider context which questions how the specific experience of being in a religious carceral institution shapes subjectivity.

I will also consider how oral history as a methodology functions in this context of epistemic practices, as a space in which the women can both convey knowledge and make sense of their own experiences, in a way which has previously been denied to them. In doing so, I position the Magdalene survivors as credible knowledge producers, challenging narratives which either portray them as unreliable narrators of their own experiences or mediate their words through a particular lens, to suit a particular framing. The analysis of this archival material will be situated in the wider context of research on post-Independence Irish society. The function of the laundries in twentieth-century Ireland is bound up in the specific context of the newly formed Irish State, reflecting well-documented ideas about gender and the role of women as reproducers of the nation. McClintock writes that 'nations have historically amounted to the sanctioned institutionalization of gender *difference*. No nation in the world grants women and men the same access to rights and resources of the nation-state' (McClintock 1997: 89). Deniz Kandiyoti (1997: 440) describes the regulation of gender as central to the articulation of cultural identity and difference – both authors here emphasize the way in which women's bodies are used to mark out the boundaries of a state. Through the control of 'their' women's behaviour, nations can separate themselves from others. Therefore, women become a 'special focus of state concerns as a social category with a specific role (particularly human reproduction)' (Anthias and Yuval-Davis 1989: 6).

As O'Sullivan and O'Donnell write, 'a pristine state required unblemished citizens and wayward women posed a threat that needed to be neutralized' (2012: 265). The institutions served as ways to *physically* control the bodies of problematic women, by removing them from wider society. In this book, I highlight the construction of certain women as both threatening and vulnerable, focusing on what this demonstrates about the justification which underpins much of the ideology behind the laundries. I describe this as a rationale of vicious paternalism, which disciplines women under the auspices of protection. Women sent to Magdalene institutions were seen as threatening to the Irish State, risking the purity of the nation through their existence and actions. However, they were also conceptualized as vulnerable, in need of care and protection, and therefore required incarceration *for their own good*, to keep them safe. In framing these actions within the context of epistemic harm, I will demonstrate the ways in which this coercive identity formation has the capacity to undermine how survivors are seen as legitimate producers of knowledge. The role of the State in maintaining boundaries of knowledge and in cultivating a deliberate epistemology of ignorance is a key concern of my work, leading to wider questions about how states and official bodies can replicate and maintain processes of epistemic injustice, keeping survivors in a state of ignorance and unknowing which mirrors their experiences of institutional trauma. Throughout the work, I prioritize questions of silence and voice, thinking not only about the silences and the voices of Magdalene survivors but also about my own instances of silence and voice. I wish to consider the ethical implications of doing work on survivors' narratives, thinking through the extent to which academic work can replicate oppressive structures through processes of 'speaking for', and considering the impact this can have on research. At the heart of this book is a desire to take the voices and experiences of survivors seriously, to position them as legitimate and expert producers of knowledge on their own narratives and to question the structures and processes which have prevented this from being the case.

Chapter outline

The overall narrative of the following chapters intends to explore the nature of women's experiences as shaped by their time in Magdalene laundries in post-Independence Ireland, focusing on the formation of subjectivity within a framework of epistemic injustice.

Before presenting this analysis, in Chapter 2 I situate my work in the social and cultural study of religion, identifying the Magdalene laundries as religious carceral institutions. I engage with what this specific context means for processes of religious subjectivity formation in particular. I then introduce Fricker's theory of epistemic injustice in more detail, exploring the ways it provides a valuable theoretical framework for research on the Magdalene laundries. I focus on particular harms of both testimonial and hermeneutical injustice, as well as the specific impact of these on a subject's sense of self. These harms are deeply rooted in the close interaction between Church and State in post-Independence Ireland, and the formation of Irish national identity in the newly created State. This chapter will therefore also look at some of the ways in which Church and State impact on gender, morality and respectability.

Chapter 3 introduces the oral history archive in more detail and sets out my methodological approach for engaging with this resource, as well as other primary source material used. I begin by presenting the archive upon which this work is based, before thinking further about the nature of oral history data as a resource for considering issues of subjectivity, agency and credibility. I engage with oral histories as instances of voice and silencing, and then consider their value as narrative constructions of the self. I then introduce some of the theoretical concepts which underpin my methodological approach, thinking through questions of bodies, gender, voice and silencing. Finally, I move on to a discussion of how I understand my practice as a researcher, as an intervention into processes of narration and silence, paying attention to issues of power and the ethics of representation in the research process. In doing this, I also engage significantly with the ethics of self-care within research, and the particular problems faced when doing sensitive and traumatic research.

Chapter 4 is the first of three chapters which present findings from my analysis of the oral history interviews and other source material. This chapter focuses on the experiences of women while they were in the institutions, exploring the processes used to discipline their voices, bodies and selves, to produce a particular type of religious gendered subjectivity. Ultimately, this was a process of stripping a woman of her agency, of the forms of meaning which are important for a sense of self, based on a religious punitive system which disciplined the female body in a very specific way. Throughout the chapter, it becomes apparent that these processes frequently revolved around the denial and restriction of knowledge and agency to the women. This chapter demonstrates how these processes formed women as unreliable subjects, incapable of being trusted with or producing knowledge about their own lives. However, this chapter also addresses examples of resistance and agency, pushing back against these processes through specific use of silence or voice, removal of labour and escape from the institutions.

Chapter 5 moves on to the experiences of the women after leaving the laundries, thinking about the ways in which the trauma of the institutions continued and extended into their later lives, as well as how they navigated this and began to negotiate different forms of subjectivity. Specifically, this chapter explores how survivors speak about the ongoing effects of institutionalization on their sense of self, the sense of shame they feel at being 'a Magdalene' and the stigma they experience as a very constant presence in their lives. Beyond this, I describe how this shame is enmeshed with a visceral terror at the visibility of a stigmatized identity. I consider the effect this shame and terror had on the production of knowledge, and the women's ability to communicate their experiences. I then address the specifically religious nature of this, and what this means for the ways in which survivors are able to navigate Irish social systems, so many of which are deeply entwined with religious ideology. Lastly, moving beyond their altered engagement with these religious relationships, this chapter explores how women found space to renegotiate their identities through finding routes to motherhood and respectability, finding new forms of agency within 'ordinary' acts.

In Chapter 6, I turn to instances of public voice on the Magdalene institutions, focusing on how processes of inquiry, apology and redress have the capacity to both address and replicate structures which create epistemic injustice for survivors. I take three key events – the publication of the McAleese report in 2013, the apology given by Enda Kenny in 2013 and the *Dublin Honours Magdalenes* event of June 2018 – and explore how these events function to produce and maintain particular subjectivities within a framework of epistemic injustice. In doing so I demonstrate the extent to which survivors are frequently still not afforded spaces in which they are respected as knowledge producers.

Chapter 7 addresses two key points which underpin much of the book. Firstly, I demonstrate how the Magdalene institutions represent a specific manifestation of the cultural and religious imaginary which existed in twentieth-century Ireland. While they can be seen as an example of disciplinary institutions, they represent an example of specifically *religious carceral* environments, which drew heavily on the sacred form of the Irish Catholic Church for legitimacy. I then consider how this was entwined with what I describe as an ideology of vicious paternalism, which runs throughout the experiences of the women, visible in both the actions of the State and the religious orders. I argue that this rationale of vicious paternalism is based on a particular understanding of gendered subjectivity, which positions women who threaten social boundaries as deeply vulnerable and in need of care, and at the same time highly threatening, a risk to those around them. In conceptualizing certain women in this way, the Magdalene institutions could be positioned as a form of social welfare, incarcerating women both for their own good and for the good of the wider society. This chapter then highlights the way in which a framework of epistemic injustice helps better understand the trauma caused by the Magdalene institutions, placing the harms caused by this ideology within a framework of knowledge production.

2

Epistemic injustice and credible subjects

As demonstrated in the previous chapter, the last twenty years have seen a proliferation of interest in, and writing on, the Magdalene institutions. However, within all of this emerging literature, there is a very specific enduring silence, namely in terms of recognition of the women themselves as knowledge producers, as reliable narrators of their own experiences. When thinking about academic work on the subject, this is primarily due to the previously mentioned lack of resources. Without a large body of survivor testimony on which to draw, it has been difficult to do any serious analysis on the ways in which these women experienced their time in the institutions. This book represents the first large-scale analysis of these voices and narratives, prioritizing a better understanding of the experiences of the women who spent time in the institutions by drawing on their own words to produce knowledge. However, in addressing the nature of this silence in the wider social and cultural contexts, it is useful to frame it within broader ideas of credibility for victims of trauma, and for women's voices in general. Both of these groups are frequently coded as unreliable, as people who should not be trusted. Arguably then, we are still trying to create the broader social conditions in which we can generate knowledge about the Magdalene laundries of a kind which recognizes the credibility of survivor voices. This book considers the question of why this specific form of silence persisted for so long. What was it about this particular instance which meant the women were not trusted to generate knowledge on their own experiences, and what can this tell us about the harms experienced by victims of religious institutional abuse in other contexts?

By examining the processes through which they were silenced, denied credibility and limited in the ways they could articulate their experiences, I demonstrate the particular forms of epistemic harm suffered by these women, and the impact this had on their sense of self throughout their lives. In this chapter, I begin by introducing Fricker's theory of epistemic injustice, addressing the ways in which it provides a constructive framework within which to better understand the experiences of women incarcerated in Magdalene laundries. I introduce the concepts of testimonial and hermeneutical injustice, and the specific harms these cause to a subject. I situate this discussion within the specific context of post-Independence Ireland, focusing on how both Church and State engaged in a project of national identity formation. In particular, I address the impact of this project on conceptions of gender, morality and respectability. In doing so, I introduce an analysis which allows for a meaningful engagement with the oral history archive, bringing together an understanding of theories of silence, voice and credibility which take into account the specific social, cultural and religious context of post-Independence Ireland. I make the case for a methodological approach which positions survivors as knowledge producers, asking why this has not previously been the case, as well as demonstrating the value this has for engaging with survivors' experiences of the Magdalene laundries.

By situating these specifically religious processes of control and discipline within a framework of epistemic injustice, I consider what it means to be discredited as an unreliable *religious* subject, particularly when one exists in a social context saturated with complex forms of religious meanings, entangled with systems of purity and morality structured by religion. Through an engagement with the religious justifications given for women's incarceration, the ways in which specific religious disciplines and bodily practices impact on the women's subjectivity, and the implications of the Church's complicated social position on contemporary public perceptions of the laundries, I situate this book firmly within the discipline of the sociology of religion. By asking questions about the impact of carceral religious institutions on a subject's sense of self, within a framework of credibility and knowledge production, I build on literature addressing the nature of abuse in religious carceral contexts, as well as broader debates about religious subjectivity and the complex ways people form, change and abandon religious relationships throughout their lives.

Epistemic injustices and the problems of knowledge communication

Miranda Fricker coined the term 'epistemic injustice' in her book of the same name. She uses the term to refer to 'a wrong done to someone specifically in their capacity as a knower' (2007:1), stating that the overarching aim of her work 'is to bring light to certain ethical aspects of our most basic everyday epistemic practices: conveying knowledge to others by telling them, and making sense of our own social experiences' (2007: 1). It is within these practices of producing and sharing knowledge that this work sits, asking questions of power – who is allowed to know, who is allowed to speak, and as a result, who is allowed to *be*. As Bev Skeggs writes, the questions which underpin this discourse are about 'how systems of knowledge, inscription and representation enable some things to be known and perspectives taken, whilst other things and perspectives are made invisible, irrelevant and lacking in importance' (2004: 45).

Fricker articulates two forms of epistemic injustice – testimonial injustice and hermeneutical injustice. Testimonial injustice occurs when identity prejudice on the part of hearers causes them to give a 'deflated level of credibility to a speaker's word' (Fricker 2007:1). Identity prejudice here is described as prejudice held against a person due to their identification with a social group that suffers discrimination. In order for something to be termed testimonial injustice, therefore, it must not simply be a credibility deficit, but one caused by prejudice relating to the subject's social identity. Throughout the oral history interviews, Magdalene survivors speak about being disbelieved and discredited, portrayed as unreliable narrators of their own experiences. To question whether these experiences can be termed testimonial injustice, then, we need to ask whether the credibility deficit they report as happening throughout their lives happen as a result of their social identity. To do this, it is important to think about the social identity they inhabited and how this identity was produced and perceived by wider social and cultural influences. Later in this chapter, I will discuss the ways in which the Church and State in Ireland functioned to produce and maintain strict gender roles, particularly around conceptions of motherhood, which worked to discredit anyone who strayed outside of them. In transgressing these boundaries, the Magdalene survivors not only inhabit the social identity of 'woman', already one with a long history of marginalization, but they exist as *bad* women, women who are at once both vulnerable and threatening. They occupy an intersection of (perceived) identities – fallen woman, victim, 'prostitute' – who are frequently coded as unreliable.

The second form of epistemic injustice described by Fricker is hermeneutical injustice, that is 'the injustice of having some significant area of one's social experience obscured from collective understanding owing to a structural identity prejudice in the collective hermeneutical resource' (2007: 155). Fricker works towards an understanding of how structural social and power dynamics constrain people's ability to make sense of their own experiences, because they have not been provided with the correct hermeneutic tools. The primary harm of this form of epistemic injustice 'consists in a *situated hermeneutical inequality:* the concrete situation is such that the subject is rendered unable to make communicatively intelligible something which it is particularly in his or her interests to be able to render intelligible' (Fricker 2007: 162). The usefulness of hermeneutical injustice in this context becomes particularly relevant when thinking about women's lives after leaving the institutions. Survivors frequently existed in a state of silence because they lacked the language to talk about their experiences. However, the interviews also demonstrate that survivors made use of a range of structures and processes to make sense of what happened to them. Placing this within the framework of hermeneutical injustice allows us to examine how these processes were successful as well as providing an understanding of why, sometimes, it may not have been possible for survivors to do so.

Fricker's work has been widely used across a range of disciplines, and in the decade since the publication of *Epistemic Injustice* in 2007, scholars have expanded the concept significantly, identifying and naming different forms of epistemic injustice (see Dotson 2011, 2012, 2014, Berenstain 2016, Scrutton 2017, Kotzee 2017, Sullivan 2017, Mills 2017, 2007, Medina 2012). It is also worth highlighting that, while the term 'epistemic injustice' has been in use only since 2007, the experience this describes has been written and spoken about for many decades, and can be traced to discussions around intersections of power, knowledge and oppression occurring long before the term was used in this way. For example, the roots of the term are evident in Gayatri Spivak's (1988) ideas of epistemic violence as a way of marking the silencing of marginalized groups. It is also visible in the words of early Black feminists such as Sojourner Truth (1995 [1867]), who spoke of the ways in which Black women's voices are consistently denied credibility. Additionally, Anna Julia Cooper opens her text, *A Voice from the South by a Black Woman of the South* (1988 [1892]), by describing practices of epistemic violence and interpretive silencing rooted in her experience as a Black woman.

By situating the experiences of Magdalene survivors within a framework of religiously motivated epistemic injustice, I work towards a better understanding of the harms caused by the Magdalene institutions specifically. Paying attention to these structural ways of knowing and not knowing allows for a deeper understanding of the trauma they caused, as well opening up the possibility of creating spaces and contexts in which to better hear the narratives of those who have been historically denied a voice, in a productive capacity.

Epistemic injustice and identity formation

This work is particularly focused on the impact epistemic injustice has on subjectivity formation, as a lens through which we can better understand the experiences of women who had their words disbelieved, who were consistently portrayed as unreliable narrators of their own experiences, while in the laundries and later in life. Fricker concludes that both testimonial and hermeneutical injustice have the capacity to cause harm to the construction of selfhood. Indeed, 'in certain social contexts, hermeneutical injustice can mean that someone is socially constituted as, and perhaps even caused to be, something that they are not, and which it is against their interests to be seen to be' (Fricker 2007: 168). This is also the case with regard to testimonial injustice – both, Fricker argues, may prevent someone from fully developing their sense of self, or as Fricker puts it, from 'becoming who they are' (2007: 168). In other words, epistemic injustice can inhibit the development of an authentic understanding of one's identity, either because you are being constituted as someone who is unreliable, unable to be trusted on your own experience; or because you exist in a hermeneutical lacuna in which your experiences are not recognized and validated. This book considers the ways that continued denial of credibility to Magdalene survivors contributes to the systematic nature of the harms caused by the institutions. It traces these from the circumstances in which women were sent to the laundries, often involving multiple instances of testimonial injustice; to their experiences of being constituted as socially worthless, as 'nothing' within the laundries; and then finally to the treatment of their narratives by the Irish State and wider public when investigations into the laundries' operations began to appear. By engaging with the impact of each of these stages on the formation of subjectivity, we can see the extent to which, as Fricker suggests, persistent epistemic exclusion inhibits the development of essential aspects of a person's identity. Fricker refers to the work of Judith Shklar (1990), who

> Develops the point that injustice is in fact a normal social baseline, while active cries of resentment and demands for rectification are the precious exception. I think that testimonial injustice is a normal part of discursive life, even though cries of resentment are relatively few and far between. (Fricker 2007: 39)

This is undoubtedly evident in many social contexts, but in the case of survivors of trauma, in particular female survivors of abuse, it becomes uncomfortably true. Their testimony exists in a society which has an embedded identity prejudice against women, particularly working-class women, women of colour, queer women, women who sell sex – against any woman making accusations which threaten the dominant cultural narrative. It is, therefore, crucial to pay attention to these cries of resentment and investigate how survivors resist processes of epistemic injustice, finding new ways to develop their identities, new forms of meaning both inside and outside the laundry. Expressions of agency allow us to explore how individuals begin to counter epistemic injustice on an individual level, which in turn gives indications of how this might be done in a more extensive, structural way. This book takes these 'cries of resentment' seriously, framing the women not as passive victims of epistemic injustice but as subjects with the capacity for agency, who frequently pushed back against the harms inflicted upon them.

The religious subject within a carceral institution

The social significance of the Catholic Church in Ireland, discussed later in this chapter, emphasizes the need to foreground the specific religious context in which this work is situated. Not only is this necessary for a thorough understanding of how women's bodies and selves were disciplined, and their value as epistemic subjects discredited, but it also allows for a better understanding of religious subjectivity in specifically religious carceral contexts, something which has yet to be fully explored by scholars working in this area. What is it about the religious nature of the discipline which worked to produce certain subjects? It is useful to consider this disciplining of bodies and selves as a practice of penance, religiously motivated discipline with the specific goal of saving the penitent's soul. Throughout the project I consider the ways in which the experience of being incarcerated within a Magdalene institution impacted on the religious subjectivity of survivors. I explore the ways in which incarceration changed how they experienced their religious identity, and the cultural forms they drew on to make sense of this. I consider how an understanding of this religious subjectivity helps better understand the complex position of survivors within the landscape of twentieth-century Ireland, in particular their shifting social identity and the impact this had on instances of epistemic injustice.

I draw heavily on Orsi's work on lived religion when thinking through these questions, in particular his understanding of religion as a set of relationships (Orsi 2005). Orsi emphasizes that thinking of religion as 'relationships between heaven and earth' within the context of particular times and places 'frees us from any notion of religious practices as *either* good *or* bad. Religions are as ambiguous and ambivalent as the bonds that constitute them, and their effects cannot be generally anticipated but known in practice and experience' (2005: 2). In this way I aim not to anticipate survivors' engagement with religion, but, instead, explore and pay attention to their religious practices and experiences. Framing religious engagement in this way allows for an understanding which makes space for the complex and shifting ways in which survivors negotiate their identities after leaving sites of trauma. It focuses not on what people *believe*, so to speak, but the way in which religion affects their daily lives and their actions. It is not religious ideas which emerge as important in this book, although there is much scope for work on the ideas which underpin the Magdalene institutions. Instead, I pay close attention to the ways in which these religious relationships are formed and fragmented, and the new shapes they take on as a result of the survivors' time in the laundries. I engage with the Magdalene institutions as specifically *religious* carceral institutions, but I am not attempting to understand the religious doctrine which underpins them, or the religious motivations of the orders who ran them. Rather, I focus on the how the religiously saturated environment of the laundries impacted upon the relationships – religious, social and cultural – of those who were sent there; how the punitive religious processes they experienced impacted upon their lives. In doing so, I wish to make space for a multiplicity of religious experiences, which may transgress the boundaries of institutional religion significantly, while still providing powerful forms of moral meaning for those involved.

The punitive *religious* nature of institutions such as the Magdalene laundries is something which has yet to be fully explored. In the last twenty years, there has been increased focus on institutional abuse, particularly in religious contexts. Native residential schools in Canada (Niezen 2017), child migration to Australia (Lynch 2015) and clerical sexual abuse scandals in America have all generated significant interest, in both the academic and public sphere. However, much of the work produced on this has, for good reason, focused on the traumatic and abusive nature of these institutions, with less work conducted on the specifically religious forms this takes. However, the religious justifications given for incarceration; the ways in which specific religious disciplines and bodily practices impact on the women's subjectivity; as well as the implications of the Church's complex social position on public perceptions of these institutions and the experiences of their wider religious communities require closer examination. Perhaps some of the most relevant literature for this project is Robert Orsi's (2016) recent work, which explores how survivors of clerical sexual abuse in America use Catholic structures and imagery to renegotiate their relationships with religion, focusing on the complex ways in which they engage with God, their own personal faith and the wider Catholic Church after this. While Orsi's work is undoubtedly important for an exploration of religious subjectivity for survivors of clerical abuse, the social geographical context of Ireland is significantly different from that within which Orsi is working, and the specific importance of Irish Church and State interactions in this context will be explored later in this chapter.

This book also considers the specifically gendered nature of religious subjectivity in this context. Recent feminist interventions into the study of religion have worked to complicate the meanings of categories such as 'woman' and 'religion', creating new understandings of the way in which these two identities interact. However, the religious and spiritual are still categories too frequently ignored by mainstream feminist literature, leading to a disconnect between secular and religious feminisms (Llewellyn and Trzebiatowska 2013). Llewellyn's later work considers how this neglect of religion by third-wave feminist movements overlooks women's experiences of the sacred and spiritual, a tendency which runs counter to the movement's 'insistence on intersectionality and the plural forms of identity, and with its concern to look beyond the privileged experiences of white, middle-class, educated, Western women' (Llewellyn 2015:5). If, as Llewellyn suggests, contemporary feminism is 'searching for ways that enable the fragmented woman, conceived as multiple and fluid, to be the grounding for feminism in community' (2015: 5), it must take seriously the experiences of religious women, and the intersecting identities they occupy.

The Magdalene laundries provide a valuable context in which to explore conceptions of gendered religious subjectivity due to the complex relationships between gender and religion which emerged in twentieth-century Ireland. The women sent to these institutions were caught up in these complex networks of religion and gender – their gendered identity was seen to threaten both the Catholic Church and the Irish State. The nature of this threat was bound up with ideas of female sexuality deeply rooted in both nationalist ideology and Catholic teaching. However, Castelli notes that many feminists

> Have tended to read 'religion' as an abstraction solely in negative terms – reading 'religion' only as a form of constraint both ideologically and institutionally, and reading the embrace of religious affiliations or allegiances primarily as a sign of false consciousness. (2001: 5)

It would be too simple to see religion as a purely constraining force in this instance, and the complex ways in which the survivors discuss their religious relationships after leaving the laundries make this clear. Feminist theology has long held that religious subjectivity is a *situated* subjectivity, that is, 'affected by various features of social context including gender, sex, race, nationality/ethnicity, and religion' (Armour 2012: 378). Armour makes the point that 'the goals of the exercise of agency are not always or simply increasing autonomy and independence' (2012: 378), which emerges as a key theme in the work of Saba Mahmood (2004). Her research demonstrates the ways in which the religious subject is continuously formed through processes of negotiation with power, showing how women involved in piety movements in Cairo are engaged in ethical self-formation, of a radically different nature than that recognized by liberal Western feminism. By disrupting traditional understandings of agency in this way, Mahmood's work could provide a fascinating potential framework with which to better understand the complex ways in which survivors of institutional abuse resist processes of discipline and inscription. If we wish to think seriously about the complexities involved in this process, moving away from a one-sided understanding of 'agency' towards one which takes account of the structural notions of power inherent in these processes, then an understanding of the complex interactions between gender, nation and the Church is required.

Gender, nation and Church: 'good' and 'bad' women within the Irish State

In the context of this work, these ideas of religious subjectivity formation must be understood within the political, religious and cultural dimensions of a particular Irish national history. Women sent to the laundries were being punished not for being women, but for being the *wrong* kind of women, as conceptualized by the newly formed Irish nation. They were an example of excessive, dangerous femininities – the 'whore', rather than the mother. Even those women who were actual mothers were the *wrong* kind of mothers, existing outside the confines of the heterosexual family and threatening the stability of that identity which was at the heart of Irish social life. Fricker (2007: 28) states that in order for something to be termed testimonial injustice, it must not simply be a credibility deficit, but one caused by prejudice relating to the subject's social identity. This social identity is necessarily dependent on the social context in which the subject exists, and therefore in this section I will consider the conceptualization of womanhood in twentieth-century Ireland, framing this within the wider literature addressing the role played by women in maintaining national identity. I then move on to an exploration of how the figure of the idealized mother was created and upheld by the Church, and how this structure allowed for certain women to access very specific types of religious and social legitimacy. I frame the experiences of the Magdalene survivors within a particular political and religious context and in doing so, I highlight structures which, while having their roots in the history of twentieth-century Ireland, continue to exist in contemporary Irish culture. The Magdalene institutions are not 'a thing of the past' as they are frequently described in the media, by the State and in some of the interviews with key informants. By understanding the contexts and processes which allowed this specific form of religious carceral institution to thrive, we can better understand the ways in which the harms of the laundries continue in the lives of survivors today.

Gender and national identity: colonial anxieties and constitutional femininity

Post-Independence Ireland witnessed what Redmond et al. describe as 'a national obsession with sexuality and sexual practice' (2015: 8). Luddy highlights the extent to which this became a preoccupation of the Irish State post-Independence, which led to a significant focus on the figure of the 'unmarried mother', who occupied an identity which, in the view of the State, was both deeply vulnerable and highly threatening. She writes of the anxiety felt by both Church and State about the unmarried mother:

> The maternal body, particularly in its unmarried condition, became a central focus in the developing welfare policies of the state and the Catholic Church. Throughout the 1920s, and later, conflicting representations of unmarried mothers abounded. They were seen as innocent victims or corrupting agents, they were 'poor girls' or potential blackmailers. (Luddy 2011: 112)

The concept of women acting as signifiers for the morality of a nation is not unique to Ireland. In setting the historical background for her detailed ethnography of working-class women in North East England, Skeggs remarks on how 'social stability was considered to be dependent upon moral purity; the moral condition of the nation was seen to derive from the moral standards of woman; woman came to signify the success or failure of the colonial project, on an internal and external basis' (1997: 42). Globally, women's bodies are formed as sites upon which the anxieties and moral qualms of nation states play out, and the figure of the 'unmarried mother' often bears the brunt of the inevitable judgements. Conor Reidy describes how prostitutes and female 'inebriates' in the early twentieth century were seen both 'as dangerous *and* vulnerable, corrupting *and* corruptible: capable of asserting influence over others, but susceptible to external influence themselves and therefore in need of care and protection' (2015: 57). This contradiction also lies at the heart of much of the discourse on unmarried mothers. They were, and to an extent still are, seen as in need of protection and rescue from dangerous influences. However, their bodies are also 'the site of sin, literal embodiment of transgressive sexual behaviour through pregnancy, and thus control of them was essential in many people's eyes in order to diminish what was seen as a significant moral problem' (Redmond et al. 2015: 8). Indeed, in many instances it was their perceived vulnerability which allowed for the control of their 'threat' – they could be incarcerated 'for their own good', as a precautionary measure to manage the threat they posed to the rest of the nation.

Broader links between conceptions of gender, the social roles of women and formation of national identity have been the subject of significant research (McClintock 1997, Kandiyoti 1997), and many writers particularly emphasize how women's bodies are used to mark out the boundaries of a state. Through the control of 'their' women's behaviour, nations can separate themselves from others. Therefore, women become a 'special focus of state concerns as a social category with a specific role (particularly human reproduction)' (Anthias and Yuval-Davis 1989: 6). This 'specific role' of women in the state means that they are allocated what Yuval-Davis (1997) describes as a 'burden of representation', resulting in the development of specific codes and regulations, defining who and what constitutes a 'proper man' and a 'proper woman', which are central to the identities of the nation and its members (Yuval-Davis 1997: 67). In the context of the newly formed Irish State, this specific role of women in public and private life in the twentieth century was explicitly defined in the draft of the second Free State constitution, made public in March 1937. No women took part in drafting this document, although many groups made formal objections to the Constitution. Article 41.1 highlights the importance of the family, creating it as a 'moral institution' within the Irish State. Article 41.2 then goes on to define the very particular role of women within this moral institution:

2.1 In particular, the state recognises that by her life within the home, woman gives to the state a support without which the common good cannot be achieved.

2.2 The state shall, therefore, endeavour to ensure that mothers shall not be obliged by economic necessity to engage in labour to the neglect of their duties in the home.

While there have been repeated calls at both the national and international levels to amend or remove Article 41.2, as of the time of writing, it remains in the Constitution. This article emphasizes the *moral* value of women remaining within the home, and in doing so, implies that there is a wider value to the State, and, indeed, all Irish people, by women choosing to stay in this domestic role. The wording slips between referring to 'women' and 'mothers' interchangeably – suggesting womanhood in this context is primarily understood through the relationship to motherhood. The success of the State, the achievement of the 'common good', is placed on the shoulders of women – they bear this burden of the project of nation building (Fischer 2017). Gardiner describes Article 41 as 'an implicit denial of freedom of choice to women in personal matters' (1993: 50), reflecting a desire by the first government of the Irish Free State to severely restrict the role of women in Irish public life (Valiulis 1995: 120). This legislation significantly undermined the Constitution of 1922 which was written in the immediate aftermath of the War of Independence and in the writing of which feminists took a prominent role. This earlier version gave women over the age of twenty-one the right to vote as well as hold office on equal terms with men. However, by 1937, 'women's political, economic, and reproductive rights had been so severely curtailed that women were explicitly barred from claiming for themselves a public identity' (Valiulis 1995: 120).

The new Constitution effectively reinforced the idea that the correct place for Irish women was in the home; and this call for women to eschew public life, conform to traditional gender roles and devote themselves to the service of their family was to become typical of the experience of the majority of women in the early years of the Irish Free State (Beaumont 1999: 94). The identity of women became dependent on their duties towards their husbands and children, and therefore women who did not fit in to this narrow category of 'good women' were conceptualized as damaging to the nation as a whole. By enshrining in law the family as the fundamental unit group of society, Article 41 of the Constitution guaranteed it special protection. However, as Mary Robinson points out:

> The family in question is the family based on a valid subsisting marriage. These provisions have been interpreted to exclude from the definition of family the single mother and her child or children. A whole jurisprudence has been built up on this concept of the constitutional family. (1993: 103)

By consigning women to the home, and tying their worth and identity to a specific conception of family, women would become 'a badge of respectability for the new state' (Valiulis 1995: 128) and women who refused, or were not able, to conform to this threatened the emerging Irish identity and the State as a whole.

Gender and the Catholic Church

Equally significant was the role played by the Catholic Church in drawing the boundaries for acceptable womanhood. Magray notes that as a cultural institution, 'the church played a powerful role in maintaining and disseminating a gender ideology that limited the power and range of social action of all women, including women religious' (Magray 1998: 12). However, within this there are a multitude of other interactions between Catholicism and gender, which together produce a more complex and nuanced picture of women and the Church in Ireland. Tom Inglis describes religious identity as historically being 'central to family life, education, health care and social welfare' (2005: 59). He emphasizes that this is not simply an acceptance of certain beliefs and teachings – being a Catholic was, and for many remains, something which was central to Irish identity, as socially significant as gender, class, ethnicity or sexual orientation. He focuses on the figure of the 'Irish mother' as a case study in Church and gender relations, arguing that it was the mother who, from the mid-nineteenth century, acted as 'the organizational link between the Catholic Church and the individual' (1998: 179). It was through the mother that the new moral and civil code could be transmitted from the Church and school into the home, and it was the mother who 'produced the Catholics of modern Ireland' (1998: 179), by handing down social and cultural practices through generations, supported by priests and the Church. This was in part because religion and morality were often the only areas in which women could find any authority. With little or no power in the public or political field, as exemplified in the limiting terms of Article 41, it was frequently in terms of morality that women were able to wield any power, with the backing of the priest. Inglis argues that 'the domination and control of women by the Church and the necessity for women to ally themselves with that dominating power if they themselves were to have any power' (1998: 198) is crucial to understanding the reproduction and maintenance of strict codes around sexual morality. With reference to Pierre Bourdieu's ideas of social capital (1977), Inglis demonstrates how Irish women worked within an inherently patriarchal system to gain a degree of authority. It was possible for women to attain religious capital through adherence to strict spiritual and moral guidelines, and so this became an important source of power for women who were unable to access other forms of capital, such as social, political, economic or cultural capital. In gaining this religious capital, they were also able to acquire a degree of honour and respect – symbolic capital – which legitimated their position within the family and community (Inglis 2005: 66).

Lindsey Earner-Byrne also explores the social role of 'mother' in Ireland, highlighting how policy affecting women was intertwined with Catholic teachings, particularly with regard to the family. She speaks of religious teaching and ideology as being

> Woven into the fabric of the development of maternity and child welfare in Dublin . . . religion and the cultural conceptualization of morality influenced not only the possibilities of co-operation between various groups, but also definitions of health. Birth control was categorically relegated to the arena of morality and consciously excluded from any health debate. Henceforth, the Roman Catholic Church regarded maternal and child welfare as a crucial issue to control in the face of either other religious or non-denominational groups or state encroachment. (2007: 51)

This is particularly relevant when considering the unmarried mother, who was seen as a significant social problem well into the second half of the twentieth century. The social role of 'mother' was legitimated primarily by marriage, which reflected 'a cultural understanding of the family as patriarchal and only *bona fide* when headed by a male obligated to the role of fatherhood by marriage' (Earner-Byrne 2007: 172). This underlying assumption informed much of the care and support that Irish mothers received during this period and, Earner-Byrne argues, was fundamentally based on religious ideas of morality.

The impact of this conception of women's identity and social role is significant – as long as the role of women in Irish society was defined primarily in relation to the institution of the family, issues of motherhood and child legitimacy would be discussed only in terms of the impact this had on family power. Earner-Byrne highlights how this view had a significant impact on all women, but to the greatest extent on the unmarried mother. Her position meant that, essentially, she was denied a legitimate identity as a citizen – 'the married mother had a husband to articulate her citizenship; a widowed woman drew her entitlement through her bereaved status; an unmarried mother was rendered voiceless' (Earner-Byrne 2007: 179).

Changing attitudes: Feminist movements and Church scandals

However, there are others, such as Roy Foster (2007), who challenge the assertions made by Inglis regarding the centrality of Catholicism in Irish society in the late twentieth century, stating that 'the notion of Catholicism as indivisible from Irish nationalism and even from Irish identity might be counted as one of the casualties of the last thirty years' cultural upheaval' (2007: 37). As the twentieth century progressed, it became clear that there was an increasing dissatisfaction with the moral structures operating in society, and while Catholicism remained important to many, the attitude of the Irish people in general, and women in particular, towards the institutional Church unarguably changed. This shift is evident throughout the interviews, particularly in the ways Magdalene survivors understand their experience of incarceration. As the twentieth century progressed, many of the women felt more able to speak about their experiences, gaining access to more hermeneutic tools outside a religious framework of meaning with which to understand the nature of their experiences. This reflected a broader change in attitudes towards women in general, and towards unmarried mothers in particular, as the twentieth century progressed. Hilliard (2004) suggests several factors at play regarding this change, but at the heart it is a shift in the location of authority, moving from relying on the institutional Church for interpretation of religious teaching to a more personalized individual faith. While there is no lessening in the seriousness with which religion and religious identity are considered, there has clearly been a shift in how this operates. In part, this is because towards the end of the twentieth-century, 'women gained access to other forms of capital and were less dependent on religious capital' (Inglis 2005: 66). However, it is also important to highlight the greater sexual and health education provided for women as a result of the growth of the women's movement in 1970, which campaigned for a change in Ireland around issues such as abortion, contraception and divorce. O'Donnell describes ideas of women's role in social life and the performance of sexuality as the 'occasion and venue where the voices of traditional and modern Ireland encountered and competed with each other' (2008: 11). This tension over the role of women, and the extent to which they can exert agency over their bodies, is still evident in contemporary Irish feminist movements, such as the recent 'Campaign to Repeal the Eighth Amendment'.[1]

The 1990s also witnessed a rapid succession of Church scandals, which undeniably led to a shift in the way the Irish people considered the position and authority of the Catholic Church. The shocking revelation in 1992 that Bishop

Eammon Casey had a secret family was followed by one sexual scandal after another, including a continuous stream of abuse allegations from young children against priests. These revelations persisted throughout the decade – in 1999, Father Seán Fortune was accused of the rape and sexual assault of twenty-nine boys. The effect of this decade of clerical abuse scandals on the position of the Catholic Church was stark. In 1990, around 85 per cent of Irish adults in the Republic attended weekly Mass, but by 1997, it is estimated that this had fallen to 65 per cent. There were 129 priests ordained in 1990; eight years later there were only forty-four ordinations with numbers continuing to fall, and in 1999 there was just one priest ordained in the Dublin diocese (Foster 2007: 57).

When considering the social landscape in which the laundries sit, it is vital to address the interactions between the Irish State and Church in twentieth-century Ireland, which resulted in the production of a particularly narrow conception of womanhood, and specifically motherhood. Gendered notions of morality and respectability, reinforced by Church power, created a situation in which those who transgressed these narrow conceptions needed to be controlled, both physically and in terms of their threatening identities. However, it is also evident that as the century progressed, attitudes towards the Church shifted as Irish society's relationship to Catholic systems of morality and meaning changed. The experiences of the Magdalene survivors should be situated within this shifting and contested context of attitudes towards women, towards unmarried mothers and reproductive health, to understand both the particular social identity which led to instances of epistemic injustice and the restrictive social context which contributed to instances of hermeneutic injustice. It is hard to say whether the changes in attitudes towards gendered identities filtered through to those still in the institutions, due to the lack of access to congregational archives, but for those who had left, the change provided them with new contexts in which they could find ways to understand their experiences and have their voices heard.

Conclusion

In this chapter, I have situated the experiences of women who were sent to Magdalene laundries within a framework of epistemic injustice, demonstrating the value of understanding the harms caused as distinctly epistemic in nature, as violence done to a subject in their capacity as a knowledge producer. A key claim of this chapter is that what Fricker describes as these everyday epistemic practices, the ways in which we convey knowledge to others, and make sense of our own social experience, are deeply enmeshed within this nationalist Catholic imaginary – in the particular way in which women's bodies were conceptualized as both deeply threatening to the newly formed Irish State, and as being vulnerable and in need of protection. In this way, religious carceral institutions such as the Magdalene laundries were able to thrive, acting as a way to both 'protect' and contain these unruly bodies. It is within this specific Irish Catholic imaginary that these questions of epistemic injustice should be considered. The particular social identity inscribed upon the women in this context positioned them as not only dangerous and vulnerable but, as a result, also unreliable. In this way, their voices and experiences could be ignored and erased. These questions of credibility, of silence and voice, spillover from the theoretical into the methodological, and in the next chapter, I turn to an exploration of how the oral history interviews allow for a meaningful engagement with these issues.

3

Silence, voice and the ethics of communication

Underpinning this book is an awareness of the ways in which everyday epistemic practices impact on identity formation, as well as the power inherent in how we communicate our experience and knowledge to others. In using an oral history archive – a form of communication in itself – the questions of silence and voice raised by this epistemic framework necessarily run throughout the work. In order to understand the methodologies employed, it is important to understand the resource upon which the work is founded. In this chapter, I will begin by introducing the archive upon which this work is based, before thinking further about the nature of oral history data as a resource for engaging with questions of subjectivities, agency and credibility. In doing so, I consider oral histories as instances of voice and silencing, as well as a method for asking questions about these issues. I demonstrate how my analysis of the data was both about the content of what was said and about how these narratives were constructed, the extent to which interviewees both spoke and did not speak. By engaging with the value of oral history interviews as narrative constructions of the self, I demonstrate the value they have for thinking through ideas of subjectivity formation and epistemic injustice. Finally, I will move on to a discussion of how I understand my practice as a researcher as an intervention into processes of narration and silence, considering issues of power and the ethics of representation in the research process. I will also think about the ethics of self-care, and the particular problems we face when doing sensitive and traumatic research. In paying close attention to these multifaceted expressions of silence and voice I work towards a methodology which makes space for survivors to be seen as credible producers of knowledge.

Understanding the archive: Oral history as a methodology

The term 'oral history' is used to refer to a wide range of resources – broadly, it is the recording of people's experiences, memories and thoughts, primarily through interviews. 'Oral history' can refer to the methodological practice of conducting and interpreting these interviews, or it can be used to define the result of this, the product of this process. While it can be useful to delineate the two, I will use the term to refer to both in this chapter. Oral history as a methodology is not a modern concept; Thompson (1988) provides a thorough overview of the premodern history of this practice, but it was not until the 1970s that the practice became firmly established in the academic historical community. However, this was not without challenges, and the methods and politics of oral history caused controversy throughout this decade (Summerfield 2004). Some saw oral history as deeply unreliable in comparison to traditional historical documentary; however, this attitude was strongly rejected by other social historians, who saw the value in oral history as methodology, particularly when engaging in research on traditionally underrepresented groups, such as women or people of colour (Thompson 1988, Lummis 1988). The cultural approach to oral history suggests that 'prevailing discursive constructions of the past "contaminate" memory, in the sense that they overlay it with later accounts and interpretations of the period of history to which a memory relates' (Thompson 1988: 66). When we engage in the act of remembering, we are distilling these memories through layers of other experiences, so that we can never simply recall something without it being influenced by prevailing dominant narratives and cultural influences. However, the idea that memory cannot be separated from external social experiences is not something which should be seen as a failing of the methodology; rather, it encourages researchers 'to understand not only the narrative offered, but also the meanings invested in it and their discursive origins' (Summerfield 2004: 67). Eva McMahan (2015: 2) echoes this cultural approach to oral history when she suggests we view oral history not as an exercise in fact-finding, but as an interpretive communicative event. When reading or listening to an oral history, the value is that it can tell us not only *what* may have happened, but *how* the interviewee experienced it, and the ways in which the event may have impacted on them and contributed to their personal narrative. During the oral history interview, the participants are 'actively coping with the communicative performance of self and other' (McMahan 2015: 2). When thinking about the value of oral histories as a resource for this project, I situate my work within this cultural approach. For the most part, I am not concerned with fact-finding, determining the veracity of the accounts of survivors to build a historical narrative of events. Instead, I see the oral history project as a way of investigating how the Magdalene survivors experienced their time in the laundries and how it impacted on their sense of selves, as well as the systems of meaning they drew upon to express and renegotiate their identities and experiences in later life. In his seminal oral history study, *The Death of Luigi Trastulli*, Alessandro Portelli writes that 'rather than replacing previous truths with alternative ones . . . oral history has made us uncomfortably aware of the elusive quality of historical truth itself' (1991: viii). This book does not aim to discover the 'truth' of the Magdalene laundries, as if there was one objective narrative of what happened, but, rather, aims to prioritize the narratives of those who were incarcerated, to produce a more complex account of both the experiences of those involved and the cultural position of the institutions in Irish society.

Knowledge production and the credible subject

This book works from an understanding of oral histories which asserts that they should not be treated simply as factual reconstructions of events, but as interpretive acts. However, a key claim of this book is that Magdalene survivors must be seen as reliable producers of knowledge on their own experiences, as communicated through these oral histories. What does it mean to be a 'reliable' producer of knowledge within this interpretive approach to oral history, and knowledge production itself? When we describe someone as credible, we imply that we consider them to have a good understanding of whatever it is that they are speaking on. We do not mean that all their memories are necessarily factually correct but, rather, that we *believe* the narrative they present, as a coherent description of the past or present. The factors which impact our understanding of a subject's credibility, or lack thereof, are hugely diverse, and rely on our own social identity as much as the speakers'. Our own gender, race and class background – all of the factors which mediate the way we see the world – impact upon the credibility we afford a speaker. Leigh Gilmore writes that 'each testimonial act follows in the wake of a long and invidious historical association of race and gender with lying that circulates to this day within legal courts and everyday practices of judgment, defining these locations as wilfully unknowing and hostile to complex accounts of harm' (2017: 2). Gilmore's work explores how 'women's witness is discredited by a host of means meant to *taint* it: to contaminate by doubt, stigmatize through association with gender and race, and dishonour through shame' (2017:2). To the categories of race and gender, I would add class – but this analogy of contagion is a useful way of thinking about how we dismiss someone as an unreliable knowledge producer. It is infrequently done all at once; rather, it is a slow process of attrition, a repetition of stereotypes again and again, until they become accepted 'facts'. Women are overly emotional, incapable of making objective decisions; working-class people are deceitful and should not be trusted – these are sticky judgements (Ahmed 2004) which are not easily washed away. Credibility then becomes linked not just to the veracity or coherence of someone's account but also to the social standing that is afforded to a speaker, the recognition of their identity as one which can be trusted.

What does it mean to assert that someone is a reliable knowledge producer? In making this statement, I do not assert that every claim made by Magdalene survivors in these interviews is true. Rather, it is an assertion that I approach these narratives with a fundamental belief that these women have the best overall understanding of their lives, of the ways in which their experiences have shaped them as people. It is a position which recognizes that believing someone, recognizing them as credible and reliable, extends beyond simply accepting what they say, but also actively working to create the conditions in which they can produce knowledge. I therefore ground my understanding of credibility in oral history narratives in the recognition that these conditions are not equal for all, that historically it has been much easier for some to speak on their experiences than others. This survivor-centred approach takes seriously the idea that if we wish to support people who have experienced trauma, we must do so on their terms, by creating space for their voices to be heard. In this book, then, I argue that under particular conditions, the oral history interview itself can be a means through which people who have experienced testimonial injustice can experience the opportunity to have their voices recognized as credible.

'Magdalene Institutions: Recording an Archival and Oral History'

The primary resources for this book are the oral histories from the project: 'Magdalene Institutions: Recording an Archival and Oral History', a Government of Ireland Collaborative Research Project, funded by the Irish Research Council. This was led by Dr Katherine O'Donnell at University College Dublin and conducted primarily between 2012 and 2013. The overall objective of this study was to contribute towards a better understanding of the Magdalene laundry system that existed in Ireland, through the gathering and study of testimonies from people who are directly or indirectly related to these institutions. The project aimed to interview survivors and their family members, religious sisters who worked at the Magdalene laundries, as well as visitors to those institutions and other key informants. Key informants referred to people who had some involvement in or interaction with the laundries, such as a doctor who visited, and someone who was employed as a maintenance man in the institution. I had access to eighty-one interviews in total. Of these, thirty-nine were taken from survivors, twenty-one from key informants, fourteen from relatives, three from activists and three from people designated as 'other'. In my analysis of the oral history archive, I was using both digital transcripts and audio files. I had access to twenty-one digital transcripts; at the time of writing, the remaining interviews are still being transcribed.

In March 2012, Dr Katherine O'Donnell, the principal investigator for 'Magdalene Institutions: Recording an Archival and Oral History', ran a pilot version of a project to collect oral histories of Magdalene women as a *Justice for Magdalenes* exercise which would record survivor testimony to submit to the IDC.[1] This was funded by the Feminist Review Trust. O'Donnell highlights how the questions moved from a focus on what would be important to know from a legal point of view to those which aimed to 'elicit life stories from the women'. She continues:

> In considering what questions to ask, I aimed to collect as full a life-story as possible. ... Early in the pilot phase ... I added closing questions that focused on the women's sense of accomplishment and pride, both to end the interview with a recollection of positive achievements and also to capture the remarkable generosity and resilience of these women. ... The aim was to capture as rich an experience as possible of the former Magdalene woman's life even if the central focus were the years of her incarceration. (2018a: 88–9)

This richness is one of the greatest strengths of the oral history archive. The interviews conducted with survivors make space for not only the narrative of their time in the laundries but also their early lives, their lives after the institutions, and the various ways in which these overlap and intersect. In doing so, the interviews allow for the women's experience of the Magdalene laundries to be situated within the wider context of their whole lives.

Throughout the book, I quote extensively from the interviews, particularly those taken with survivors. I have struggled with the best way to introduce the interviews in a way which also introduces the woman whose words I am using. I want to make clear the context for each interview with each woman, giving space for details of her life, and at the very least the details of her incarceration – how old she was when she first entered a laundry, which institution it was, how much time she spent there. However, to do this for each interview throughout the text would be impractical. I have therefore included a list of all the interviews from which I have quoted, giving more information about these relevant details when known, which can be found in Appendix B. Even this at times felt lacking – but there is no way that it would be possible to fully make the readers aware of the complexity of each woman's life, without exhorting them to read the whole interview. There are some interviews from which I quote much more than others; and many which I read, listened to and coded which do not appear in the final book. In part, this is due to the nature of oral history interviews – some are very long, containing detailed descriptions; others shorter, more tentative. Some women spoke more about parts of their life which this book did not focus on, and others went into much greater details about ideas and events which sit more firmly within the broader narrative of my work. I would like to stress that all the interviews were invaluable in allowing me to work towards a better and more nuanced understanding of the Magdalene institutions, whether they are directly quoted or not.

Finally, I wish to clarify the issue of referencing the interviews from the oral history archive. Because of the nature of the two forms of resource, my referencing style necessarily changes when quoting from a transcript, or an audio file. For transcripts, I use the page number (e.g. MAGOHP/4/ANON, Mary: 24). For audio files, I reference the timestamp when the quote begins (e.g. (MAGOHP/06, Patricia Dervan: tape 6, 00:09). For some interviews, there are multiple audio files, and I have made this clear by referring to tape 1, 2 and so on, as in the previous example.

Other sources: From State documents to personal interaction

Moving past the specific experiences of Magdalene survivors as told through the oral history interviews, this book also engages with instances of public voice on the institutions. In doing this, I focused on three key events – the creation and publication of the IDC report in 2013; the apology given by Taoiseach Enda Kenny shortly after this; and the *Dublin Honours Magdalenes* (DHM) event in June 2018. My analysis of these instances of public voice focused on exploring the ways in which they both addressed and maintained the processes of epistemic injustice as experienced by survivors. To do this, I drew on the oral history interviews with survivors, activists and family members, as well as the IDC report itself; the text and audio recording of Enda Kenny's speech; and finally, my own experiences of attending and volunteering at the DHM event.

The final instance of public voice addressed by this book was the DHM event, which took place in June 2018. This was the only event for which I could not use any data from oral history interviews. Instead, I drew on my own experiences and observation of the event, as a volunteer, note-taker and attendee. I made the decision to focus on four specific incidents from the two-day event, thinking through how I had experienced them, and then considering how they might have been experienced by the survivors in attendance. For three of these incidents, my conclusions on the latter question are necessarily vague – there was no way of asking the women who took part in the event for their thoughts on what was happening. I was there as a volunteer, not a researcher, and so my interactions with the women, the questions it would have been appropriate to ask, were necessarily limited. I could draw only on the brief conversations I had had with the women, and the rushed notes taken over the two days. However, a key aspect of the event which informed my analysis was the listening exercise, which took place on the afternoon of the second day. This was a group interview session, designed to facilitate a discussion between small groups of survivors, asking the question, 'what do you think people should know about the Magdalene laundries?' During this, I took notes, working alongside a facilitator, while also recording the voices of the women on my phone. It was a stressful process – the room was noisy; the women's voices were quiet; and I was unsure if the technology would work. Once we started, comprehensive note taking was almost impossible – the women spoke quickly, often two at a time, over each other, their words spilling out. I tried to keep up as best as I could but inevitably, I got drawn into their narrative, responding when they asked me questions, rather than staying silent and simply taking notes.

Some of them were very keen to make sure they were helpful – they asked us if they were answering the questions correctly, saying the right things. We tried to reassure them that there was no right answer – this was a chance for them to speak their mind, to say whatever they wanted to. The uncertainty in their voices mirrored some of the interviews, but as the exercise moved forward, most of the women in my group gained confidence in their words, the solidarity provided by proximity to others who shared their experiences evident in their increasing strength of conviction. This process, while difficult at times, both emotionally and practically, allowed me a level of engagement with the women which I had previously not encountered throughout the project. It gave me an opportunity to listen to them speak about their experiences directly, to hear them articulate their frustrations and their hopes. I had access to the final transcript from my group which provided a valuable resource in my analysis of the event, but it was the process of sitting and listening to the women speak which gave me a richer sense of their feelings and experiences of the event. This transcript will be made available to the public at a later date, and in quoting from it I am mindful of the dual role I occupied – both academic and volunteer – throughout the process.

Other sources

My analysis of the IDC report focused primarily on the ways in which the committee engaged with and presented survivor narratives, and what this tells us about how we are encouraged to think about the survivors. At over 1000 pages, the report is a lengthy resource, and it was not possible to conduct an in-depth analysis on the whole document within the confines of this project, although there is great scope for further research that addresses the document in this way. With this in mind, I chose to focus on particular sections, such as the chapter on living and working conditions, as a way of considering how the women's experiences are presented to the public. I looked at the physical space given to survivor testimony throughout the report, as well as the specific wording used when speaking about these voices. In doing so, I considered whose voices were being conceptualized as credible, whose narratives were given the space to be heard in a meaningful capacity and what this tells us about those which were not. The apology and statements from religious orders are significantly shorter resources than the IDC report, and therefore I was able to do a closer analysis of these texts, thinking not only about the specific words used, but also the imagery employed by the speakers and the forms of meaning these created.

Speech and silence in survivor narratives

This book works towards a methodology which takes seriously the idea that Magdalene survivors are credible producers of knowledge on their own experiences. Oral history as a methodology allows for a meaningful engagement with the voices of the survivors, and in this section, I further explore some of the theoretical concepts which underpin my approach to this style of research and analysis. Firstly, I think about how silence and voice is conceptualized in the context of the oral history interview, drawing on ideas of survivor testimony as a form of 'excluded speech' (Alcoff and Gray 1993). I then move on to a discussion of oral history and subjectivity, thinking of the interview as an event in which the respondent draws on her environment to construct particular identities.

The powers of silence and voice

The oral history interviews taken with women who spent time in a Magdalene institution are examples of survivor testimony. In describing them as such, I do not just mean that they are testimony from survivors. I use this term to describe their function, as well as the content. Alcoff and Gray describe how, 'in attempting to speak out, survivors must not only tell their story of abuse but counter the abuser's version that is typically normalized by dominant cultural narratives about victimhood, the family, and relationships between parents and children' (1993: 175). In a similar fashion, Zur highlights the extent to which survivor testimonies, and particularly the testimony of women and other marginalized groups, turn 'private thoughts into unobtrusive political acts. Whatever the person's intentions, these actions reinterpret the political domain and challenge the "natural order of things" proposed by State discourse in which the official historical past is a coherent, unified and self-explanatory narrative' (Zur 2004: 49). Survivor testimony is therefore by its nature political, pushing back against dominant narratives which shore up norms around acceptable identities. As Leydesdorff et al. highlight, 'speaking out – telling one's own story about the traumatic past – is both a personal necessity, and inescapably social in its significance' (2004: 11).

In thinking through my understandings of silence and voice, I draw extensively on work done by Linda Martín Alcoff and Laura Gray-Rosendale (previously known as Laura Gray) in their paper 'Survivor Discourse: Transgression or Recuperation', published in 1993. Writing in 2018, in an introduction to a chapter which represents a revision of this paper, Alcoff says that in this paper, she and Gray-Rosendale were 'speaking out publicly as survivors. This sort of activism felt quite at odds with the climate of postmodernism . . . where subjectivity was something to be deconstructed rather than expressed' (2018: 176). Alcoff discusses how, in the initial paper, they wished to create something which would work as a way to 'think through the relation between these theories and our activist practice', creating a 'mutual interrogation in which the theory itself would be put to a real world politics test' (2018:176). I was particularly drawn to this approach because of the balance between theoretical work and practical application, something which has been a constant concern of my work. In this section, I explore my understanding of silence and voice with reference to their writing, thinking through the ways in which theories of speech and silence work in the lives of survivors, and the implications this has for my methodological choices.

Alcoff and Gray, drawing on the work of Foucault, highlight two key points which appear at first to be contradictory: firstly, the idea that 'speech is not a medium or tool through which power struggles occur but itself an important site and object of conflict' (1993: 260). Secondly, they foreground the claim that

> Bringing things into the realm of discourse, as the confessional structures of the Church brought bodily pleasures into discourse and thus 'created' sexuality, is not always or even generally a progressive or liberatory strategy; indeed, it can contribute to our own subordination. (1993:260)

There is a tension, then, between the idea that movements for social change should focus on speech as a central locus of power, that 'the act of speaking out in and of itself transforms power relations and subjectivities, or the very way in which we experience and define ourselves' (1993:260); and the warning that by speaking out, necessarily bringing things into the realm of discourse, we help 'inscribe them into hegemonic structures and to produce docile, self-monitoring bodies who willingly submit themselves to (and thus help create and legitimate) the authority of experts' (1993:260). It is within this 'contradictory space', as Alcoff and Gray describe it, that I situate my understanding of speech and silencing, alongside an awareness of how the form of speech and context in which it is uttered impact upon the way in which power functions. Much of the discourse around voice and silence rests on the assumption that giving voice is inherently positive and silence/silencing is therefore inherently problematic. While there are many contexts in which these assumptions are valid, my work aims to further question these understandings of silence and voice, exploring the liberating potential for silence as well as its role in oppressive structures. In doing so, I work towards a more nuanced understanding of speech, contributing to a methodology which is equally sensitive to the possibility and value of silence in certain instances, as well as its oppressive function.

'Giving voice' as an act of liberation has a long history in feminist research, and there has been a strong focus on demanding the 'unseen and unacknowledged be made visible and heard' (Ryan-Flood and Gill 2010: 1). Early feminist work highlighted the importance of emphasizing women's voices, lives and narratives in history, writing their contributions into history:

> The very act of treating women's experiences as worthy of academic research was in itself a revolutionary concept in the face of much theory by the 'founding fathers' of social science and generations of empirical work that assumed male perspectives and experiences were universal. (Ryan-Flood and Gill 2010: 1)

In the context of trauma and survivor discourse, 'speaking out' has been adopted as a crucial part of the movement. Survivors are encouraged to disclose their trauma, either in public or in private, and 'the strategic metaphor of "breaking the silence is virtually ubiquitous throughout the movement"' (Alcoff and

Gray 1993: 261). Judith Herman discusses the power of speaking out in the introduction to her work, *Trauma and Recovery*, stating that 'remembering and telling the truth about terrible events are prerequisites both for the restoration of the social order and for the healing of individual victims' (1992:1). She recalls her work on abuse in the 1970s, describing how

> The speak outs of the women's liberation movement brought to public awareness the widespread crimes of violence against women. Victims who had been silenced began to reveal their secrets. . . . My first paper on incest, written with Lisa Hirschman in 1976, circulated 'underground', in manuscript, for a year before it was published. We began to receive letters from all over the country from women who had never before told their stories. Through them, we realized the power of speaking the unspeakable and witnessed first-hand the creative energy that is released when the barriers of denial and repression are lifted. (Herman 1992:2)

There is no doubt that this is a powerful mode of activism, with the potential for an intensely positive impact not only on an individual's understandings of their personal trauma but also on wider conceptions of social dynamics of abuse, the way in which it functions to keep survivors in a state of silence. However, Parpart makes the point that, although the willingness and ability to speak out and name oppressions and oppressors is a critical factor in challenging injustices and gendered power imbalances, 'the assumption that voice equals agency needs to be rethought' (Parpart 2010: 15). As Tanya Serisier highlights in her pioneering work on this topic, for survivors, 'speaking out' is an experience 'fraught with vulnerability and risk' (2018: 11). This is not to imply that speaking out is a 'wrong' way to go about activism, but to recognize that if we privilege voice over silence as the pinnacle of empowered agency, we risk ignoring the transformative potential of a complex mix of choices (Parpart 2010: 25).

Sara Ahmed writes:

> Sometimes silence can be a tool of oppression; when you are silenced, whether by explicit force or by persuasion, it is not simply that you do not speak but that you are barred from participation in a conversation which nevertheless involves you. Sometimes silence is a strategic response to oppression; one that allows subjects to persist in their own way; one that acknowledges that, under certain circumstances, speech might not be empowering, let alone sensible. (2010: xvi)

Here, she makes the distinction between the process of choosing to be silent, and the process of being silenced, being prevented from participation in a discourse.

Therefore, it is vital to interrogate the reasons for a person's silence, the context in which their words are (not) being uttered. We must ask similar questions about speech as well – to whom are they speaking, and where is the locus of power in the interaction? In working with survivor narratives, we must pay close attention to the conditions of speaking, to look at where 'the incitement to speak originates, what relations of power and domination may exist between those who incite and those who are asked to speak, as well as to whom the disclosure is directed' (Alcoff and Grey 1993: 284). Within the specific context of the Magdalene laundries, O'Mahoney makes the point that we can consider the silence of survivors 'from a personal, cognitive level (as a form of survival for the survivor) as well as in terms of broader societal processes, which encourage survivors of trauma to stay silent around topics that are prohibited from being discussed openly in society' (2018: 463). In carefully thinking through these various understandings of silence and voice, I work towards a methodology which takes notice of these relations of power, in order to reflect on how framing these within the context of epistemic injustice helps one to better understand the complex nature of the harms done.

Oral history and subjectivity

This book posits the oral history interview as an event in which these relations of power can be explored, specifically in the context of the production of a credible self. Skeggs writes that 'access to the self is limited by the means and techniques of telling and knowing' (2004: 124). For a project which draws extensively on oral histories, these techniques must be thought about not only in a theoretical context but also as part of an exploration of methodology. In what way can we understand the oral history interview as a 'technique of telling', and how does it present the subject with access to the self? Through processes of speaking and being listened to, we present ourselves and are understood in particular ways. The social position, identities and roles of the speakers and hearers will all contribute to the power relationships involved in any speech act, and so it is important to consider the various configurations of speakers and hearers involved in any particular context. Abrams describes the oral history interview process as such that, 'in an interaction with the interviewer . . . the respondent actively fashions an identity' (2010: 33). In this section, I explore the production of self and knowledge through these processes, and how they overlap with questions of credibility. I also question the impact of speaking out and the significance of articulating experience for the recognition of the self, and how the perception of speaker credibility by social audiences plays into this process. Abrams writes that

> Decades of oral history practice have taught us that interrogation of an individual's life history does much more than offer us empirical evidence about past events. The telling of a life story is a complex narrative performance which requires attention to the use of language, the deployment of narrative structure, the articulation of memory, the context in which the life is narrated; in other words, all the devices by which a person represents the self in oral fashion. (2010: 34)

Examining questions of subjectivity in oral history methodology requires us to consider the interview not simply as a vehicle for information-gathering, but as a process which facilitates the telling of memory stories. This allows for a wider understanding of how oral history projects can be part of a bigger agenda, 'that of liberating voices and validating experiences and understanding how people construct retrospective versions of their lives' (Abrams 2010: 63).

Building on these ideas surrounding the importance of articulation of experience, it is also useful to think about the significance of having these accounts publicly recognized as credible as part of the process of self-formation. It is not enough that we are able to articulate our experiences, although this is important; we must be visible and credible to those we are speaking to. In a keynote speech written for International Women's Day in 2016, feminist philosopher Pamela Anderson (2016) said that 'the vulnerability of a (woman) speaker follows from her dependence upon an audience; if she is to be heard, her dependence requires an audience who is both willing and capable of hearing her as a speaker and a knower'. She quotes Jennifer Hornsby (1995), who explains the function of reciprocity between speaker and audience in her essay, 'Disempowered Speech'. Hornsby writes, 'the existence of reciprocity is actually a perfectly ordinary fact, consisting in speakers being able not only to voice meaningful thoughts but also to be heard' (Hornsby 1995: 134). What does it mean to be 'heard', meaningfully, in this context? It is not just the act of having someone hear your words in a physical sense, although being given the platform in which to speak about one's experience can be an important first step. However, it is also being afforded credibility when speaking, trusted as a knowledge producer, being viewed as a subject with epistemic value. The absence of these conditions in the social experiences of Magdalene survivors is a fundamental claim made by this book, and therefore any methodology that wishes to engage with the epistemic harms inflicted on these women must think through the various functions of silence and voice. This brings us back to the conclusions drawn by Alcoff and Gray (1993) – it is not just the act of speaking out but also the conditions of speech, which impact upon the formation of subjectivity in these contexts. These conditions of speech, and the power dynamics inherent within them, remain at the forefront of the methodology for this book, particularly when considering the wider questions of epistemic injustice which I turn to in subsequent chapters.

As previously discussed, this book considers the oral history interview as an interpretive event, in which people who have experienced testimonial injustice may have the opportunity to have their voices recognized as credible. It is a format in which they can be positioned as reliable producers of knowledge, a chance for the interviewer, and those doing secondary analysis on the interviews, to create a space in which their voices can be heard in a meaningful capacity. The oral history interview becomes a way in which people may be able to speak out, but it also can be a space in which they struggle to speak, or struggle to overcome entrenched silences and instances of epistemic injustice in relation to past experiences of abuse. In this way, patterns of speech and silence themselves become a form of data, as much as the content of the speech itself. In paying close attention to these patterns throughout the process of listening to the interviews, I aim for an understanding of how epistemic injustice is produced and addressed which does not rely simply on what is being said or not said but also on the contexts in which these utterances or silences occur.

Power dynamics in the research process: From interview to analysis

When thinking through these theoretical understandings of silence and voice, I wish to stress that it is not just the silences and voices of the interviewees which emerge as concerns for this project. The impact of my own voice, and my own silences, are also significant. Finally then, I turn to ethical questions which underpin this work, thinking through questions of power in the research process, and how we as researchers can attempt to navigate these, particularly when doing work on survivor narratives. I also want to think about the questions faced by researchers doing work which deals heavily with traumatic narratives, the impact on the researcher and the importance of attention to the ethics of self-care.

Since this project involved secondary analysis of interviews which had already been conducted, issues of informed consent and avoidance of harm in the interview process itself did not manifest in the same way they would have done had I been conducting the interviews myself. However, I do wish to highlight the ways in which these ethical issues were addressed in the original recording of the interviews, which laid a foundation for the ethical stance of the project. Everyone who participated in the oral history project had consented to do so and had consented to have their words put in the public domain, to an agreed upon extent. Most interviewees use pseudonyms. At the start of the interviews, participants were asked to confirm if they understood the consent process. An example of a typical exchange between interviewer and interviewee might be as follows:

> **SP** So I just want to ask Mary, if you consent to participate . . . that I just want to confirm that you agree to participate in this interview voluntarily and that you are familiar with the information and consent forms.
>
> **M** Yeah I am.
>
> (O'Donnell, K., Pembroke, S. and McGettrick, C., 'An Oral History of Mary', MAGOHP/4/ANON, 2013: 1 [hereafter MAGOHP/4/ANON, Mary])

These exchanges were generally fairly short – participants had clearly been given information before the interview regarding the future use of their interviews and most of the more in-depth discussion was not recorded. However, there were a few interviews in which extended examples of this process can be seen. For example, at the start of the interview with Bridget O'Donnell (O'Donnell, K., Pembroke, S. and McGettrick, C., 'An Oral History of Bridget O'Donnell', MAGOHP/45/ANON, 2013: tape 1 [hereafter MAGOHP/45/ANON, Bridget O'Donnell]), the discussion regarding release of material lasts about eight minutes. The discussion is allowed to unfold; she is not rushed in her verbal working through of the significance of her decision.

Moving beyond the interview process itself, I also wish to consider the specific ethical implications of working with survivor narratives as a researcher. Thinking through my research practice as an intervention into processes of narration and silence opens up broader questions about power and ethics in the research, some of which are echoed in the interviews themselves. Towards the end of her interview, Samantha Long, whose mother spent time in a Magdalene laundry, speaks about her anxieties around co-opting her mother's story:

> I suppose ever since I processed all the information over the years, it has been a huge part of my identity, but I don't like talking about it out loud all the time,

because it was her pain not my pain, although her pain has translated to me as you can hear from my words, I think. I'm always conscious of not taking advantage of her story because it's her story, but the reason I'm speaking is because she can't speak. I'm speaking for her and I know she'd be very happy for me to do that.
(O'Donnell, K., Pembroke, S. and McGettrick, C., 'An Oral History of Samantha Long', MAGOHP/74 2013: tape 3, 23:42 [hereafter MAGOHP/74, Samantha Long])

As an academic researcher whose work draws on narratives of trauma from survivors of institutional abuse, I am cautious of 'taking advantage' of these narratives, misrepresenting their words through the lens of my own identity and experience. I do not understand this project as an attempt to 'give voice' to a group who have suffered the effects of institutional silencing, but to emphasize the importance of listening to and giving credibility to their *existing* voices. It is important to draw attention to the epistemic harms which have prevented them from being seen as valid producers of knowledge, and in doing so, work towards creating the conditions in which their voices can be heard and believed. However, this necessarily entails interpretation and analysis of their narratives, and so the question emerges as to how it can be ensured that this intervention is done with as much attention to implicit power relations as possible. Riessman highlights the need to ask of our research: 'whose voice is represented in the final product? How open is the text to other readings? How are we situated in the personal narratives we collect and analyse?' (1993: 61). The difficulty then becomes how to balance my voice as researcher with the voices of my research subjects. The aim of the project is obviously not just to reproduce their voices with no analysis, but equally, not to overshadow their narratives. Hollway and Jefferson ask us to consider: 'what do you, the researcher, assume about a person's capacity to know, remember and tell about themselves?' (2013: 1). When we hear someone speak, or read their testimony, we make assumptions based on what we *think* we know about the subject. These assumptions will frequently be gendered, classed and racialized, and will also depend on the nature of what we are reading or hearing. Therefore, when working with testimony from people who are frequently coded as unreliable narrators, who have been repeatedly denied credibility in their narratives, it is particularly important to examine these assumptions, and consider how they impact on the ways in which we engage with their narratives.

Hollway and Jefferson highlight that

> Treating people's own accounts as unproblematic flies in the face of what is known about people's less clear-cut, more confused and contradictory relationship to knowing and telling about themselves. In everyday, informal dealings with each

other, we do not take each other's accounts at face value, unless we are totally naïve. (2013: 3)

As discussed previously in this chapter, I do not see this approach as naïve; rather, I think that accepting these accounts 'at face value' helps to build a more nuanced and complex understanding of the nature of the interviewees' experiences. By accepting their accounts in this way, I provide a space within my work for their words to speak for themselves. Instead of trying to solve ethical issues around power dynamics in the research process, I argue it is more important to remain aware of them throughout the work, remaining open and engaged with the impact they have, occupying a position of conscious and mindful reflexivity. In addition, I suggest that Fricker's concept of testimonial virtue as a methodological tool has value as a way of addressing some of the epistemic issues at stake. To cultivate this virtue, the hearer must 'be alert to the impact not only of the speaker's social identity but also the impact of their *own* social identity on their credibility judgment' (Fricker 2007: 91). In the context of analysis and research, it is important to employ this alertness to try and work towards a reflexive knowledge production. In my research practice, this involved a continual (re)evaluation of my own identity and positionality in this project, particularly recognizing when it was productive to dwell on the impact this had in the work, as well as when it was not. Often, this coalesced around my affective experience of the work, and so I will now turn to a discussion of emotionality in my research, and the impact this had in both personal and academic contexts.

Ethical care for the self: Doing traumatic research

As someone working in the field of what is frequently termed 'sensitive research', I have found myself writing extensively about the particular issues which arose as a direct result of the nature of the archive. Throughout the research, reading the transcripts and listening to the audio of the interviews was an incredibly difficult process. The interviews frequently reference domestic and intimate partner violence; child abuse; and sexual, physical and psychological abuse. They affected me in a very visceral way – visibly and immediately – as well as in the context of my broader emotional state. The issues faced by qualitative researchers doing sensitive research are not new, but it is only recently that significant attention has been paid to the emotional impact of this type of work. Work done by Campbell (2002), Johnson and Clarke (2003) and Dickson-Swift et al. (2008) has emphasized the value of paying attention to the ways in which doing traumatic research affects the research process, but many people engaged in this still struggle with a complex array of feelings, and lack the necessary coherent practical support. While this is not a primary aim of the book, I believe that attention to the ethics of self-care, particularly when doing research around trauma, is a necessary part of the work. My methodology aims to take seriously these ethics of self-care, and in doing so, contribute to discussions about the role emotionality plays in research, how it impacts upon the work and the researcher, and how it can be managed in a way which allows it to be a productive part of a research practice. From the start of this project, I was aware that this would be an emotionally difficult process. In this section, I will discuss how I understand the more personal emotional aspect of this work, as well as the importance of engaging with the affective nature of doing traumatic research. I also suggest strategies for managing the difficulties of work such as this.

I struggled with the emotional content of the interviews from the beginning of the analytic process. As I began to read the interview transcripts, the idea of the Magdalene institutions as traumatic spaces became more focused, presented in the lives of individuals rather than as wider social phenomenon. Women's names and experiences fused together in my mind to paint distinct portraits of those involved, and the temporal realities of the ongoing abuse became starkly apparent. However, the reactions I was having to the written material were manageable – I had experience of reading traumatic material, and I made sure the pace of my work was such that I could take breaks when I needed. As to be expected, the more I read and re-read the transcripts I had initial access to, the less immediate emotional impact they had. As I moved forward with the project, I – naively – assumed that I had done most of the difficult emotional work at the start of this process. I now knew what to expect from an interview, the kind of content which might be distressing, and I saw myself as more prepared for the difficult task of listening to the narratives. However, as I began to listen to the audio files, I realized that this would be significantly more difficult than reading the transcripts. In the following sections, I focus on two distinct affective responses I had – anger and grief. Both of these responses resulted in feelings of deep shame at the levels of emotion I was experiencing, and towards the end of this section I address the ways in which this gendered shame manifested itself in my research process.

Anger and disruption

When I began working with the audio recordings of the interviews, one of the most difficult things to manage was the level of uncertainty in the work. Before listening to a particular audio file, I had no information about the nature of the interview except for the name of the interviewee, and whether they were a survivor, a relative and so on. Therefore, there was no way to do any specific emotional preparation for particularly distressing topics, no way to manage the ongoing impact of the work by alternating the more traumatic interviews with those which did not touch on difficult issues. I initially assumed that interviews from survivors would be the most taxing, because they would be direct narratives of abuse and trauma. However, while these interviews were very hard to read and listen to, those which produced the most intense reactions were often with relatives of survivors and key informants, in part because they provoked different and less expected emotions in me, which I had not prepared for.

Throughout the process of interview analysis, I expected to feel a certain level of sadness and grief and I address the ways in which this impacted the work in the next section. However, I also often experienced waves of anger, sometimes to a level which made me feel deeply uncomfortable. My anger usually followed one of two directions. Unsurprisingly, I frequently felt a generalized anger at the existence of the Magdalene laundries. This usually overlapped with feelings of grief, and was sometimes impossible to separate – while difficult, this was manageable, as not only did I expect to feel this way, I could also share these feelings easily. Anyone to whom I spoke about the work sympathized, and therefore I felt less shame around this reaction. However, at times, I found myself feeling anger *towards* the interviewees, and it was this emotional reaction I found significantly more difficult to manage, resulting in a more fractured process of analysis. There were times when I felt unable to continue because of the level of anger I felt, and I found it necessary to stop working and spend time processing my own feelings, exploring where these came from and what they could tell me about my place in the research. I often felt deeply uncomfortable with this reaction – I was ashamed at not being able to approach the material from a more 'objective' standpoint.

One of the most striking examples of this can be seen in my reaction to the interview with PJ Coogan (O'Donnell, K., Pembroke, S. and McGettrick, C., 'An Oral History of PJ Coogan', MAGOHP/68, 2013 [hereafter MAGOHP/68, PJ Coogan]). Coogan is a journalist who became involved in issues around adoption in the mid-1990s, which led him to start engaging with the Magdalene institutions. He reviewed the film, *The Magdalene Sisters,* and took an interest in the subject as a journalist after that. Halfway through the interview, Coogan tells the (younger, female) interviewee that she is, in fact, using the tape recorder the wrong way. While this may have been a well-intentioned piece of advice, I cannot deny that it stuck in my head while listening to the audio file. The first file ends just as he says this, and a new file begins – we never hear the interviewer's reaction to this comment, and the new file starts with her laughing politely. Hearing this distinctly masculine piece of unsolicited advice, and the all-too-familiar tone of the interviewer, set the tone for some of his next comments and undoubtedly contributed to the anger this interview prompted in me.

Coogan's father was a Garda, who remembers being called by the nuns to deal with 'runaway' women from the laundry in the late 1960s and early 1970s. Coogan speaks at length about this, positioning the Gardaí as compassionate actors who were put in a difficult situation, but ultimately, had to do their job:

> I don't think any Gardaí ever brought a woman back willingly, but many of them did it because they had to. (MAGOHP/68, PJ Coogan: tape 2, 14:55)

> I think there was a knowledge, particularly in the experienced Gardaí, that something behind those walls wasn't right. But there was also a duty that if, that the girls had to be brought back if they were caught. (MAGOHP/68, PJ Coogan: tape 2, 16:37)

> He [Coogan's father] doesn't feel good about doing it, but at the time he was doing his duty, and I know that it would trouble him deeply to think that he ever brought a girl back to face physical abuse or violence of any kind. I think deep down he knows that it probably happened, he hopes that it didn't, but I think deep down he knows that it did. I don't know much about whether there was a lot of brutality in the Good Shepherd, I know some places were terrible. From what I know, there wasn't a lot of physical brutality in the Good Shepherd. (MAGOHP/68, PJ Coogan: tape 2, 19:04)

After listening to these excerpts, which all occur in the space of about five minutes, I had to stop the interview, and stop work for the day. I remember feeling hot waves of anger at the sentiments expressed here, at the attempt to induce sympathy for his father and the idea that while his father 'didn't feel good' about what he did, he still returned women to an abusive environment out of obligation to his job.

They do not read as particularly shocking, now that I have some distance from them. However, in order to understand my intense response, it is important to position this in the wider social context of my work, and the events which surrounded me as I did the research. I listened to this interview on 17 October 2017, at the height of the sexual abuse scandals in the media which led to the #MeToo movement. Personal accounts from survivors of sexual trauma were unavoidable if you spent any time on the internet or read a newspaper. In this context, listening to Coogan defend his father's actions in returning women to

Magdalene institutions, because of 'law' and 'duty', was extremely challenging. For the previous few weeks I had been faced with a constant wave of men avoiding responsibility for their actions and eliding those of others, cover-ups upon cover-ups and outpourings of male guilt just slightly too late to make a material difference. I felt angry, and I had no sympathy for either Coogan or his father – What difference does it make that he didn't 'feel good' about what he was doing, when the end result was the same? Coogan describes his father as being in an impossible position – but I struggled to find sympathy for him when his actions resulted in the continued incarceration and abuse of women. Coogan tries to mitigate the situation by suggesting that the particular institution his father would have been returning women to was not as brutal as others, but this framing of physical abuse as occurring only in the context of beatings or violence from the nuns is one I find troubling. As this book demonstrates, the very nature of the laundries constitutes physical abuse – being forced to do intense and dangerous unpaid manual labour is in itself physical abuse and had long-term effects on the women's bodies. To say otherwise demonstrates an underlying understanding of violence which fundamentally erases much of the trauma experienced by the women.

While it is important for me to hold my reactions as legitimate and valid for the sake of mental well-being, it is crucial to investigate them rigorously in the context of this project, and to think about why I had such a strong, disruptive and deeply unsympathetic, emotional response. Working towards a reflexive knowledge production means being aware of the external factors which influence my understanding of an interview, as well as the influence of my own specific social identity. As highlighted earlier, the wider discussions around responsibility for abuse which were taking place in the media played a big part in my response to this interview. However, Coogan's description of his father's job and related feelings on this play into wider questions about the responsibility individuals have towards care for vulnerable community members, as well as the responsibility the State has for this. In many of the interviews with key informants, we hear assertions that the laundries were hidden away, that members of the public were not aware of what was happening, the implication being that if they *had* known about these places, if they had known what was happening there, something would have been done. Here, we can clearly see that the Garda's duty to his job, to the State and to the Catholic Church was placed above the desire to stop abuse against women and girls. This gives great insight into the social priorities of Ireland even in the 1970s. It is this stark rendering of the public's knowledge and subsequent disinterest in the Magdalene institutions, with weak lip service paid to 'duty' which, I feel, caused such an intense reaction in me.

The second example of this type of affective response comes from an interview taken from Bridget Flynn, who visited the laundries in the early to mid-1990s. In this decade, the women with whom she engaged were likely to have been in the laundries for many years, and so would have been older. She says:

> I remember one day talking to one of the women, she was remembering the day that she had come into the laundry, and she said the date and the year, and I said to her, oh gosh, you've got a great memory, oh, that's really good. And she just said, 'why wouldn't I, it was my eighteenth birthday'.
> (O'Donnell, K., Pembroke, S. and McGettrick, C., 'An Oral History of Bridget Flynn', MAGOHP/17, 2013: 12.07 [hereafter MAGOHP/17, Bridget Flynn])

I found this passage incredibly distressing and, as with the interview with PJ Coogan, had to stop listening and pause the interview for a while. However, the interviewee's voice barely changes, and she continues speaking with almost no hesitation. I felt an overwhelming grief which moved me to tears, but this shifted rapidly into an anger at the *lack* of emotional reaction from the interviewee. When I later tried to think about this incident, and process my reaction, there are two things which I see as contributing to my reaction. Firstly, the content of the statement itself, and the temporal reality it conjures. The fact that some women spent their entire adult lives in the Magdalene laundries is something that I 'knew', theoretically, but having it explicated in this way made evident the horror of the situation in a very immediate way. Secondly, the tone of voice taken by the interviewee made a deep impact on me. Clearly, I felt this should have been something she 'cared' more about – something which, like me, 'should' have caused her to stop and reflect on the fact that this woman had spent *her entire life* in an institution.

In both of these examples, I believe that I would not have had the reactions I did if I had simply read the transcripts, without listening to the audio files. It was the tone of both of the interviewees, far more than the words, which struck me, and provoked strong reactions of anger and sadness. It is also worth noting that in both of the examples, it is the *absence* of the emotion I *expected* to hear in their voices which I found troubling. I wanted them to feel the same as me, and to express that feeling in a way which I could identify. With this in mind, it is important to note that I have no idea what this Bridget Flynn thought about this exchange. All I have is the way she decided to speak about it at this particular time, in this particular interview. Similarly, it is understandable that Coogan wants to paint his father in a sympathetic light – it is evident he is working through his thoughts on this and should not be expected to instantly be able to separate a desire to present one's family in a positive light from a wider commentary on state responsibility. Listening to these passages was a difficult process, as was managing my subsequent reactions. However, by paying close attention to these reactions, rather than ignoring the affective responses they produced, I was able to confront the extent to which my own personal politics, and the social context in which I exist, impacted on my research. Before discussing *why* this attention to affective responses is so valuable, I address my feelings of sadness and shame, considering the specific impact they had on how I worked.

Tears and shame

While the anger I felt towards the work was perhaps a more difficult response to manage, my overwhelming emotional reaction to reading and listening to the narratives was one of deep sadness. The emotional impact of this was a significant part of how I experienced the process of the work; however, in this context my primary focus is on the somatic, rather than psychological, reactions. This was most evident in a physical manifestation of sadness – crying. My experience of crying in the context of listening to these interviews was extremely different to that caused by personal sadness. Rather, it was frequently an uncontrolled physical reaction to hearing the traumatic narratives of the women. Often, I would not realize I had started crying until I noticed tears falling. Whenever this happened, I noticed an immediate impulse in myself to hide this reaction, particularly if I was in a public space such as a library. I, and I suspect many others, shy away from showing vulnerability in an academic setting, with good reason. In an essay on vulnerability and compromise in feminist research, Griffin writes that

> After all, as researchers we are either learning the trade of how to conduct research, or once trained and in possession of our PhD, we are meant to exercise our trade, conduct research, as masters, or should I say mistresses, of what we do. There is therefore not much room for vulnerability, and, in so far as we show it, or it is attributed to us, we make ourselves vulnerable not only within our research but also within our profession. (2012:333)

Throughout the process of listening to the interviews, I felt, and continue to feel, a sense of guilt and embarrassment at my 'overly emotional' reactions, at my vulnerability. Both my anger and my sadness have at times felt deeply inappropriate. My reaction to the work, especially the reaction of tears, feels self-indulgent, unhelpful and, above all, shameful. This is not an isolated feeling; Drozdzewski and Dominey-Howes (2015) explore this response at length as part of a special issue on the impact of traumatic content on the researcher. Drawing on work by Cameron et al. (2009: 272) and Lorimer (2003), they highlight the ways that expression of emotion in research has not only been silenced and ignored, but also sometimes penalized. They suggest that 'this omission may be because often we do not have the time to insert ourselves into our own research practice but more likely is that we are taught firstly to think about our participants and that such self-reflection might seem indulgent' (Drozdzewski and Dominey-Howes 2015: 17). While Drozdzewski and Dominey-Howes are working primarily within the field of geographical research, the concepts and experiences they discuss are easily transferred into other disciplines in which we come into contact with traumatic spaces and stories.

What is it about caring for our own mental and emotional health as researchers working with traumatic narratives, thinking of ourselves as subjects within the work we do worthy of consideration, that is 'self-indulgent'? Ethics and care for our participants is such an integral part of our research, but if we do not also care for ourselves in the process, can we perform the appropriate duty of care for those whose stories we are responsible for? There is a risk that the listener becomes a receptacle for the emotional material, constantly repressing the effects it has on her own self with serious consequences for mental and emotional health, a process often referred to as 'vicarious trauma'. O'Donnell articulates her concerns around this in a discussion of the process of collecting the oral histories, asking, 'if I could not stay healthy, how was I going to be able to do the necessary work?' (2018a: 89) While my proximity to these traumatic narratives was significantly less than that of the interviewers, the effort of attempting to hide my feelings due to the shame I felt was visibly disruptive to the flow of work. It made the process of listening to some of the interviews fractured and slow. It is, unsurprisingly, very difficult to write, code interviews or even continue to listen to them, while also attempting to stem the flow of tears. The nature of the interviews had an impact on places I chose to work in – I found myself working from home more frequently, working in isolation, so that if I did have this reaction, I would not have to explain it to my colleagues or hide it from strangers. Ironically, this meant that I was moving away from structures of support which are vital for dealing with work of this type, working less frequently in groups or with friends. My shame around my feelings caused me to isolate myself, and as a result, I had no one to discuss the shame with, no one who could reassure me that these feelings were normal and reflected the deep level of involvement I was feeling towards the project.

Rosalind Gill discusses similar feelings, writing that

> This individualizing discourse devours us like a flesh-eating bacterium, producing its own toxic waste – shame: I'm a fraud, I'm useless, I'm nothing. It is (of course) deeply gendered, racialised and classed, connected to biographies that produce very different degrees of 'entitlement' (or not). This affective response is in turn profoundly silencing and isolating – and how could it be otherwise; we don't want to 'show' our ugly failure, any more than it might already be evident, so we are careful about who we tell of our rejection. (2010: 240)

As I thought more about traumatic research as a category, the importance of being open about the intensity of my thoughts and feelings became increasingly clear. On a writing retreat I attended where I wrote extensively about the process of listening to the interviews, I deliberately discussed the nature of my research with the other writers in advance, letting them know that I might be upset throughout the weekend. By doing this, I was able to tell them what kind of support would be useful – I therefore did not feel I had to suppress emotional reactions and if I did have them, I felt supported and able to manage them far more effectively than when I was working alone. The retreat had a strong focus on mutual support, attempting to create a space where we could freely discuss things like this; the experience of being in an environment like that was incredibly beneficial and has allowed me to focus on ways to navigate this work in a more sustainable way.

These questions are also deeply gendered. There is undeniable pressure on women to try and diminish or obscure the personal emotional impact of the work we are doing, in order to try and maintain the image of the 'objective researcher', for fear of being dismissed as 'oversensitive', itself a hugely gendered term. But what does this achieve? Is there an expectation that as (female) researchers, we should simply engage in the necessary emotional labour of managing this vicarious trauma ourselves without letting it affect our work, the underlying assumption being that all these feelings would make us incapable of clear and analytical thought? In the introduction to her work, *The Cultural Politics of Emotion*, Sara Ahmed writes:

> It is significant that the word 'passion' and the word 'passive' share the same root in the Latin word for 'suffering' (*passio*) . . . the association between passion and passivity is instructive. It works as a reminder of how 'emotion' has been

viewed as 'beneath' the faculties of thought and reason. To be emotional is to have one's judgment affected, it is to be reactive rather than active, dependent rather than autonomous. Feminist philosophers have also shown us how the subordination of emotions also works to subordinate the feminine and the body ... emotions are associated with women, who are represented as 'closer' to nature, ruled by appetite, and less able to transcend the body through thought, will and judgment. (2004: 3)

How can we begin to move past this disinclination to address emotionality in research? Echoing the suggestions of Drozdzewski and Dominey-Howe, I would turn towards Bondi's argument for the emotion we feel in our work to be treated as a 'relational, connective medium in which research, researchers and research subjects are necessarily immersed' (Bondi 2005: 433). We cannot avoid this; if we are doing research with people, intense emotions are an inherent part of their narratives and life experiences. It is a mistake to imagine that letting emotion and feeling into our work, letting it shape *how* we work and *what* we produce, will only result in less effective research.

Instead, it is more useful to focus on developing methodologies that embrace these affective responses, which allow us to manage these emotions in a way which is sustainable for our mental and emotional health, as well as being positive and productive in a research capacity. What does it mean to think of emotion as 'a relational, connective medium'? How can this help us to place ourselves within the work, without letting it overwhelm us? What conceptual frameworks can we use to make sense of these emotions in the context of academic research, making it a useful and productive part of our work? Speaking of her own experiences of the process of interviewing the Magdalene survivors, O'Donnell describes feelings of confusion, grief and horror, alongside a sense of discomfort with her own ignorance. 'After all', she writes, 'I turned 30 years of age just months after the closure of the last Magdalene institution in Dublin, but never noticed that event. I needed to face the structure of my ignorance and the complicity of this ignorance in my unawareness' (O'Donnell 2018a: 91). It was only by bringing a 'curious attention' to these feelings that she was able to have the affective response which allowed for a deeper understanding of her own positionality in the interview process, particularly her feelings of complicity in a culture which allowed the Magdalene laundries to flourish.

O'Donnell describes bringing what she calls a 'reparative' awareness to the process as a way of navigating the feelings she was experiencing. Drawing on the work of Eve Kosofsky Sedgwick (2003), O'Donnell describes a 'reparative reading' as one which

Places an accent on noticing what is immediately present, on being affected, on taking joy in an ability to be affected and be partial. A 'reparative reading' seeks to incorporate the contagion of emotion, by acknowledging feelings and their somatic impact. Such a reading feeds theories that are rich in description and attentive in local and minute ways. It enables us to work towards representing the felt affect and construing knowledge that is informed by considering the emotions. (O'Donnell 2018a: 92)

It is by seriously acknowledging these moments of profound emotionality, of anger and sadness and shame, that we can begin to cultivate sustainable methodologies for doing work of this kind. These moments force us to confront our prejudices and the impact of our social identities on our work; they reflect the way in which research spills over into our personal lives, and vice versa. As O'Donnell and Sedgwick demonstrate through the methodology of 'reparative reading', acknowledging the affective dimension of work leads to research which can sit with these feelings, and use them in a productive and positive way.

Conclusion

In this chapter, I introduced the oral history archive upon which this project is based, thinking about oral history as a methodology as well as the specifics of the archive. I considered the ways in which this particular methodology creates space for nuanced engagement with questions of credibility and knowledge production which lie at the heart of this book. Specifically, I suggested that the oral history interview can be a means through which people can experience the opportunity to have their voices recognized as reliable, to be meaningfully heard as credible knowledge producers. I considered the theoretical underpinnings of this methodology, thinking through questions of silence and voice, and how both of these processes can bring forth particular types of subjectivity. In doing so, I work towards an understanding of silence which moves past a simple binary between speaking out and staying silent, making space for a broader understanding of the power structures within which these processes are situated. This book is concerned with questions of epistemic injustice – how it is produced and maintained in the lives of survivors, and the way in which the harms caused have prevented survivors from being seen as credible producers of knowledge. In order to focus on these epistemic practices of communication, it is necessary to focus on the nature of the communication itself. Research is itself a communication style, an epistemic practice, and so when considering the manner of the research itself, we must necessarily think about the issues of knowledge production, of silence and voice, which are created by the practice of *doing* the research. As highlighted in the previous section, O'Donnell has articulated how, after a period of intense emotional discomfort brought about by the process of interviewing Magdalene survivors, she had a realization about the need to understand her own positionality and complicity within the work. 'Simultaneously', she writes, 'I changed my focus in approaching the Magdalene women and began to regard them as authors, creators of their life stories' (O'Donnell 2018a: 91). In this chapter, I have demonstrated the ways in which my work is strongly aligned with this change in focus, positioning the Magdalene survivors on whose stories I draw as expert producers of knowledge on their own experiences. In adopting a methodology which has this claim at its heart, I also address questions of how to work with survivors' testimony in a way that makes space for their narratives to be heard in a meaningful capacity.

This is a process which requires a close attention to the ethical, building on the work done by those involved in the interview process. This should be understood not only in the context of how to approach the interviews themselves but also with reference to the ethical dimensions of care for the researcher, an awareness of the emotional nature of the work. In doing so, I work towards a reflexive approach which considers not only the impact of my own positionality on the research but also the impact of the research on my own identity. However, as Skeggs (2004:129) highlights, the ability to be reflexive in this way is itself a privilege, demonstrating a position of power and perceived authority. Reflexivity is 'made possible through access to resources, and the technique of telling for the middle class depends on accruing the stories of others' (Scharff 2010: 92). It is with these questions of silence and voice in mind, and the necessary power structures inherent within them, that I turn to the next chapter, engaging with the experiences of women at the point of entry to, and during their time in, the Magdalene institutions.

4

Inside the institution: Discipline and penance

> SP And can you give... describe your daily routine at all?
>
> B Not really. I know that we would have had Mass in the convent... every morning before breakfast and then we would have had breakfast and then we would have gone to our chores, you know, make our beds... whatever our chore was.... I would have went straight to work, and we worked until probably half-past-five, six o'clock in the evening. We had dinner at lunchtime, an evening meal... and then we sat around... knitting... or... I don't remember a library of any sort; I don't remember books of any sort so I'm pretty certain we didn't have any. There was nothing in the form of education ... of any sort. The whole thing was numbingly bland and it was deliberately so, because if it were in any way exciting it would get you thinking. By being mind-numbingly bland you just went from day to day to day and in that way you went through twenty and thirty and forty years, and you coped with it because it was so bland... it was so grey.
>
> (O'Donnell, K., Pembroke, S. and McGettrick, C., 'An Oral History of Bernadette', MAGOHP/12/ANON, 2013: 22–23 [hereafter MAGOHP/12/ANON, Bernadette])

> *All you did was you prayed, you cooked, you cleaned.*
> (O'Donnell, K., Pembroke, S. and McGettrick, C., 'An Oral History of Celine Roberts', MAGOHP/22, 2013: 35:18 [hereafter MAGOHP/22, Celine Roberts])

In starting this chapter, I tried to find a passage from the interviews with survivors which would give a sense of life in the institutions, the routine and day-to-day experiences as presented by the women themselves. The huge diversity in the interviews makes this almost impossible – they stretch across almost fifty years, drawing on stories from ten different institutions run by four different orders of nuns. There is, of course, no universal experience to describe, no description of a routine which can tell us how these women experienced their time in the institutions. However, the aforementioned passages stood out to me because of the focus on the mundane and repetitive nature of the institutions. The desired effect of this blandness – days running together, the routine itself almost disappearing into the dullness – was to create a subject who had no will to push back, who would be docile. Foucault defines a docile body as 'one that may be subjected, used, transformed, and improved. And that this docile body can only be achieved through strict regimen of disciplinary acts' (1977: 137). This chapter focuses on the experiences of the women at the point of entrance to, and while they were in, the institutions, looking at these disciplinary acts as they impacted on voices, bodies and self-identities, working to 'improve' these women and produce a particular type of religious gendered subjectivity. Ultimately, this was a process of stripping a woman of her agency, of the key things which are important for a sense of self – but this was based on a religious punitive system which targeted the female body in a very specific way. However, this chapter also addresses women's resistance to these disciplinary acts, pushing back against the processes and identities inscribed on their bodies.

Bernadette's assertion that this was an intentional process is also something I want to draw out as I start this chapter. Her words demonstrate recognition of a deliberate intent – the cultivation of compliance, of lack of resistance. The routine as described by Bernadette and Celine, and many of the other women, shows some of the ways in which this dullness and routine had an attritional nature – it slowly wore the women down, eroding their sense of self in a gradual, drawn-out manner. Through the descriptions given by survivors of daily life in the laundries, of the routine, the punishments and the slow erosion of their selves, we can see how the institutions served 'to discipline the body, optimize its capabilities, extort its forces, increase its usefulness and docility, integrate it into systems of efficient and economic controls' (Foucault 1980: 139), with the aim of producing the correct type of female body, that of the penitent, a religious woman who not only recognized her sins but also saw incarceration and hard work as the only way to be absolved.

Throughout the interviews, it is apparent that these processes frequently revolved around the denial and restriction of knowledge. Therefore, in this chapter, I consider how a framework of epistemic injustice can help to understand the ways in which these women were formed as unreliable subjects, incapable of narrating their own experiences or making decisions about their own lives, holding in mind the question of how the various forms of epistemic injustice were produced in these institutions. I foreground the specifically religious nature of these processes, as well as considering how the religious nature of the environment worked to produce a certain form of religious subjectivity. I have chosen to delineate these processes into three sections. Firstly, I explore how women's voices were silenced, either through the imposition of a rule of silence or through a lack of credibility or through denial of information. I then think about the specific methods by which the physical bodies of the women were disciplined, through restriction of freedom and movement, and through physical abuse. Finally, I engage with the impact these processes had on the development of a self within the boundaries of this carceral religious environment. Throughout these three sections, I also address women's resistance to these processes, the various techniques by which they exerted agency and pushed back against the specific identities they were ascribed. By making these distinctions, I do not wish to suggest that these processes can be fully separated from each other, that there is no overlap. Indeed, I would argue that they are very much entwined, working together to produce specific subjectivities. The disciplining of voice and body, the constant denial of credibility, all impact on the formation of self within the laundry. Silencing of voice is fed by the physical boundaries placed on the women, and the erosion of identity through psychological abuse is heightened by denial of credibility.

Disciplining voices: From coercive silence to rebellious noise

In the two preceding chapters, I discussed the importance of issues of silence and voice for this book, both theoretically and methodologically. Throughout the work, questions emerge regarding who has been allowed to speak, and in what way; who has been silenced, and how this silence has been experienced by survivors; as well as the best ways to engage with the voices and testimonies of survivors of trauma and abuse, to avoid speaking over or speaking for them. Silence in many forms is present throughout this book. In this section, I will explore the specific instances of silencing for women at the point of entry to, and while they were in, the Magdalene laundries. This will include exploring the insistence on forced silence in the institutions, as well as silencing achieved through lack of credibility and denial of information. I will consider the impact that these forms of silencing had, both immediate and in the longer term. I will also think about the various ways this silence was subverted and resisted, and to what end.

Silence in the institution

When thinking about the ways in which a person can have their voice controlled, one of the most obvious is that of forced silence. Foucault describes silence as one of the 'forms of coercion, schemata of constraint, applied and repeated' (1977: 128), which characterized new forms of punishment towards the end of the eighteenth century. Silence as a tool is used throughout institutions of confinement and has a long history as a disciplinary process, in settings from schools to prisons. In the Magdalene institutions, this is evident in the silencing of physical voice, as well as limitations on the ability of the women to speak out about their experiences while in the institutions, to communicate the nature of their experiences accurately to others and therefore begin to make sense of it themselves.

Silence as an experience is distinctly gendered. Throughout history, 'the talk of women has been regarded as unnatural, irrational, hysterical, a cost to their wombs and the next generation, and an immodest and punishable offense' (Patterson 2000: 669). I have previously discussed the relationship between gender and nation which permeated twentieth-century Ireland and influenced the way in which 'bad' women were conceptualized and managed. When considering the various reasons given for women's entry into the laundries, some of which will be discussed later in this chapter, it is evident that they were frequently seen as being a threat to the national identity of Ireland. They were the 'wrong' kind of woman, embodying an excessive hyperfemininity – through their visible pregnancies outside of the confines of marriage; speech against men; or refusal to comply with patriarchal authorities.

Silencing women then has different social and cultural implications in comparison to silencing men. It is used to control them twofold: to ensure they do not pose a risk to the public but also to prevent them from *causing harm to themselves*. As Patterson highlights, public speech from women has historically been considered something by which they damage themselves and their reputation as good and morally productive citizens, and specifically, as reproducers of national identity through their role as mothers. Patterson goes on to highlight the links between women's speech and morality, emphasizing that

> Women who talk publicly still risk moral assessment. 'Public women', an historical reference to prostitutes, find tickets to the language game unevenly distributed, on bases other than deliberative merit or dialogical engagement; let your women keep their silence in the churches, for it is not permitted unto them to speak. . . . Historically, folk culture has held, and continues to hold, that

it is women who talk too much, despite an enormous quantitative literature that contradicts that folk wisdom. Perhaps then ... any female talk is normatively 'a lot' or 'too much', morally suspect. (2000: 670)

The link between public speech and sexual immorality, in the historical framing of prostitutes as 'public women', is also relevant here. Although in the twentieth century it seems few women were sent to the laundries for selling sex, the association with prostitution remained, along with the enduring stigma.

Throughout the interviews, silence within the institutions is a fairly consistent theme, and it is evident that many of the laundries maintained a strict rule of silence, particularly while the women were working:

> I asked one of the girls something and the nun, she says to me, 'stop talking in the laundry, it's not allowed'. We weren't allowed to talk or do anything.
> (O'Donnell, K., Pembroke, S. and McGettrick, C., 'An Oral History of Pippa Flanagan', MAGOHP/46/ANON, 2013: 2 [hereafter MAGOHP/46/ANON, Pippa Flanagan])

Not only were women discouraged from speaking to each other but their interactions with nuns were also monitored. Patricia Burke Brogan, who, as a novice nun, briefly worked in a Magdalene institution, describes being forbidden from speaking to the women, during her interview:

> I wasn't supposed to talk to them or listen to their stories, the only thing was to tell them what to do and check their work.
> (O'Donnell, K., Pembroke, S. and McGettrick, C., 'An Oral History of Patricia Burke Brogan', MAGOHP/72, 2012: tape 2, 5:12 [hereafter MAGOHP/72, Patricia Burke Brogan])

The only form of permitted speech is that which relates to work. She could tell them what to do, but nothing more. This immediately forecloses the possibility of conversation, of reciprocal speech which might result in a productive exchange of experience. What does living under this enforced rule of silence do to a person, to their sense of self? At the most basic level, being forced to be silent means being prevented from engaging in speech with others, which makes for an isolated existence. To return to Fricker's basic everyday epistemic practices of conveying knowledge to others (2007: 1), being silent makes this very difficult. With few or no opportunities to speak to each other, building relationships was almost impossible in Magdalene institutions. It is through this communication with others, this relationship building, that we make sense of our social experiences; therefore the rule of silence had significant consequences.

Mary Creighton speaks about this silence between the women, describing how she was with

> All old women, and they wouldn't talk, none of them . . . not one of us talking to the other, because we never conversed . . . I don't know, they weren't talking, even to each other. Even when they were working they weren't talking to each other, you weren't allowed to talk at the breakfast table . . . you never talked to each other.
>
> (O'Donnell, K., Pembroke, S. and McGettrick, C., 'An Oral History of Mary Creighton', MAGOHP/40, 2013: tape 1, 1:38:02 [hereafter MAGOHP/40, Mary Creighton])

In part due to this insistence on silence, it appears that the potential for friendships in the laundries was fairly limited and was certainly something strongly discouraged by the nuns. Evelyn speaks about friendship during her interview, saying she

> Made a nice friend in there . . . she was there for a couple of months before I left, I made a nice friend, she was a lovely friend. We got on well, her and me. And behind the nuns' backs when we thought they weren't looking we'd have a little giggle. But the majority of the time we really didn't – especially working – we d . . . really didn't speak . . . but we couldn't let the nuns know that we were good friends because that wasn't allowed. You weren't there to make friends, you were there to be punished.
>
> (O'Donnell, K., Pembroke, S. and McGettrick, C., 'An Oral History of Evelyn', MAGOHP/10/ANON, 2013: 35–36 [hereafter MAGOHP/10/ANON, Evelyn])

Friendship emerges here as something with the potential for radical disruption – and is described by Evelyn with specific reference to noise. Giggling behind the nuns' back, a small subversive act of rebellion, forms the basis for her description of this friendship. It is perhaps then easy to see why speech and noise were banned in the institutions – it had the potential to disrupt the everyday working of the laundry. This is further elaborated upon by Lucy, who makes a direct link between silence and productivity – if you were talking, you were not working, again disrupting the carefully maintained discipline of the laundry environment:

> You know, if you stopped to talk, if you were kind of . . . like because like you were slowing . . . you were actually slowing down productivity by . . . by stopping to talk like, there was no . . . you could never have a conversation or anything in th . . . in . . . in the laundry because you . . . you would actually . . . I remember this woman Emily [pseudonym] I . . . I turned around to speak to her and she'd go, 'sssshhhh!' like that, you know, she . . . she shut me up straight away.

(O'Donnell, K., Pembroke, S. and McGettrick, C., 'An Oral History of Lucy', MAGOHP/07/ANON, 2013: 39 [hereafter MAGOHP/07/ANON, Lucy])

Patricia Dervan, whose mother-in-law was in a Magdalene institution, and who was one of the founding members of the Magdalene Memorial Committee, demonstrates another aspect to the disruptive potential of noise, suggesting that

> The reason they were kept in this silent atmosphere was because the nuns were of the opinion, if the women were allowed to talk that they might just organise, they might talk about plotting, a plot to escape, so therefore, they lived in a silent world, except for their prayers.
> (O'Donnell, K., Pembroke, S. and McGettrick, C., 'An Oral History of Patricia Dervan', MAGOHP/06, 2013: tape 1, 1:08:48 [hereafter MAGOHP/06, Patricia Dervan])

The noise as well as speech of women was, to the nuns, a dangerous thing. It also posed a risk to the women's morality, as evidenced by Bernadette's words:

> One of the things that I remember was that you were discouraged from having friends ... because friendships bred ... problems for the nuns. I've always felt there's only one sin in Ireland and that's sex. And although I did ... I never saw any lesbianism, if you had a friend it could progress into a lesbian relationship and they weren't going to have that so you didn't have friends. You ... you ... your free time ... well all your time ... was ... was ... was supervised. And if they saw you being too friendly with one particular person they ... they parted you and ... and ... you ... you had to move away from them and have less contact with them. (MAGOHP/12/ANON, Bernadette: 21)

Friendship was seen by the nuns to be problematic – a path to either unproductivity, or sin, or perhaps a combination of the two. By maintaining a strict rule of silence, the nuns could attempt to limit the interactions between women as much as possible. Some women do recall making friends during their time in the institutions:

> **SP** Did you make any friends?
>
> **M** I would say I did yeah, but once you got out you didn't want to see anybody ... y ... just in case you'd ever end up back ...
>
> **SP** Yeah.
>
> **M** Yeah I did I think I made a lot of friends but ...
>
> **SP** Would you say you were close to them while you were in the laundry?

> M The girls I worked with on the lace ... probably because we had nobody else ... but just as friends. (MAGOHP/4/ANON, Mary: 37)

However, Mary's assertion that these relationships were rarely continued after leaving the laundry seems to ring true across other interviews. This was often due to practical difficulties as well as the fear of going back to the laundry expressed by Mary.

Pippa Flanagan says that she

> Made a few friends, but when I asked ... when I got out, if I could have their address they said no I can't. I just wanted someone from either Loughrea or the Magdalene Laundry to be a friend when I went outside. (MAGOHP/46/ANON, Pippa Flanagan: 9)

She goes on to say:

> Yes, it would be lovely to [make contact with other survivors] ... because I feel comfortable in their company because they went through the same as I did and that's why I would really like if we could all get together and kn ... know each other. (MAGOHP/46/ANON, Pippa Flanagan: 9)

Later in this chapter, I argue that the withholding of information by the nuns was another way in which silence functioned as an oppressive structure for women while within the laundries. This quote from Pippa further demonstrates the way in which the continued denial of information, in this case, location of other survivors, contributes to enduring isolation. Even after leaving the enforced silence of the laundries, survivors are denied the networks and structures in which speaking about their experiences might be possible, or comfortable. The implications of this kind of continued silencing through information withholding for Magdalene survivors after they left the institutions will be discussed in more detail in subsequent chapters.

These examples demonstrate the many ways enforced silence was enacted in the institutions, and how it was conceptualized as necessary – to increase productivity, to avoid friendships from forming, to avoid the dissent caused by excessive feminine speech. It is also important to think about the types of speech which were allowed, and what this tells us about processes of subjectivity formation. Primarily, the most encouraged form of speech was prayer – women speak about this as a near constant experience during their time in the laundries:

> Oh you prayed before you had your lunch, oh goodness me yeah, yeah that's all we ever done was pray, pray, pray. Yeah we'd ... yeah we'd have to say prayers before

lunch, and then after we finished and before we went back to work we'd have to say prayers again.... And then, of course then you'd have your tea break then at about three o'clock, more prayers. It was always prayers in the morning, afternoon, night time whatever, there was always prayers before and after a meal, and then when we'd have our tea break, prayers and then again after we'd had our tea break, and then just before we finished work, before the laundry closed, more prayers. And then you'd go and you'd have your main meal in the evening and more prayer ... ah I was forever praying, forever praying yeah. (MAGOHP/10/ANON, Evelyn: 24)

She [Patricia's sister-in-law] complained, always, of the fact that they had to pray so much, because I think, she never expressed this to me, but I think she thought it became meaningless because of the repetition, it was just like ... sort of parroting out things rather than the prayers having any meaning, it was just something they parroted. (MAGOHP/06, Patricia Dervan: tape 2, 29:48)

This authorized form of speech served to further discipline their voices, forming them as religious, penitent subjects. They are actively being shaped into this religious subjectivity by forced speech, which worked in conjunction with the forced silence. It is interesting that whilse the frequency and volume of prayers is something many of the interview subjects reiterate throughout their narratives, the content of the prayer is almost never discussed, suggesting that it is the verbal *act* of prayer, rather than the religious meanings it contained, which stayed with the women. It was a process of discipline, rather than one which held spiritual significance for the women who took part in it.

The discredited subject as silent subject

Moving beyond the specific experience of forced silence, I turn to a consideration of how women were silenced by having their voices ignored, suppressed and discredited. It was not simply through lack of voice that women experienced oppression – the experience of having one's speech disregarded and discredited also emerges as a recurring theme throughout the interviews. As Patterson highlights, 'both voice and silence pose risks' (2000: 671) – harm may be done both when a subject does not speak openly, as well as when they are not heard meaningfully. This process is one which can be seen throughout the lives of survivors, from their entrance into the laundries until the recent processes of apology and redress. It is therefore an idea which I will discuss further in later chapters, considering the cumulative nature of this. However, it is particularly evident in the interviews when women are speaking about their early lives, and their experiences at the point of entry into the laundry.

'Routes of entry' are also examined in the McAleese report over three chapters, and so this is a specific event in the narratives of the laundries where it is possible to compare the way in which survivors speak about their experiences, and with the ways these experiences are presented by the Committee. Throughout the women's discussions of their routes of entry, it becomes apparent that they were routinely lied to, disbelieved and deceived about the circumstances of their entry. The McAleese report, and previous government statements such as that made by Sean Aylward, the then Secretary General of the Department of Justice, to UNCAT Committee Members in May 2011, suggest that some women entered the laundries under their own volition. Aylward in particular highlights his conviction that 'as far as we can establish, on the facts available, the vast majority of women who went to these institutions, went there voluntarily, or if they were minors, with the consent of their parents or guardians' (2011). However, it is important to investigate this idea of voluntary entry further. Rose Brien Harrington, whose great-aunt Esther was in a laundry, raises some important points regarding choice in this matter. When speaking about a nun who claims Esther entered voluntarily, Rose states:

> I daresay a lot of women went in voluntarily . . . were they told beforehand what was going to happen to them, were they told they were going to have their clothes taken off them and their hair cut short, were they told they weren't going to be able to use their own name . . . were they told they were likely to be beaten, were they told they weren't going to be paid for anything they did, were they told they'd never be able to own anything, were they told all that before they went in there? I can't see anyone going in there voluntarily if they knew all that.
> (O'Donnell, K., Pembroke, S. and McGettrick, C., 'An Oral History of Rose Brien Harrington', MAGOHP/14, 2013: 1:03:48 [hereafter MAGOHP/14, Rose Brien Harrington])

To what extent can it be said someone does something 'voluntarily' if they are given no information on the subject? Denial of information is used to place restrictions on the agency of these women, limiting the extent to which they were given the opportunity to make informed choices, and coercing them into specific forms of behaviour. Other interviewees link their entry to the laundries to more specific events, particularly experiences of being abused by family members. Lucy states very early on in her interview that she was sent to the laundry because she was abused at home – 'I was abused at home and I was put into the Magdalene Laundries by social services because of the abuse at home' (MAGOHP/07/ANON, Lucy: 1). This is not in response to a question about her entry to the laundry; rather, she is asked by the interviewer – 'So the first question I just want to ask is could you tell me something about yourself?' (MAGOHP/07/ANON, Lucy: 1). It sounds very much like something she feels is important to say, a crucial point about her experience in the laundry which she wishes to immediately have recorded.

A version of this question is asked at the start of almost every interview with a survivor. The responses vary hugely – some interviewees talk about their family, identifying themselves as a mother, or a wife; others talk about their early lives and place of birth; while others appear to interpret the interview as a space in which they are expected to talk only about their experiences in the laundries, and so begin there. The question was left deliberately vague to encourage participants to bring up what they felt as important. Later in the interview, Lucy gives more details about this statement – she describes being offered food by a teacher, feeling like she had to refuse it because accepting help would show something at home was 'wrong':

> So, she [the teacher] obviously got a sense of something wrong and reported it. But the next thing I know was there was a knock on the door and I was taken away from the home. I was put into Sean McDermott Street [Sisters of Our Lady of Charity Magdalene Laundry] and I thought I was going to prison because I had maybe said something that I shouldn't have said to somebody and . . . (MAGOHP/07/ANON, Lucy: 4)

Lucy fears she has engaged in the wrong kind of speech – that she has 'said something that I shouldn't have said'. She immediately assumes it is her fault that she was being sent away, because of this. Lucy is not the only respondent to describe being sent to a laundry after reporting abuse by a family member. Early on in her interview, Evelyn says:

> My father was very abusive like I said, and then when Mum went into hospital to have the baby, he got really, really bad abusive wise. Liked his drink, he did drink . . . he did drink a lot. And then when mum died then things got even worse. More . . . more than you can imagine. So I would run away from home and the police would always come find me, and so . . . and I'd go up to the police and tell them my father was abusing me, but it was ignored. And then one day I went up to the police on a Saturday afternoon and told them what was happening and then the next thing I knew I was on my way to High Park, and I was . . . I hadn't even had my fifteenth birthday at the time . . . (MAGOHP/10/ANON, Evelyn: 1)
>
> . . . They didn't tell me where I was going; they just said to me when I went up to the police that Saturday afternoon and told them that you know, I'd had enough

of my dad abusing me, they had to do something, they just told me to sit in a room and... and wait there. So I did, what felt like an hour, it could be two hours I really don't know. Then they came back and said right, they were going to take me into care. (MAGOHP/10/ANON, Evelyn: 2)

Unlike Lucy, Evelyn tries to make her abusive environment clear to authority figures, rather than hiding it. However, the end result is the same – they are forcibly taken somewhere they did not choose to go. Later in her interview, Evelyn says that throughout her time in the institution, she was told she

Was stupid... I was... what was it they... they classed it as, I was making unfavourable... beha... it was unfavourable behaviour towards my father. So, in other words I was telling lies and that was why I was in there because I was a sinner. (MAGOHP/10/ANON, Evelyn: 30)

In both of these examples, the interviewees report seeking care and protection from authority figures, and instead of receiving this, they are taken to Magdalene institutions. In both cases, it is insinuated by authority figures that the women are being sent to the laundries as a protective measure – Evelyn is told she is being taken into care; Lucy is taken from her home by social services. This raises several questions – Did these authorities genuinely believe that the Magdalene laundry would be a safer environment for these girls? Did they think the girls were lying, and therefore needed to be confined for their own safety, or the safety of others? Or did they simply have no other option? The idea that they were places of protection and care is an idea articulated by some of the key informants interviewed as part of the oral history project, as well as appearing to underpin some of the few statements by members of the religious orders. For example, Patricia Dervan, a founding member of the *Magdalene Memorial Committee*, describes how

I've heard so many nuns look me straight in the eye and tell me, we rescued these people, we rescued them, rescued them by subjecting them to cruelty and heartbreak and taking their children... I mean it's just... sometimes words fail me. (MAGOHP/06, Patricia Dervan: tape 4, 31:06)

The ideology which conceptualizes the Magdalene institutions as places of care will be explored further later in this book. However, the obvious hypocrisy of this situation is made apparent in Evelyn's case when she is later told that her 'unfavourable' behaviour towards her abusive father is the reason for her incarceration. Obviously, we have no way of knowing the 'actual' reason Evelyn was sent to a laundry. Indeed, I would suggest that, in this context, such a line of inquiry is counterproductive. What would count as the actual reason? That stated on her convent record? We have no way of verifying this, as all convent archives are currently closed. Instead, I would argue that what is significant is the way in which Evelyn was made to feel, the impact that this information had on her, which we can infer from the last line of the previous quote – 'in other words, I was telling lies and that was why I was in there because I was a sinner'. She is made to believe that it was her fault that she had been sent to this place, that it was something she deserved. This raises further questions about her process of response to this – Did she initially believe what she was told about herself, and if so, how and when did she start to question this? She speaks about how she felt in the laundries, saying:

> I felt lonely, isolated and the main part of the feeling ... how I felt there was I felt rejected. I was put in there through no fault of my own and like, I was rejected, and it was a lonely, lonely time ... (MAGOHP/10/ANON, Evelyn: 6)

Later, she says:

> ... you know and [they would] tell you how dirty you are, and only babies wet the bed. And there was ... and ... and you felt degraded as it was you know, without them making you even worse, you know, and, 'you need to grow up' and stuff like that and, 'God doesn't like people who wet beds'. And, you know, it was all these stupid sayings that they had and thinking back now you think, yeah it was stupid but they would make you feel really, really, really they ... they would degrade you. You know, and you'd get, 'oh you're wetting the bed, stupid girl' and all that, you know and ... and to keep being told you're stupid all the time it does really ... (MAGOHP/10/ANON, Evelyn: 36)

It is clear that while she may not have believed she deserved to be there, the repeated assertions of the nuns about her lack of credibility, and her shameful identity, had a significant impact – Evelyn does not seem to be able to find the words to describe the effect it had on her, but her phrasing suggests it was a deep and degrading hurt.

Other women speak about being directly lied to when they entered the laundry. Julia Brown (O'Donnell, K., Pembroke, S. and McGettrick, C., 'An Oral History of Julia Brown', MAGOHP/11, 2013 [hereafter MAGOHP/11, Julia Brown]) was told by nuns that the convent would shut down if more people didn't go for further education there. At the age of twelve, she agreed to enter a convent run by the Good Shepherd Sisters, Limerick, in 1952, and spent two years there. She did not receive further education. Sadie O'Meara states that she was working in a B&B, when two women came in and told her they could get her a better job:

So I didn't know what to do, because as I was raised, you didn't say no in them days, in the 50s, you didn't say no, you'd be afraid to say no. So I said OK. So they took me off in this car . . . brought me into this room and said, 'we're the Legion of Mary, and we're putting you in here for your own safety'. And the nuns accepted me . . . they were looking for cheap labour, of course.

(O'Donnell, K., Pembroke, S. and McGettrick, C., 'An Oral History of Sadie O'Meara', MAGOHP/80/ANON, 2013: 10:41 [hereafter MAGOHP/80/ANON, Sadie O'Meara])

In this instance it is important to think about whether Sadie would have considered the financial motivations of the nuns in this way at the time, or whether she was more immersed in the moral assumptions of the Laundries, and came to frame her experiences as an exploitation of labour later in her life. Her interview does not give much indication of this; however, it is important to bear these questions in mind when thinking about the impact of wider social systems and discourse around morality on the lives of the women.

These examples demonstrate the continuous obfuscation and deliberate confusion which accompanied the women's entrance to the laundries. They show how little credibility or importance was attached to the voices of the women involved – when they raised concerns or made allegations of abuse, their testimony was not heard. They were effectively silenced through this total lack of credibility. Their identity as young women in a country which operated within a strict system of religiously motivated gender roles meant that their testimony was classed as unreliable, especially when it was consisted of accusations against, or was contradicted by, older men.

Institutional silence and the state of 'not knowing'

Patricia Burke Brogan's interview suggests that the nuns were discouraged from speaking to women in the laundries, again highlighting the ways in which any kind of connection was made difficult. However, beyond this, women were given almost no information by the nuns about the conditions of their stay. In this section, I consider how the silence of the nuns was itself traumatic for the women. Specifically, I argue that the constant lack of information given to the women about being in the laundries contributes to a wider instance of epistemic violence, in which women are prevented from being conceptualized as knowers, as subjects with agency and capacity to make decisions on their own lives. I consider the impact that being in a constant state of 'not knowing' can have on the self, and how this can be seen as a form of epistemic violence.

During the interviews, survivors were asked a specific question about information and rights:

> Were you given information such as the length of time you would spend, your rights etc.? (O'Donnell, K., Pembroke, S. and McGettrick, C., 'Topic Guide for Survivors', 2013: 2)

Throughout the interviews, women answered this in a consistent way:

> SP Yeah, okay. And so you weren't given any information about rights etc. or? . . .
>
> E No. . .
>
> SP No.
>
> E . . . nothing, no, no. (MAGOHP/10/ANON, Evelyn: 4)
>
> SP Yeah. And were you given information . . . like when you were put in, like . . . sent . . . like . . . like the length of time you would spend . . . your rights.
>
> M Nothing at all! You . . . said, 'if you be a good girl', and more or less, 'you can get out soon'.
>
> SP Okay so it was just like, 'soon'. (MAGOHP/4/ANON, Mary: 15)

Similar responses are given throughout the interviews, and it is apparent that the women were almost never given any information regarding how long they would be staying in the institutions, whether they would ever be able to leave, and why they had been sent there in the first place. Many survivors refer to this constant sense of 'not knowing', of being consistently denied information, as one of the most difficult things about being in the laundries, particularly with regards to the length of stay. Bernadette discusses this on two occasions during her interviews:

> SP Okay. And . . . were you given any information like the length of time . . . ?
>
> B Hmm. No. That is one of the things that I found very, very difficult to cope with was . . . that . . . in boarding school was not unlike prison except that you knew when term was going to end and you knew when your education was going to end. In prison you . . . you know when your term is going to end. (MAGOHP/12/ANON, Bernadette: 10)
>
> SP Okay. Okay. I'm just going on now to ask you about your individual experience, did you have any fears or anxieties while you were there?
>
> B Yes, the not knowing when I was going to get out . . . was I going to be there for the rest of my life? If so how would I cope? I would cope on a day to day basis, but on a long term basis? That was very scary . . . and

> totally helpless; could do nothing about it if that was what my mother had decided ... totally helpless ... did not know that my brothers and sisters. (MAGOHP/12/ANON, Bernadette: 59–60)

Bernadette emphasizes that this lack of information made her feel 'totally helpless' – she repeats this phrase twice, making clear the sense of powerlessness which this denial of information caused. The comparison made by Bernadette to prison is one repeated again by Mary Smith:

> What ... you ... what crime did I commit? What crime did any of us commit to be in there? And to be honest, as I said it was worse than any, any prison, you had no visitors, no one came to visit you, the doors never opened and like that when you were in there, you nev ... you never knew you were going to come out of there. (MAGOHP/31, Mary Smith: 61)

Phyllis Morgan also draws on this comparison, when describing her experiences of working with Magdalene survivors:

> **SP** And in terms of ... yeah, so in your survivor group, just to ... I know we don't distinguish, but just to bring with the Magdalene ... Laundry survivors, what kind of problems do you encounter amongst ... or feelings or ...?
>
> **PM** Frailty. Frailty's the word that comes into my ... when I look around at ... at them when we ... how frail they are. Some of them quite broken, broken women even though there's a ... a dignified manner about them all. They ... they have a lovely manner, very dignified ... but frailty is ... I see because of the hard work and the trauma of being locked away, never knowing when you were going to get out. Because if you went to a prison you knew the date you were going to come out. These ladies never knew. I've ... you know I heard some of the women say, 'God, I was watching women dying around me thinking "oh my God, is this how I ... is this how I'm going to end my life?" I don't want this, I've ... I've got to get out of here!' And some of them did escape and managed to get away and come over to England, you know, you ... lucky that luck was on their side.
>
> (O'Donnell, K., Pembroke, S. and McGettrick, C., 'An Oral History of Phyllis Morgan', MAGOHP/27, 2013: 57 [hereafter MAGOHP/27, Phyllis Morgan])

Being denied any information about one's situation, especially if the boundaries of the situation are already out of your control, works to increase a sense of powerlessness within a person. By denying women information about their rights, they are being denied the ability to be in control of their own experiences. They are not allowed to become knowers, denied basic information which would allow them to plan ahead and make decisions. They are constructed as subjects unable to make sensible decisions regarding their future – they need others to do this for them. In this way, women are stripped of agency by being denied the capacity to make choices.

What does being forced to exist in a constant state of not knowing do to a person's sense of self? What does planning for the future allow us to do, specifically, and what does an inability to plan prevent? Being trusted with information makes people feel valued and valid. We trust people we see as reliable, and so to be trusted with knowledge tells a person how they are viewed by others. Therefore, the experience of repeatedly *not* being trusted with information, being told nothing about your circumstances, emphasizes the extent to which you are viewed as unreliable and untrustworthy. Women are kept in a state of stasis, fixing them with their trauma more firmly by denying them a timeline of progression or escape. As Doris says:

> You weren't told anything about anything, doesn't matter what, you weren't told. You just thought you were an orphan, you had nobody and that was it.
>
> (O'Donnell, K., Pembroke, S. and McGettrick, C., 'An Oral History of Doris', MAGOHP/37/ANON: 21:25 [hereafter MAGOHP/37/ANON, Doris])

After emphasizing the lack of information given, she makes a link between knowledge and identity – the lack of knowledge is, for her, tied up with being an orphan, having nobody – 'that was it'. This demonstrates the ways in which lack of information then impacts upon identity formation, interacting with other strands of a stigmatiszed identity to repeatedly hammer home the idea that you were not epistemically valuable. It is important to note that for many survivors, and family members, this state of not knowing is still in existence. The continued refusal of religious orders to open their archives ensures that survivors and their family are denied information which might shed light on family histories which have until now remained shadowy and unclear. Requests for information are frequently treated as unimportant and the State continues to delay with regards to information about redress. This will be explored further in subsequent chapters, but at this point it is important to note the continual nature of this, and many other forms of trauma endured by survivors of the Magdalene institutions.

Resistance to silencing: From noise as rebellion to active silence

It is clear that the various uses of silence functioned in a distinctly oppressive way for women who spent time in the laundries. From preventing the formation of meaningful relationships to the trauma inflicted by being kept in a constant state of 'not knowing', silence penetrated many aspects of the women's lives, forming them as unreliable and untrustworthy, not valued enough to be given the basic knowledge about their current or future circumstances. However, while it is clear that silence was a deeply traumatic part of many of the women's experiences, to imply that survivors willingly submitted to this forced silencing is incorrect. Women describe resisting this silence in many ways, both by using their voice to disrupt the silence and by using silence to create space for their own agency.

The use of *noise itself* as a method of resistance to coercive silencing appears as a theme throughout some of the interviews. In this context, we can think of the voice as a tool, focusing less on the content of the utterance, and more on the very act of making any kind of noise. This has a long history as a form of protest, from protest chants to noise demonstrations outside prisons and detention centres; noise can be understood as both a form of resistance and support. It allows us to demonstrate our agency with a tool which is available to almost all people, either through the voice or through makeshift instruments, pots and pans, banging, stamping. There are specific examples of noise as resistance throughout the interviews:

> The first day when I went to Gloucester Street I refused to take off my clothes, I refused to do anything. I just sat and cried and wailed and screamed, nobody took any notice of me. (MAGOHP/4/ANON, Mary: 13)

> **SP** Can you describe to me, like an example of how you rebelled?
>
> **E** I would shout! Yeah. I would shout at nuns, I . . . if they said something to me.
>
> (MAGOHP/10/ANON, Evelyn: 46)

> I screamed and I screamed and I kept screaming, because that was my only power.
> (O'Donnell, K., Pembroke, S. and McGettrick, C., 'An Oral History of Margaret Burke', MAGOHP/18/ANON, 2013: 11:08 [hereafter MAGOHP/18/ANON, Margaret Burke])

Noise disrupts the environment in a very immediate way. It demands attention, although as Mary's account demonstrates, not always successfully. However, the relative 'success' of women's resistance is less important in this instance than the fact that they chose this particular way to exert their agency. In an environment which attempted to silence women's voices, both literally and metaphorically, noise-making demonstrates their desire and capacity to push back against this.

However, it is important to remember that silence has meanings 'other than consent, compliance, agreement, or ignorance' (Lewis 1993: 134). To suggest that those women who did not actively make noise were not resisting silencing in other ways ignores the complexity of resistance in these spaces. For example, Martina Keogh states:

> I've seen them holding women down and beating them, so you wouldn't win with them, no matter what, so I learned to shut my mouth and just call them names under my breath behind their back.
> (O'Donnell, K., Pembroke, S. and McGettrick, C., 'An Oral History of Martina Keogh', MAGOHP/44, 2013: 44:46 [hereafter MAGOHP/44, Martina Keogh])

By withholding her voice, or significantly reducing its volume, Martina makes space to engage in a quieter, subtler form of resistance: silence in the presence of the nuns, but whispered names behind their back. The content of her quiet speech here is also significant – later in the chapter I discuss the significance and power of names in more detail, but it is useful here to take note of the overlap in forms of resistance and exertion of agency.

Disciplining bodies: Prayer and productive subjects

The focus on literal silence, on the closing of the mouth, demonstrates not only the desire for control of speech but also the emphasis on bodily control within the institutions. From the structure of the day to the physical limitations of their movements, the whole experience of the laundry was designed to discipline the body. In this section, I will explore the ways in which this bodily control is further exercised in the laundries, returning to Foucault's ideas around the production of 'docile bodies' through discipline, surveillance and punishment. In particular, I focus on the idea of docile bodies as productive bodies, and how conceptions of gendered productivity shape ideas about what constitutes physical abuse. I will focus on the processes used in the laundries to discipline the body, to make it productive and docile, and thus produce the desired Irish Catholic female body, penitential and obedient. I also address how these processes of bodily discipline produced the Magdalene survivors' sense of identity, as well as how they resisted these processes.

Locked doors and windows: Restricting the physical environment

Firstly, it is evident that the women in the institutions experienced bodily control through significant loss of freedom of movement. They were rarely allowed to leave the convent building or surrounding grounds, although some women in the later part of the century speak about occasionally going into the local towns. Throughout the interviews, survivors refer to the doors and windows of the institutions being locked:

> **SP** Hmm. Yeah. Actually one question, in terms of being trapped is, were the doors and windows to the laundry locked?
>
> **M** Definitely locked. There was no escape. (MAGOHP/4/ANON, Mary: 13)

Mary instantly links the locking of doors to a loss of freedom, an inability to escape. This is echoed by Margaret Burke, who adds a temporal quality to the lack of freedom:

> That was the thing about the Magdalene laundry – the doors are locked behind you . . . once you're there you're there for life. The only time you get out of there was if somebody with some kind of respectability would take you out. (MAGOHP/18/ANON, Margaret Burke: 33:15)

Lucy's description of the laundry on Sean McDermott Street focuses more on the material properties of the constraints:

> **SP** And were the . . . were you locked in?
>
> **L** Oh yeah, yeah, yeah.
>
> **SP** And w . . . and you said actually already that there were bars on the windows?
>
> **L** There was bars on the windows and over the walls there was barbed wire and it was kind of like . . . there was kind of bar . . . steel bars and in between all them steel bars there was barbed wire . . . (MAGOHP/07/ANON, Lucy: 26)

Bernadette's interview shows how the freedom of the women, the ability for them to come and go, or even open a window, was controlled by the nuns:

> **SP** Can you describe to me what the building was like in terms of say, were the doors locked, the windows?
>
> **B** I don't remember the windows. We certainly wouldn't have opened and closed them without going to a nun to ask for permission. The outer doors

were certainly locked because on the Christmas morning that I was allowed home a nun brought me to the front door and she unlocked it for me and when I came back that evening, we had to phone her before we arrived and she had to come and unlock the door to let me back in, so yes the doors were locked. (MAGOHP/12/ANON, Bernadette: 36)

This forcible restriction of bodily movement by bars on the windows and locks on the doors, by necessitating women to ask to be allowed to go outside, or open a door, was not only designed to limit the physical freedom of women in the laundries; it also worked to produce a sense of powerlessness. This is reflected in some of the aforementioned interview extracts. For example, Margaret Burke links the locking of the door with the realization that 'once you're there, you're there for life'. Margaret makes the explicit link between moral respectability and the power to move past these physical restrictions. In order to leave the laundry, someone with 'some kind of respectability' had to take you out, the implication being that the women did not have this kind of moral capital.

Other women describe the effect that being locked in had in a more visceral way. Sarah describes how

> Once I heard that bolt going on that door, I was hysterical.
> (O'Donnell, K., Pembroke, S. and McGettrick, C., 'An Oral History of Sarah', MAGOHP/36/ANON, Sarah, 2013: 31:05 [hereafter MAGOHP/36/ANON, Sarah])

Before this statement in her interview, Sarah had been discussing her perception of other, older women in the laundry, who are described as being 'different':

> They didn't communicate, they didn't talk to us, they weren't allowed to talk to us. (MAGOHP/36/ANON, Sarah: 29.46).

It is unclear who Sarah is referring to when she speaks of 'us', but it seems likely it is younger women who had not spent a significant amount of time in the institution, in comparison to the older women, many of whom would likely have been in the laundry for many years by that point. The sound of the bolt in the door stands out as a key point for Sarah, a realization that she was destined to become one of these 'different' women, because she was trapped in the institution. This interplay between the physical and temporal nature of the confinement is one which appears in other interviews, with reference to the ways in which the perception of age impacts on the women's experiences. This is repeated in the interview with Mary Smith, who, when speaking about her entry to the laundry, says:

I seen all these elderly ladies there and I knew that once the door ... what really traumatised me more, to hear that door locking behind you and you were never, never, never to walk out that door again, never! ... And that's what traumatised me so much, that that door was never going to open and that was a fact. I was in Sundays Well in Cork and it was the Magdalene Laundries.
(O'Donnell, K., Pembroke, S. and McGettrick, C., 'An Oral History of Mary Smith', MAGOHP/31, 2013: 20 [hereafter MAGOHP/31, Mary Smith])

Again, the sound of the door locking functions as an enduring memory for her, but this also intersects with the temporal nature of her fears, that she would never leave. Several of the women speak about seeing the older women in the laundries and feeling scared, or seeing them as alien, strange creatures. Again, this can be linked to the denial of information, the trauma of not knowing. When looking at older women in the laundries, women were seeing the physical manifestation of their fear of never getting out. Just as the sound of the door closing reminded them that they were physically confined in the institution, the presence of older women who had very visibly spent decades here reinforced the temporal aspect of their confinement.

Noise features again as a focal point for traumatic memory in interviews with Pippa Flanagan and Lucy:

Oh there was big bars on the windows. I would no mind, the first day that I went in, it was a big brown door and Sr Frances went out first and ... Mother . . . whatever you call them, that's what you called them in the laundry, she says, 'you go on now,' she says, and all I could hear was the big bang of the door, and that bang stays with me. (MAGOHP/46/AN ON, Pippa Flanagan: 9)

And (pause) we knocked on the door and she didn't come in with me ... I was just taken in on my own ... and it was a big creaky door, I'll always remember it I can still hear the creak of the door, you know, and the door creaked and I turned around and she was gone. (MAGOHP/07/ANON, Lucy: 9)

What is important about these sounds? They provide a very clear point on which the traumatic memory of being incarcerated seems to focus upon – both women emphasize the enduring memory of these sounds, suggesting they occupy a particular space in the women's experiences. They are sounds of enclosure, emphasizing the reality of the women's physical context. This focus on sound also reinforces the significance and stress the women experienced when realizing they were physically confined within the institution. Sound shapes an awareness of spatiality – for example, you might become aware of confinement, of the limits of your environment, by the way that sound echoes around a room. It functions as a marker of their bodily confinement.

Physical abuse and work as discipline and punishment

I now turn to the issue of physical abuse within the laundries, thinking through how this shaped the experiences of the women and acted as a form of disciplinary process. In considering this, there are two points I wish to focus on. Firstly, I consider the prevalence of physical abuse, and how it has been conceptualized by the State. The McAleese report makes it a point to stress the lack of physical abuse in the Magdalene institutions, as opposed to the industrial schools, where physical beatings were far more frequent, stating that 'a large majority of the women who shared their stories with the Committee said that they had neither experienced nor seen other girls or women suffer physical abuse in the Magdalen Laundry' (McAleese 2013: 932). I contend the accuracy of this statement. Even if we limit our conception of physical abuse to violence and beatings, which I will later argue is an inadequate definition, many of the interviewees, both survivors and key informants, report that the nuns were frequently physically violent towards women. Trevor Heaney, a maintenance man employed in the Good Shepherd Laundry in Limerick in the mid-1970s states:

> There was one nun that used to be outside the workshop at the laundry, where my workshop was, and when she got angry she thought nothing of pulling the strap out. She pulled the strap out and hit them to get them to speed up – physically hitting. Now she was old school.
> (O'Donnell, K., Pembroke, S. and McGettrick, C., 'An Oral History of Trevor Heaney', MAGOHP/61, 2010: 5 [hereafter MAGOHP/61, Trevor Heaney])

He describes the nun as 'old school', perhaps implying that her behaviour was not the norm during his time in the laundries, but suggesting that this had been acceptable behaviour previously. Mary O'Mara was a Girl Guide Leader for many years. Through this work she came in contact with children from the Good Shepherd orphanage, one of whom eventually came to live with her for a time. Speaking of the same institution as Heaney, she states:

> And there was one nun – she was a serpent. She used to kill the 'in girls'. She used to just catch them by the back of the hair and turn them around and hit them across the back of the knuckles, right down across the back of the knuckles. You know those sticks, bamboos. You could be walking along and you'd get it across the back of the legs.
> (O'Donnell, K., Pembroke, S. and McGettrick, C., 'An Oral History of Mary' O'Mara, MAGOHP/64, 2010: 5 [hereafter MAGOHP/64, Mary O'Mara])

Violence is also frequently described by the survivors themselves, often as punishment for minor perceived wrongdoings:

> If you forgot . . . lost a sock or something, you'd be beaten to a pulp for this because like you know, your job . . . you had to do your job right and this was the job you had to do. If you did it wrong you . . . you . . . hell to pay . . . (MAGOHP/07/ANON, Lucy: 5)

> **SP** And can you tell me how you were . . . how you and the other women were disciplined and punished?
>
> **E** Well, if you can visualize a belt or a big cane, that's how we were punished. You'd get grabbed by the hair, dragged into the office to see the Mother Superior, and you'd have to explain yourself – there again you weren't always given a chance to explain yourself – and you'd get the cane across the backside, across the legs or the belt, depending on who . . . depending on who is in charge to give you . . . (MAGOHP/10/ANON, Evelyn: 27–28)

These examples, among others, trouble the assertion made in the McAleese report regarding the frequency of physical abuse. This book does not use quantitative analysis to determine what percentage of women experienced violence of this nature; indeed, such a task would be impossible unless one spoke to significantly more women than either the oral history project or the McAleese report has done, and so I cannot state with authority that either a majority or minority did or did not experience violence. However, does it require a majority of women to have experienced physical violence for this to be a serious issue?

Secondly, and I would argue more importantly, I contest the idea that violence in the form of beatings is the only way women could have experienced physical abuse in the institutions. This is a deeply flawed conception of violence and physical abuse; it fails to address the *inherently violent* nature of the laundries. Forcing women to work long hours, doing physically demanding manual labour, for no money, with a severely limited diet, should be considered physical abuse. You do not need to beat someone to inflict actual physical harm on them. As Patricia Dervan highlights:

> She [her sister-in-law] never complained of physical abuse in the sense of being beaten or physically attacked, but of course there was physical abuse through starvation and overwork etc. (MAGOHP/06, Patricia Dervan: tape 2, 32:00)

The most common form of work done by those in Magdalene institutions was laundry. This ranged from pressing clothes, to filling and emptying washing machines, to cleaning soiled nappies. Other women describe making lace and knitting jumpers. This work is frequently described by interviewees as extremely tiring; many women speak about working six days a week, the hours were long and the food not sufficient to sustain this level of physical exertion. Pippa Flanagan describes her first day in the laundry:

> Now, my first day was in the laundry room sorting out the clothes and I was very sick because with the way the ... all the white coats and brown coats, and they were covered with blood and that ... we had no protection for our hands, no nothing, we had to lift the dirty clothes up and sew them. They had a special number for each place that they were from. So we were at that from about six o'clock in the morning and then we ... I was in the laundry then in the afternoon and it was back-breaking, completely back-breaking. (MAGOHP/46/ANON, Pippa Flanagan: 2)

There are similar descriptions throughout the interviews – the work the women were forced to do was hard, painful and physically demanding. It was, in itself, a form of violence. In thinking about the work done by the women, I argue for a conceptualization of it not as 'work' but as another example of bodily discipline and, specifically, punishment. Alongside the physical abuse described previously, this work should be considered as another form of disciplinary process, designed to produce a docile and penitent body.

One of the reasons that the work itself is frequently not considered to be a form of physical abuse is our conception of work and the value of productivity in contemporary society. 'Work' is considered by many to be an objective good – we are encouraged from a young age to get a job, to contribute and to be a productive member of society. Work provides us with a sense of identity, and certain forms of work are seen as better, more productive and valid than others. Morality is deeply connected to productivity. In the context of the laundries, this becomes apparent when we consider the nature of the work being done by the women. As they washed and sorted laundry, they were considered to be literally washing away their sins, cleansing their souls through hard work, which both gave them a purpose and had a materially productive outcome – namely, clean laundry. Women who had previously posed a threat to the moral fabric of society were now not only confined for the public good, preventing them from causing harm to others; they could also make amends for their sins by physically cleaning dirt, doing good for their communities. It is also pertinent to remember that they were doing a highly feminized form of labour which they would have been expected to do in domestic settings as part of their gender role for free. They were working hard, but they were also doing 'women's work'

– productive and reproductive labour, which would benefit society as a whole, and equip them with skills to become good wives and mothers, helping maintain the heterosexual family which was at the heart of the Irish State in the twentieth century.

I would argue the fact that the work being done had such a 'legitimate' and productive outcome, as well as fitting into traditional gendered labour norms, also made a difference to the way that people perceived the institutions. Modernity is focused on productivity – we ascribe value onto bodies through their capacity to be productive, to contribute to society. Bodies which may lack this capacity for productivity – disabled people, old people, people with mental health conditions – have frequently been conceptualized as less valuable, because they cannot contribute to the same standard. Even now, we require people who wish to claim benefits to make efforts at productivity – they must demonstrate that they wish to be useful, be valuable, get a job. Patricia Dervan continues to think about this focus on productivity, saying that there was

> No value being put on her life, you know, in our society we tend to value people in terms of their contribution to society through their work, and we tend to reward that work with payment, but in her case there was no value put on herself. (MAGOHP/06, Patricia Dervan: tape 2, 32:38)

The laundries occupied a certain space within this discourse of productivity – as well as having religious moral symbolism, the work could be conceptualized as good and valuable for both the women and society as a whole.

Bodily resistance: Escape and strike

We can see resistance to these processes of bodily control and discipline in several ways. Two ways that stand out in the interviews are narratives of women running away from the laundries; and instances in which women simply refused to work. These two examples are particularly interesting because they neatly demonstrate the wide variety of ways women exerted agency and engaged in processes of resistance. The first is very 'active' – women were breaking the physical boundaries of the space to which they had been confined. In the second, they are resisting through passivity – they are literally *doing nothing* but still causing disruption and conflict.

Escape from the laundries was not something which seemed to happen very frequently, and only a handful of interviewees report attempting to run away from Magdalene institutions, with varying degrees of success. Some were apprehended by the Gardaí fairly rapidly, while a few managed to escape the confines of the convent permanently. Mary was at the Sean McDermott Street laundry in Dublin, and after escaping she was brought back by the police, before being sent to another institution in Limerick:

> I remember the day ... the day that I did run out and I really, really, really had to plan it because remember I wouldn't go into the uniform. ... So I knew that if I didn't go into the uniform that I wouldn't be recognised when I came out, and the other girl had the uniform on, so we ... but it was her aunty who told the police that we were there. And I remember seeing, I said to her two ... I think it was at two o'clock the door used to open, and I said to her, 'watch ... watch the door at two o'clock, be ready', and we were ready. And as I was running and running th ... all these women knew what I was doing and they tried to push ... push me back. So I got one of them and I pushed her, I did! ... And she fell over and I ... we just kept legging, legging it. And Sean McDermott Street I think has got like cobble stones ... remember ... I always remember that. I remember running and thinking, 'oh I wish it wasn't cobble ...'. (MAGOHP/4/ANON, Mary: 14)

The vivid description she gives of her escape focuses on physical sensations – the cobble stones beneath her feet, the feeling of being pushed back by the other women. She also stresses the importance of the uniform as a signal to the public that she and her friend were from the laundry, this very visible marker of difference as a factor in being recognized and returned by the guards. The escape attempt is resisted by both the women *in* the laundry and those outside, in the form of Mary's friend's aunt, who appears to have reported them to the police. The surveillance and discipline by the nuns is supported by the actions of the general public, as well as other women in the laundry, demonstrating the many ways in which the ideology underpinning the laundries permeated the wider social landscape.

Lucy was also in the Sean McDermott Street laundry, although she entered in 1977, fifteen years after Mary, representing one of the latest experiences of incarceration in the archive. Lucy's escape was successful. Unlike Mary, who describes planning out her escape carefully, Lucy speaks about her decision to run away as spontaneous:

> And how I came to run away was ... one of the girls had a visitor and I remember she was going out the door and I was watching for the door and when ... when they had disappeared ... they were c ... I think they were coming in or something, but the door was open – I don't know why – because I remember trying the door a couple of times and I couldn't get out, but this

particular day the door was open, and I got out. And I said, 'I'm never going back there again'. But I didn't know where I was going to go. (MAGOHP/07/ANON, Lucy: 41)

Kathleen describes thinking about running away in advance of doing so; again, the importance of uniforms is emphasized – even in a large city like Dublin, on one of the busiest streets, this was enough to make them visible as 'other', and identifiable to the guards:

> K I ran out of the place with other girls and we were brought back by the guards.
>
> SP Do you want to tell me about that actually?
>
> K I do remember queuing up outside the . . . the conv . . . the church was up near . . . was nearer to the Industrial School, which meant you had the easier way to get out, because you were on . . . you were out in the open . . . and the Industrial School was there, the church was near the Industrial School, the Magdalene Laundries was further down so you had no way of running out of there, but once you got up near the church you had an easier way. And I remember we had it planned the night before, and there was three of us and we ended up on O'Connell Street, we just ran out and the gate was open and we ran out. You see the gate would have been open because the laundry vans were coming in and out. . . . And we ran out and we thought we were great. We were down the middle of O'Connell Street, didn't know what we were going to do, but we'd run away and I remember the guards coming to us on O'Connell Street, because the clothes were a giveaway anyway.
>
> SP Because you would have been wearing the uniform?
>
> K We were wearing the uniforms . . . and they would have been a given away [giveaway] and I remember the guards bringing us back . . . bringing us back to High . . . to the Magdalene Laundries in High Park – I don't mind mentioning High Park – and brought us back. (MAGOHP/34/ANON, Kathleen: 37–8)

Again, the guards feature in this account of an unsuccessful escape, and this is repeated in the interview with Mary Merritt, who says:

> On Saturday we used to have to go up to the farm . . . and I ran out, I ran out of the big gate, because the gate was open in the farm, into Griffith Avenue, and before I knew it the police were picking me up and bringing me back.
> (O'Donnell, K., Pembroke, S. and McGettrick, C., 'An Oral History of Mary Merritt', MAGOHP/43, 2013: 20:10 [hereafter MAGOHP/43, Mary Merritt])

Finally, we have an account of escape from Mary Currington, in which the importance of not being visibly 'other' is once again emphasized:

> Anyway, myself and Hazel . . . although she was still out in the laundry working and I was in the sewing room, and she said . . . I said to her one day I said, 'Hazel' – she was a city girl – and I said, 'how about us trying to run away?' And she said, 'Imelda, are you serious?' I said, 'I am, I can't get out of this place any other way'. And she said, 'But how are we going to get out, Imelda? What about our clothes?' I said, 'you work in the laundry, you can nick a couple of dresses for us, hide them behind a machine and nobody will know they're there'. It took us two months to arrange this between the two of us (MAGOHP/15, Mary Currington: 29–30)

Mary Currington also reports being returned to the laundry by the guards, after being spotted in an arcade:

> Anyway, this guard [Irish police] suddenly this guard appeared and he . . . he seemed ever so tall and he said, 'oh good evening'. And, 'oh hello,' like that and I put my head back down. And he said, 'now who are you?' I gave him a different name to what I was and I thought, 'here we go, he's looking for a couple of people now'. As soon as anybody disappears, the nuns alert the cops you know, the police, the guards what you call them . . . over here. Anyway, and he said, 'are you on your own?' I said, 'yes I am' – lies, white lies – 'I am'. 'Are you sure you're on your own?' I said, 'yes I am'. And he said, 'and why are you standing out here?' Of course I slipped up, I said, 'I'm waiting for someone'. 'Well let's go and see if we can find that person in there', you know. And I saw Hazel out [of] the . . . the left eye and I thought, please, please don't let her see me now. And I was walking around with the guard, you know, this big fella and suddenly I heard my name – 'Imelda!' She should have known better, she saw the guard with me, she shouldn't have said my name, you know! He said, 'oh, so you're Imelda are you? (MAGOHP/15, Mary Currington: 31)

Mary Currington's narrative of her escape is particularly interesting because, when asked about methods of survival, she later states:

> **MC** Not into . . . not to get into bother. You couldn't answer them back and you didn't do so, you know.
>
> **SP** Yeah.
>
> **MC** That was my survival, way . . . way of coping with it, you know.
>
> **SP** Yeah, yeah. Although you did try to run away once . . .
>
> **MC** Oh yes, yes . . . (MAGOHP/15, Mary Currington: 89)

Mary Currington does not, it seems, conceive of her escape as a method of survival – perhaps this was because it was unsuccessful, lasting only about two hours. However, when thinking about bodily strategies of resistance, I would argue that even unsuccessful escape attempts could be seen as an exertion of agency.

From these extracts, we can see how escape presented itself as a way for the women to very distinctly resist the disciplining of the body enforced by the nuns. However, running away was not as simple as escaping the physical confines of the laundry. Ireland in the twentieth century operated a system of very specific social networks, and if you did not have somewhere to go when you escaped the institution, you would immediately stand out as someone 'other', who did not belong, even if you were able to alter your appearance through a change of clothes. An interview with Maureen Sullivan demonstrates the complexity of escape as a method of resistance:

> **SP** And if a nun turned around to you tomorrow and said, you weren't there held against your will, that you could leave whenever you want, what would you say to her?
>
> **MS** How could a twelve-year-old leave a building on her own and not know even where she . . . I was never in New Ross before, I didn't even know it was in Wexford . . .
>
> **SP** Is that true, could you have left?
>
> **MS** No, you could not leave the building, even your dormitories was locked. everywhere was locked. You were watched 24/7, not only did the nuns watch you, but you had trustees watching you as well. They'd watch you in the bathroom.
>
> (O'Donnell, K., Pembroke, S. and McGettrick, C., 'An Oral History of Maureen Sullivan', MAGOHP/38, 2013: 1:05:59 [hereafter MAGOHP/38, Maureen Sullivan])

Maureen highlights the barriers to escaping from a laundry – not only her age but also the unfamiliar geographical location. Women were frequently sent to institutions far away from their birth towns – you not only had to escape the physical confines of the institution but then you would likely also find yourself in a town where everyone knew everyone else. You couldn't say where you had been, and who would help you, without knowing this? Finding employment as a complete stranger in a new place was unlikely – who would take you on without a reference? The chance for you to reinvent yourself was incredibly slim, unless you moved beyond the geographical confines of Ireland and made it to England. This complexity in escape further demonstrates the interconnected nature of the laundries to wider structures in Irish social life. They were able to operate in Ireland until the very end of the twentieth century because they were supported not just by the State and the wider Catholic Church but also by the very social fabric of Ireland. They were not anomalies, existing outside of the wider social and moral code, but very much part of it, woven into the fabric of twentieth-century Ireland.

Other women resisted this bodily discipline by simply refusing to work. Removal of labour, or striking, is one of the most universal forms of protest:

> Laundry, washing machines . . . they had the contract with the laundries all over Dublin, terrible . . . I know I refused to do it and I was always, always in trouble and always doing something because I . . . I wouldn't do it for them. (MAGOHP/4/ANON, Mary: 7)

> I'd go on strike, I wouldn't do what the nuns wanted, loads of things I wouldn't do. (MAGOHP/4/ANON, Mary: 46)

Mary specifically describes her actions as going on strike. She also highlights that this kind of behaviour got her in trouble, further reinforcing that not only was this a personal act of agency, it was recognized as such by the nuns. Kathleen R also speaks about removal of labour as a way of resisting bodily discipline:

> I didn't want to spend the rest of my life there, so I rebelled again, I went up the stairs, sat on the stairs, I wouldn't do no work, I wouldn't eat nor nothing . . . And I was rebelling all the time, I wouldn't do nothing, nothing . . . nothing for them, I done nothing, wouldn't do no work nor nothing for them, I wanted to be out in a job.
> (O'Donnell, K., Pembroke, S. and McGettrick, C., 'An Oral History of Kathleen R', MAGOHP/73/ANON, 2013: 2 [hereafter MAGOHP/73/ANON, Kathleen R])

Interestingly, for Kathleen R, her unwillingness to work is very much confined to the institution – it is not that she does not want to work, just that she does not want to work *for them*. Later in the interview she says, 'all I wanted was to have a job, that was all I wanted' (MAGOHP/73/ANON, Kathleen R: 26). Getting a job is a priority for her, but crucially, a *paid* job, rather than the unpaid labour she is expected to do in the laundry. Work is a key way in which people develop a sense of self-worth, and productivity was a clear focus of the institutions, a way in which the women could surpass their sinful natures.

Therefore, refusing to work, refusing to be productive, carries a particular significance – through this they were not only resisting the bodily discipline that work enforced, but also the religiously motivated moral ideology which underpinned the institutions.

Disciplining selves: Shameful subjects and the power of names

This final section will address the ways in which the women's sense of identity was disciplined, specifically how the women were produced as shameful subjects, through processes of blame and dehumanization. I explore this through two particular experiences which emerged as significant throughout the interviews. First, I engage with the experience of depersonalization, being repeatedly told you are nothing and nobody. Secondly, I look at the practice of forcible renaming, something reported by many of the interviewees. Both of these practices work to dehumanize the women, removing their agency and sense of identity so they could be coercively formed into a new, penitent subjectivity.

Being a nobody

Throughout interviews with survivors, women speak about being referred to by the nuns as 'nobody' or 'nothing':

> We used to have to line up in Clonakilty and they used to make us hold our hands and the nuns used to say to us, 'say after me, "I am a nobody. I am a nobody"' – they used to keep telling us to say that, 'I am a nobody'. And they used to brain wash us with this and I was actually talking to a girl and she keeps onto this day saying . . . she thinks she's a nobody. She keeps on . . . she has herself brainwashed that she's a nobody. (MAGOHP/31, Mary Smith: 14)

In this section of the interview, Mary is talking about her experience in an industrial school, rather than a Magdalene institution. However, these institutions were run by the same orders of nuns, and many of the survivors went to a Magdalene laundry as a direct result of being in an industrial school. While it is important to be mindful of the distinctions between the two institutions, to separate out experiences completely is unhelpful. The trauma they suffer in the industrial schools overlaps and accumulates as they move from one institution to another. Other interviewees give similar descriptions of their time in Magdalene institutions:

Yeah, you were always being told that you were . . . you were useless and that you'll never make anything of yourself and you're there because nobody wants you. (MAGOHP/04/ANON, Mary: 31)

An awful lot of name-calling with me was because I was abused by two uncles and the nuns knew it so I was treated like . . . as if I was nothing and told me I was nothing, and I'd never lead to anything.
(O'Donnell, K., Pembroke, S. and McGettrick, C., 'An Oral History of Jane', MAGOHP/16/ANON, 2013: 07:51 [hereafter MAGOHP/16/ANON, Jane])

I used to hear them say to me, 'oh you'll never be anything, you'll be nothing', you know . . . you know, the way I used to hear them say to other girls about . . . 'you'll be walking the streets like your mother, you'll never be anything. You'll be walking the streets with a shawl around your shoulders'.[1] (MAGOHP/27, Phyllis Morgan: 7)

Mary, Jane and Phyllis all describe a similar narrative within this experience – that they would never amount to anything, never make anything of themselves, with the threat of prostitution – 'walking the streets' – looming large as the inevitable result of amounting to nothing. This forcibly constructs them as subjects without social value, with nothing to contribute to society, because of the sinful nature of their identity. Again, the value of productivity as an identity feature emerges here – these women's productivity is being directly linked to their perceived moral failing. Through this process of dehumanization, the laundries emerge as institutions designed to strip women of their agency and identity. They suffered a constant attrition of their sense of self through a process of verbal and psychological humiliation:

There was a . . . you were nothing, you . . . you were just nothing. You belonged to nobody, as far as they were concerned. You were a . . . a sinner . . .
(O'Donnell, K., Pembroke, S. and McGettrick, C., 'An Oral History of Bernadette and Francis Murphy', MAGOHP/13/ANON, 2013: 70, Bernadette speaking [hereafter MAGOHP/13/ANON, Bernadette and Francis Murphy])

And I had no idea what . . . what was that about, because I w . . . I wasn't allowed to speak, I'd no . . . no . . . what would you say, they never gave me a chance to speak for mesel', to ask questions . . . you were just a nobody. (MAGOHP/46/ANON, Pippa Flanagan: 14)

But there was no-one ever nice, you know. You, you'd have to pull out of the way when they'd pass, they were better than every . . . you . . . you were a nothing, you were there and th . . . and that's the way they had it, you were nobody and you felt a nobody.
(O'Donnell, K., Pembroke, S. and McGettrick, C., 'An Oral History of Martha', MAGOHP/48/ANON, 2013: 58 [hereafter MAGOHP/48/ANON, Martha])

Being repeatedly told you have no worth, that no one cares about you and that you have no legitimate identity clearly had a significant impact on many of the women, on their sense of identity and self, as shown by Martha's final few words. You were told you were a nobody, and, for her, this translated into feeling like a nobody:

> Getting told you know, 'you're a dirt . . . you're dirty like, we have to do this because you have the devil inside you, you . . . you're this horrible child and nobody wants you and we're the only ones there', and I mean they *drummed* it into us . . . *drummed* it into us and it . . . it got to the stage where I believed it. (MAGOHP/48/ANON, Martha: 2)

Returning to the interview with Mary Smith, we can see how this process continued for her, from the Clonakilty Industrial School to the Sundays Well laundry in Cork. Speaking about the day she was brought there by Keane, 'the cruelty man', she says:

> So with that, he left me there, he said, 'we have another one', that's what he says to the nun. He said, 'I have another one for you', they were his very words, 'I have another one'. You would think of him talking about a piece of furniture or something! (MAGOHP/31, Mary Smith: 20)

This process of dehumanization, removing agency from women by literally assigning them a status of less than human, is described throughout the interviews. The end result of this process is summarized by Patricia Dervan:

> I think the oppression and suppression of the personalities of these women is something we perhaps don't talk enough about . . . you have to admire the nuns, it sounds a terrible thing to suggest, but I have a certain admiration for them in that they succeeded in their objective of making nothing of these people, of making them cogs in a wheel, they somehow did succeed. (MAGOHP/06, Patricia Dervan: tape 4, 55:08)

While I would be wary of making the argument that the nuns were successful in making the women into 'nothing', the frequent and repetitive assertions by survivors that this experience not only took place but also had a significant and lasting impact on them demonstrates the intentionality and efficacy of this. As Mary Smith says:

> they took your freedom, they just . . . they took your identity . . . (MAGOHP/31, Mary Smith: 48)

Changing names and house numbers

This process of identity stripping was not only achieved in this very direct manner; it also occurred through the practice of giving women a 'house name', usually that of a female saint, or a house number. Interviewees were asked a specific question about this:

> Were you given a house name or number and a uniform? (O'Donnell et al. 2013)

From the responses, it appears that this was not something which happened in every institution, although having one's name changed was significantly more common than being given a house number. This forcible name change often happened at the point of entry to the laundry; as the earlier extracts demonstrate, this was frequently a very traumatic time for the women, and the coercive renaming and/or assigning of a house number is mentioned as something survivors found deeply distressing:

> So you went upstairs, took your clothes off, got into this big, long dress (laughs) given your name . . . change . . . and they said, 'your name now is going to be Theresa [pseudonym] . . . and your number . . . is going to be 59'. (MAGOHP/13/ANON, Bernadette and Francis Murphy: 3, Bernadette speaking)
>
> **SP** And you were given a house . . . a name like a new name?
>
> **E** Yeah, yeah, yeah, I was given a name . . .
>
> **SP** Which was . . .
>
> **E** Evelyn. [Interviewee's house name and chosen pseudonym] Yeah, yeah I was given a name. You had numbers on your clothes . . . (MAGOHP/10/ANON, Evelyn: 17)

How does the experience of being coercively renamed impact on a person's sense of self? Being stripped of one's name has a long history of use as a dehumanizing punishment; for example, prisoners are frequently identified by numbers rather than names. Names carry a heavy significance that is difficult to pin down – unless you have experienced the pain of being misnamed, of having such an integral part of your identity taken away, it is perhaps difficult to fully understand the specific distress this can cause. From birth, our name is one of the few things which stays constant – we hear it multiple times a day, it becomes enmeshed with our identity. When we hear someone's name, we make certain assumptions about their identity based on this – for example, their gender, their race, their class. Rightly or wrongly, names are a key way in which we discern social facts about each other. Giving someone a nickname can be an act of love, or of humiliation. Naming holds a degree of power over someone – it is seen as a privilege, for example, to be asked to suggest names for a child. You are helping shape their (perceived) identity.

People change their names when going through major life events – for example, changing your name is frequently an important step for people going through a process of gender transition. The new name signifies a shift away from an old identity, one which no longer fits with how the person experiences their subjectivity. Renaming yourself is a deeply powerful act because it takes the power away from the person who originally named you, forming yourself in a certain way, choosing how you wish to present yourself. To change someone's name without their consent can therefore be experienced as a violation of personal autonomy, a denial that someone's experience of themselves is valid. It positions the 'namer' as epistemically superior, placing themselves in a quasi-parental role above those they name – they know you better than you know yourself, and therefore they know what your name *should* be. In a specifically carceral environment, especially one presented as without a clear end in sight, to forcibly rename someone makes a clear distinction between the old life and the new – in giving someone a new name, it is implied that the old one will not be used again, the old life will not be returned to because that person no longer exists. Each time the new name is used, this identity is further reinforced, the new subjectivity inscribed on the bodies of the women through this practice.

It is not insignificant then that the women were almost always given the names of female saints. If we understand the process of renaming as one of a wider coercive formation into a particular subjectivity, then the name someone is given sheds light on how they are to be viewed. By assigning 'sinful' women the names of saints, we can assume it was hoped they would leave behind their previous life and come to embody the qualities of the woman they were now named after – the penitent as an idealized subjectivity they would come to inhabit, through hard work and incarceration in the laundries. To build on this, calling somebody by a number, as described in some instances, is even more dehumanizing, because it is outside the frame of reference for what human names are. It therefore takes that person outside the frame of what human beings are, removing them from a widely understood symbolic framework and placing them into a new one, a jarring and uncomfortable process. To be a number is to be less than a whole human – a nobody, a nothing. Examples from the interviews illustrate what a painful experience being coercively renamed was for these women; they all express distress at the experience and listening to the audio files, the discussions on names are often fraught with emotion:

SP Did they take your name away?

NS I wouldn't let them take my name away! My name is Nancy Shannon, and I'm holding on to it. They'd have to kill me first, to get it.

SP They wanted to take your name away, didn't they?

NS Yes . . . they'd have to kill me first to get my name. No-one's going to get it.

(O'Donnell, K., Pembroke, S. and McGettrick, C., 'An Oral History of Nancy Shannon', MAGOHP/30, 2013: 10:02 [hereafter MAGOHP/30, Nancy Shannon])

Throughout her interview, Nancy's voice is shaky, and she sounds like she is frequently on the verge of tears. The previous exchange is vehement, she sounds angry. Shortly after this, however, she breaks down and there is a pause in the interview while her son comforts her. Later, she repeats:

> I was told not to be using my name . . . I'm not going to give up my name for nobody. (MAGOHP/30, Nancy Shannon: 22:58)

Mary also describes this process as one she found uncomfortable:

> They . . . they insisted that my name would be Elizabeth [pseudonym of interviewee's house name], would be . . . would be Elizabeth and that there was another . . . Sr Angela [pseudonym] and that . . . that would be . . . and I said, 'I'm not having . . . don't want another name, I'm not doing it'. (MAGOHP/04/ANON, Mary: 15)

Both Nancy and Mary stress how they did not want to change their names, emphasizing the discomfort this caused them. Mary Currington also describes this process:

> And the next minute I know I'm standing in this parlour and there was about four nuns surrounding me and all I could hear them saying was, 'now what shall we call her?' And I said . . . 'I'm . . . my name is Mary'. And another nun is saying, 'no, and what's your second name?' 'It's Mary Josephine'. 'Oh we can't, we can't . . .' They were talking between themselves, 'we can't call her Mary Josephine, or Mary Jo, we've got one of them already'. (MAGOHP/15, Mary Currington: 20)

The language in the final remark – 'we've got one of them already' – is deeply dehumanizing. She is reduced to an object, 'one of them'. She is being talked *about*, rather than spoken *to* – not only does her real name not matter, she does not exist as a subject but simply as a thing which needs processing and differentiating from others. Speaking later in her interview, Mary Currington says:

> People often asked me afterwards why was our names changed, you see and I've got two ideas on that. One, I was told by one of the nuns that . . . to protect the identity of a lot of the local girls, because if they got into trouble outside in the city it would be in their papers you see. And if we got hold of the papers and we saw say, Hazel McDermott or whatever, had stolen . . . something or . . . like that, that would be in the papers and everybody in the . . . S . . . in the Magdalene side would know why she was in there. They said they were protecting the identity of the people in there. My other idea is that . . . so that whenever we left there or were put out of there we'd never be able to trace our friends . . . (MAGOHP/15, Mary Currington: 30)

The repeated emphasis on this process of forcible renaming being done to 'protect the identity' of the women is a recurring theme. The McAleese report tells us that

> In relation to the practice, in some Magdalen Laundries, of giving 'House' or 'Class' names to girls and women on entry in place of their given names, the Sisters explained that they did not intend to undermine the identity of the girls or women involved. They state that the practice was adopted from the very first days of the institutions in the 1800s, in order to preserve the anonymity and privacy of the girls and women who were admitted – in other words, that the intention of the practice was that every entrant would be protected from discussion of her past. They said that they regret the impact which this practice had on some women. (McAleese 2013: 959)

Again, we see repeated the assertion that this practice, experienced by the women as distressing and traumatic, was, in fact, done *for their own good*, to save them from the stigma of their own identity. Their experience is presented as posing a danger to themselves – they are both threatening and in need of protection. There is another discussion to be had about the way in which the assertions of the nuns are taken at face value throughout the report, with no interrogation. In this context, though, it is enough to engage with the alleged aim of this practice, as an indication of the disconnect between the intention and how the practice is experienced by the women.

Pippa Flanagan also discusses being told similar things when speaking about her experience of having her name changed:

> And Sr Frances just sat with me and then she turns around and she says to me, 'now, you have to get your name changed because we don't want any people knowing who you are, you're a n . . . a number'. I . . . I couldn't understand, I thought . . . I just didn't. So she rang a bell for another woman to come and get

me and she took me to . . . up to the bathroom and took off all me clothes and I had to get into a bath of . . . it was disinfectant. Because they said . . . to wash me s . . . me sins away and I didn't understand what that meant. (MAGOHP/46/ANON, Pippa Flanagan: 2)

Two reasons are given here for the practice of renaming – 'we don't want any people knowing who you are' and 'you're a number'. The first speaks to the use of shame as a method of self-regulation – similarly to Mary Currington, Pippa Flanagan is made to feel like she *should* be ashamed of what she has done, that it would be harmful *to her* if people knew who she really was. This idea that the very act of being in a Magdalene institution was enough to make a woman shameful, to inscribe her with a sinful identity, is one repeatedly expressed throughout the survivor narratives. Underlying all of this is the idea of one's name as a locus for shame, something for the stigma to 'stick' to – the idea that there is something so deeply contaminated about you that it has infected everything about you, even your name, and so for your own sake, it needs to be changed and obscured.

However, this idea is also found in the interviews with key informants and others outside of the institutions who describe their conceptions of the laundries as places where sinful or wilful women and girls were sent. If this is how the institutions are positioned in society, then the women who exist within them are necessarily marked with this stigma, even when they leave. Returning to Pippa's statement and the latter reason given – 'you're just a number' – this once again demonstrates the use of renaming as a way of stripping women of their identities, of their sense of selves. They are constructed as objects, numbers, not whole people. This process of coercive renaming is, of course, linked to the process of identity erosion discussed in the previous section. It was a way of disciplining and controlling a perceived deviant identity, of marking the boundaries between a woman's past, sinful life and her new existence in the Magdalene institution.

Reclaiming a name

Margaret Burke sums up the overarching result of these processes as that of a dehumanizing identity erosion – 'we were never allowed to be . . . human, really' (MAGOHP/18/ANON, Margaret Burke: 54:38). However, Margaret then goes on to use the association between names and identity in a different way. When speaking about her life after leaving the laundry, she says that 'I hated who I was in Ireland . . . I felt a deep depression there' (MAGOHP/18/ANON, Margaret Burke: 1:34:13) – so she changed her name to cleanse herself of everything from her time there:

> It was like it was washing it away from me, Ireland, the Magdalene laundry . . . Margaret Burke belonged in Ireland, not me. So I changed my first name . . . I changed it to Marina. (MAGOHP/18/ANON, Margaret Burke: 1:34:40)

Margaret is, similarly to the nuns, using the power of renaming as a way of forming a particular identity, but rather than as a coercive tactic for the erosion of identity, she is producing a new one, which allows her to distance herself from 'who she was' in Ireland. This demonstrates the potential productive power of naming, regaining control of one's identity through a rejection of the past persona. Nancy Shannon also touches on this when she speaks about changing her name after getting married. She states:

> I'm not going to give up my name to nobody, the only one I gave my name to is Pat Shannon. (MAGOHP/30, Nancy Shannon: 23:08)

In the next chapter I will discuss the ways in which women worked within frameworks of 'traditional' femininity, using social identities like mother and wife to regain the credibility which was denied to them through their time in the laundries. I feel that the power of changing one's name when married has a role in this, although it is not explicitly discussed by many of the women. However, by taking on this new name, voluntarily, and in a highly socially legitimate context, the women are again exerting agency which was so frequently denied to them in their earlier lives.

Conclusion

This chapter has explored the experiences of the women at the point of entry to, and during their time in, the laundries, drawing on their own narratives as expressed during the oral history interviews. I have focused on how their voices, bodies and sense of identities were controlled and coercively shaped by practices of discipline and penance; as well as considering their resistance to these practices. The processes which worked to achieve this were not limited in operation to the social and symbolic worlds within the institutions but reflected those in wider Irish society.

These processes of discipline represent clear incidences of testimonial injustice, whereby the women's social identity resulted in a lack of credibility, both as they were entering the institutions and throughout their time there. Throughout the interviews, they speak about experiences of being disbelieved and discredited, their testimony discounted and their voices silenced. It was their social identity as mostly young, working-class women, existing in twentieth-century Ireland, which resulted in these instances of testimonial injustice. Many of these women were perceived as a threat to the moral fabric of the newly formed Irish State, either by their actions or simply by their existence as women outside the norms of the heteropatriarchal family. Their incarceration could then be framed as for the good of the nation, because they were seen as unreliable narrators, liars whose testimony threatened those in power. Throughout this chapter, I have demonstrated not only the ways in which their experiences can be conceptualized as instances of testimonial injustice, but also the effect this had on their sense of self. In this context, being consistently denied credibility can be seen to have a significant effect on the women's subjectivity. In combination with a deliberate erosion of agency through processes of humiliation and name changing, it is easy to see how, as Mary Smith says, 'they took your freedom, they just . . . they took your identity . . .' (MAGOHP/31, Mary Smith: 48).

I have emphasized the distinctly religious nature of this epistemic injustice. It was not just the women's identity as *women* which led to this credibility deficit, but also the way in which this identity was produced in the specific context of post-Independence Ireland, a country in which the interactions between Church and State worked to create very specific boundaries of acceptable womanhood. After leaving the institutions, the women existed in a society where these interactions, and the structures they produced, were still deeply significant. I now turn to an analysis of the women's experiences after leaving the institutions, thinking about the ways in which these instances of testimonial and hermeneutical injustice endured and increased.

5

Fractured endings and new meanings: Religion and respectability

I think sometimes I hardly know who I am, really, who I really am, because, you know, I spend my life, more or less, trying to be what I think will be acceptable to other people rather than, to hell with everyone else, I want to do this for me . . . that's the biggest part of the fallout, I suppose, from it.

(MAGOHP/22, Celine Roberts: 1:16:05)

When I first went out, I was not able to cope at all as I told you, and I always felt I was a nobody, which they made you feel all the time, they always told us we were nobodies anyway . . .

(MAGOHP/15, Mary Currington: 87)

The nature of trauma is that it does not end with the traumatic event – it continues, shifting and changing, but for many people, an ever-present experience. While in the laundries, the women experienced a process of identity erosion, a gradual attrition of their sense of self through punitive discipline and mundane routine. This did not stop once they left the institutions – as Mary Currington and Celine describe, the damage caused by the trauma of institutionalization lingered. Thinking about the processes of disciplining minds, bodies and selves in the laundries as contributing to an instance of epistemic injustice allows us to then explore how the harms of this continue and are replicated in the women's lives after the institutions. In this chapter, I focus on the experiences of the women after they left the institutions, and how these processes of discipline persisted, as well as focusing on the ways in which survivors renegotiated their identities after the traumatic experience of being in a laundry.

In this chapter I make three broad points. Firstly, I argue that on leaving the laundries, women experienced ongoing shame around their incarceration, because the cultural system of meaning underpinning the institutions was present in wider Irish society. The stigma of being a 'Magdalene', inscribed upon their bodies during their time in the laundries, persisted and impacted on their behaviour and sense of self significantly. Secondly, I argue that this sense of ongoing shame was borne out by a cultural system of purity and impurity structured around religious relationships, beliefs and practices – the women's experience of trauma frequently left them unable to continue to live in that system of meaning without some sense of alienation or distance, through either rejecting God or rejecting the Church but not God or finding some way of accommodating themselves in a society that remained structured around religious organizations. I consider the various ways in which women renegotiated their religious relationships, and the new forms of meaning which emerged as a result of this. Lastly, moving beyond their altered engagement with religion, I explore the ways women found space to renegotiate their identities, either through finding routes to motherhood and respectability, and/or finding relief in the mundane acts of everyday life, which provided a framework of symbolic meaning in which to exert and explore new types of agency. Again, I situate these experiences within the wider framework of epistemic injustice, thinking about how the processes of discipline which produced these forms of injustice while they were in the laundry continued and were augmented by the social and cultural context of post-Independence Ireland.

Leaving the institution: Abrupt endings and conflicted feelings

In the previous chapter, I drew out the women's descriptions of entering the laundries – particularly the confusion around this, and the trauma it caused. Many women described the deliberate obfuscation by the nuns, social services and other authority figures, about what was going on, how long they would be there, what they had 'done' to end up in such a place. If we think about beginnings, we must then also think about endings. Before engaging with the ways in which processes of epistemic injustice continued in the lives of the women after leaving the laundries, I first consider the process of leaving itself, particularly the extent to which this kept women in a state of 'not knowing'.

The act of 'ending', of finishing something, leaving somewhere or someone, comes with its own set of complicated social meanings and rituals. Frequently, we commemorate endings in some way – a graduation ceremony, a leaving party, an exit interview and so on. We do this to provide a boundary between the old and the new, allowing us time to prepare for what might be a challenging event. Without this, endings can be traumatic – if your partner breaks up with you with no warning, leaving suddenly with no further communication, the pain is likely to be greater than if there was a gradual and mutual agreement to end the relationship. We seek closure and clarity. Even in more difficult circumstances, there are often clear steps towards an ending. For example, when being released from prison, there are procedures and steps in place, processes to go through which are intended to allow those involved to prepare for what will happen next, even if functionally this is not always the case.

The circumstances of leaving the institutions varied significantly across the interviews. Most commonly, it seems women were sent to work in religiously run hospitals or for a family; or they were collected by a family member. However, a common theme throughout the sections of interviews which discuss leaving the institutions is that of abruptness. The women were almost never given any prior warning; they were simply told on the day they were going home or going to a job. They were in the institution, and then they were not. Mary Currington gives a clear account of the day she left, demonstrating this complete lack of notice given:

> I remember . . . oh no, I'll . . . I'll tell you about leaving the . . . the laundry first. 1969, January 1969, it . . . actually it was the first day of the troubles of Northern Ireland and I got up that morning at half past six to get ready for church and so on. I had my towel and my flannel and my toothpaste with me and my little round tin of toothpaste. It was a cake, a very hard cake of toothpaste. And I was just about to go and have my wash in cold water as usual, and Monica, [pseudonym] . . . she came out into the dormitory and said, 'Imelda, my zip's broken, can you fix it for me?' You know, being a sewing lady. I said, 'Okay M . . . Monica,' I put my washing things on my bed, and once I was behind that door she said, 'come on Imelda, you're leaving'. Those were her very words! Well, the butterflies that went in my tummy that very moment, I said, 'well hold on a minute', I said to her, 'I'll just go and say goodbye to my friends'. 'Imelda, you're leaving, did you hear what I said?' And I started crying, I wanted to go all those years I was in there, suddenly I was being plucked from the security I had in there for those six years and I was going out – where I don't know, they didn't tell me. They put me in clothes [identifying details removed] very poor-quality clothes, ill-fitting clothes. I think the coat I had on me wasn't fitting me at all. (MAGOHP/15, Mary Currington: 41)

This day is one which made a lasting impact on Mary Currington, evidenced by the levels of detail present in her description. She expresses the conflicting emotions she feels when she is told she is leaving – joy at the prospect of finally being able to escape a place she had wanted to leave for so long; mixed with the anxiety of having no idea where she was going next, or what would happen; and the sadness at leaving her friends without being allowed to say goodbye. It is not surprising that this conflict resulted in tears. While she is obviously pleased to be leaving the laundry, the fact that this 'leaving' is so sudden, forcing her out of a situation in which she has a level of security, into one where she has no control over what will happen to her, causes an intense reaction. There is no acknowledgement of what has happened to her, of the past six years, and she has no time to prepare for the future. Even in leaving, she is stripped of agency and dignity, forced to leave behind the few small possessions she has – her flannel, her toothbrush and toothpaste – and given ill-fitting clothes to wear.

Pippa Flanagan also speaks about the day she left as being filled with uncertainty, confusion and sadness:

CMcG Something I meant to ask you actually . . . the day you left the laundry, like, did you get warning that you were leaving or . . .

PF No, no.

CMcG . . . how did you know you were leaving?

PF No, you'd get no warning, they just would call you into the office that you went into that day, you were met and just told [inaudible], yeah, the people were waiting on me outside in the car, the ones I was going to work for.

CMcG On the same day that you were leaving?

PF On the same day. And I went out with the clothes I had on me back, no money, not even a toothbrush, just straight to [name of town removed] in Co. Mayo to work.

CMcG But did you get a chance to say goodbye to your . . .

PF No.

CMcG . . . friends or anything?

PF No, we . . . we . . . not even in the orphanage, we always had to go out the back and never say goodbye. And that's why, this is the part that I am missing, is to meet up and . . . you know . . . to get to know the girls again . . . because we never said goodbye.

CMcG Okay. Yeah.

PF Never said goodbye. I was very, very sad; very sad. You know.
(MAGOHP/46/ANON, Pippa Flanagan: 32)

Again, Pippa's interview highlights the indignities inflicted on the women as they left. She mentions being forced to leave without her toothbrush – this small item operating as a symbol of one of the few things women *had* while in the institutions, which they could not even take with them when they left. Similarly to Mary Currington, she had no warning about when her exit would happen, no way of preparing for the future or marking her time in the institutions, no way of saying goodbye. Much of the sadness which is expressed by women when speaking about their experiences leaving the institutions centres around this prohibition from saying goodbye to their friends, from letting anyone else know what was happening to them or where they were going, continuing the themes of 'unknowing' explored in the previous chapter. While in the laundries, women were deliberately kept in a constant state of ignorance about what was happening to them. It is unsurprising then that these features of their experience continue when they leave the institutions. In being prevented from saying goodbye to their friends, they are not only kept in ignorance themselves but this state is replicated in the other women too. Your friend does not leave, she is simply gone one day. You cannot say goodbye or prepare for her departure in any way. It is hard to overstate the real terror this would have caused the women. A fear repeated throughout the interviews is that of growing older in the laundries, typified in the interviewees' descriptions of seeing older women in the institutions, a visual representation of their worst fears. To add to that the confusion of your friend simply disappearing, leaving you to grow old alone and forgotten about, would have instilled a real fear in the women. The abruptness of leaving then has an impact beyond the removal of agency for individuals – it is a continuation of processes of deliberate ignorance designed to produce a docile and subdued body, full of fear.

Bernadette Murphy's interview contains an extended description of the day she left:

> **BM** I was . . . I was in the packing room and the auxiliary came in and said, 'can I see you?' And we went to this . . . along this big corridor and down near the . . . the main entrance and she said, 'there's a dress there, put that on, there's a coat there, put that on'. And then the nun came and said, 'you're going to B&B . . . and the auxiliary will come back for you in the morning to take you to Waterford. You're on your way to Galway'.
>
> . . ..
>
> **SP** And you never got . . . did you get to say goodbye to anyone?
>
> **BM** Oh no.

SP You were just brought out . . .

BM Brought out.

SP . . . and that's it.

BM Gone!

SP Okay. Jesus.

BM Yeah, it was . . . there was . . . that, yeah . . . that . . . that does stick with me a lot.

SP Yeah.

FM Were you given changes of clothing or anything like that – a case to take with you?

BM No, there was no case. There was this little . . . no, honest to God I'm sure I was like a gypsy. I was.

FM Just in what you stood up in?

BM Yeah . . . yeah. (MAGOHP/13/ANON, Bernadette and Francis Murphy: 89–90)

Again, there are significant similarities to the previous two extracts. One day, she is told by an auxiliary to come with her, and then told to leave – she is denied the opportunity to mark her departure by saying goodbye to anyone, nor is she given a change of clothes or anything to take with her.

The focus placed by survivors on the pain caused by the lack of opportunities to say goodbye also raises questions about the extent to which it was possible to build important relationships in these institutions. Some women speak about this as something which was almost impossible, the conditions of the laundries being such that communication with the other women was extremely difficult, as discussed in the previous chapter. However, excerpts such as the previous one suggest that the relationships between the women had the *potential* to be significant and meaningful. It is difficult to fully know the extent to which women were able to make friendships, because it is not something many survivors have spoken about. However, I argue that the sentiments around friendships expressed by Mary, Pippa and Bernadette speak to the human need to mark relationships, particularly the ending of them, even if they were fleeting or created in difficult situations. Perhaps the extent of the friendship does not really matter; when we are removed from a site which has had a significant impact on us, we try to mark that in any way possible. Saying goodbye is a clear ritual of leaving, and so the desire to say one's goodbyes, even to people we may not feel particularly connected with, is strong.

Some of the women also describe difficulty in remembering the day they left the institution:

> I'm trying to remember; they came up to me and said to me that, 'your father's coming to take you home'. I remember that bit and I was delighted, but at the same time I was apprehensive about going because I was going back to what I'd left, as to the reason why I was in there. And I knew I would be going back to it, but I was going back to my brothers and sisters. As . . . and as much as I actually wanted to get out of there, I didn't want to go back to that abuse again. So, it was the chance you took I suppose. But yes, they told me that and I was . . . I think he was coming up the next day to pick me up, and that was it. And I . . . I don't . . . I don't remember leaving there, I don't remember saying goodbye to the girls and I don't remember how we got home. (MAGOHP/10/ANON, Evelyn: 47–8)

Again, Evelyn describes feeling a complex mix of emotions on hearing she was leaving – although in this instance, it is linked to the circumstances to which she is returning. The abusive situation which contributed to her entry to the laundry would not have changed, and so in that moment, she is forced to consider whether the laundry is a preferable option to her home life. Bernadette also describes having little to no memory of this day:

> **B** The day I left was the day I would have been told, there would have been no build up, there would be no . . . no 'I'm going home tomorrow' thing . . . I would have been told, 'you go upstairs right now, pack your bags and then come down this ex . . . this different corridor so that you don't see anybody to tell them that you're leaving', you just get out . . . and go. And I know that would have happened, but I don't remember it happening.
>
> . . .
>
> **SP** Okay. And can you describe what happened the day you were leaving and where . . . where you went?
>
> **B** No.
>
> **SP** No.
>
> **B** No.
>
> **SP** Okay.
>
> **B** No memory. (MAGOHP/12/ANON, Bernadette: 64–6)

Both Bernadette and Evelyn describe how the day they left is one which they cannot really remember – Bernadette's repeated 'no' stressing her inability, in conjunction perhaps with a disinclination, to remember. When contrasted with the level of detail given in previous extracts – Mary Currington's emphasis on her toothbrush, her hard cake of toothpaste – this paints a picture of the wide range of experiences caused by the abrupt nature of women's departure from the laundries. For some, the day is rendered in sharp detail in their memory, for others it slips away, or is pushed from their memory. Whether this is due to the nature of the ending process, the trauma experienced during their time in the laundries, or simply the natural difficulty we all have in remembering events from a long time ago is impossible to say.

However, it is important to note that for some of the interviewees, the experience of leaving seemed to be characterized overwhelmingly by joy:

> **M** When I was leaving, the nun just said to me, 'have I anything to say for myself?' And I told her, 'no, I'm glad to be getting the hell out of here'. But that's not where it ended, you know, you had to go through life knowing you had all of that – you couldn't tell anybody about it because nobody really wanted to know. And so therefore you were left with the whole thing yourself.
>
> **SP** Yeah. So yeah we'll talk about you leaving now, so what word or phrase best describes the way you felt the day you were leaving?
>
> **M** Absolute ... overjoyed ... overjoyed and I left with the same clothes I came in two-and-a-half-years before. I couldn't wait to get the hell out. (MAGOHP/04/ANON, Mary: 50)

Unsurprisingly, leaving the laundry was a significant event for many of the interviewees, and their description of how they experienced this reinforces several of the themes discussed in the previous chapter. For many of the women it was deeply painful to be taken out of the laundries so immediately and abruptly; there was no opportunity to prepare themselves for a sudden shift in circumstance. Even the most basic of leaving rituals – saying goodbye – was denied to them, and they were forcibly moved yet again from one circumstance to another, without being able to make their own preparations. They had no agency in this event. The time spent in the institutions was marked by routine and strict rules, and so the complete lack of ceremony around their departure is at odds with this, a jarring end to their experience in the institution. Women were caught in a system of ritual and powerful symbolic meaning, and then thrust out of this into an unknown and uncertain future which they had no chance to prepare for. It is unsurprising that some of them could not remember this, or spoke about it as a deeply painful experience, despite it being ostensibly the end of their incarceration.

Most importantly, though, this denial of information and removal of agency further demonstrates the way in which these women were not seen as important or capable enough to warrant information about their own lives. Their experiences in the Magdalene laundries are consistently characterized by uncertainty – uncertainty about length of stay, about the reasons they were in the institutions, about what the institution was, whether they could leave and so on. The end of their time in the laundry was no different. It was not seen as important for them to be able to prepare for their future lives because not only were their lives seen as unimportant – they wouldn't amount to anything anyway! – but they were also considered incapable of making the correct decisions. It was up to others – the nuns, the State, their parents – to decide where they should go, from an industrial school, to a laundry, to a suitable employment. This continued infantilization of the women, even as they leave the physical confines of the institution, speaks to the vicious paternalism which characterizes much of the ideology underpinning the Magdalene institutions, which removed choices from women 'for their own good'.

Shame, stigma and the terror of visibility

Even in the act of leaving the institutions, the women were denied the capacity to make decisions about their lives, to exert agency over their own experiences, to be credible subjects. This ongoing instance of epistemic injustice contributed to long-lasting feelings of shame and stigma, which are present in many of the survivor narratives. The ongoing shame around their incarceration in the institutions was in part due to the cultural system of meaning underpinning the laundries, which operated in society more generally when they left. The stigma of being a 'Magdalene' persisted and impacted on their behaviour and sense of self significantly. In this section, I explore how survivors speak, or do not speak, about the ongoing effects of institutionalization on their sense of self, the lingering shame they feel at being a Magdalene woman and the stigma which they feel as a very constant presence in their lives. However, within this framework of shame, I also emphasize how this experience can be considered as one which was *beyond* shame, characterized by feelings of terror and fear (O'Donnell 2018: 90). I demonstrate how, when women left these institutions, they had no way of expressing what had happened to them without the risk of *becoming* a shamed person, of making visible this spoiled identity which was so coercively assigned to them during their time in the laundries. They lacked the vocabulary and language to both make sense of their experiences and meaningfully communicate them to others. Doing so would have also risked further taking on the stigmatized identity, and so there was a real terror surrounding the discussion of their experiences. Situating these experiences within this framework allows for an understanding of this as an example of hermeneutical injustice – survivors were unable to make sense of their experiences because they had no hermeneutic resources to draw upon which would not have further inscribed them with a stigmatized identity. Remaining silent meant they could, to an extent, avoid this, or at least exert some level of control over their own narratives. In the previous chapter, I explored the ways in which various manifestations of silence in the laundries worked as oppressive structures in the formation of idealized subjectivities. Silence is a continual feature of many of the survivors' experiences after they have left the institutions, and in this section I will explore how silence functioned in their lives after leaving the institutions.

Many of the women speak of feeling intense shame around their experiences in the laundries, which often was closely linked to an inability to speak about their experiences to others, particularly their families:

> I didn't want to tell them [her family], because I was ashamed of my life. (MAGOHP/30, Nancy Shannon: 39:01)

Nancy's voice breaks as she says this, and the lingering pain caused by this shame is clear. Another interviewee, Pearl, when asked why she had not spoken about her experiences to anyone, answers, 'I did [feel ashamed] to be put in there' (O'Donnell, K., Pembroke, S. and McGettrick, C., 'An Oral History of Pearl', MAGOHP/19/ANON, 2013: 1:17:57 [hereafter MAGOHP/19/ANON, Pearl). It is notable that Pearl did tell one person, her neighbour Nuala, who had also spent time in an institution – someone whom Pearl saw as sharing the same identity as herself, who would not judge her. Much of this shame focuses on the identity of a 'Magdalene' woman, at once both a fallen, shamed woman and a dangerous threat to social stability. It was a stigmatized identity, and marked out those who held it as other, wrong, bad. Within the laundries they had been forcibly inscribed with the identity of a penitent, and this did not leave them once they left. Kathleen describes how she

> Never spoke about the Magdalene laundries until I heard it on the radio programme, I had never . . . nobody knew anything because I was ashamed, and the word ashamed is very strong with me, to tell anybody I was in the Magdalene laundries because of the stigma that it had. Nothing wrong with being an unmarried mother, I'm not an unmarried mother and there's nothing wrong with it, if it happened, but it was the way it was portrayed, and people, that they were fallen women, they were prostitutes and this is what was said, I'm

certain ... I was none of them. I was just a child who was born out of wedlock. (MAGOHP/34/ANON, Kathleen: 1:10:34)

Kathleen puts a heavy emphasis on the word 'ashamed'. For her, this shame appears to revolve around the stigma associated with the idea of what a 'Magdalene' woman was, rather than the actuality of her experience. Again, this shame is a relational one – her concern is people finding out that she had been in the laundry, and the shame is constructed by the visibility of the identity. The construction of this identity is rooted in the use of women's bodies as markers of purity and national identity in post-Independence Ireland, and the complicated relationships between gender, nationhood and morality in this context. As discussed earlier in this book, women in twentieth-century Ireland became a measure of the nation's morality, with the post-colonial anxieties of the newly formed Irish State played out upon their bodies, their behaviour and identities controlled through a rigid system of ideas around purity, endorsed by the Catholic Church. This climate of morality created an environment in which the bodies of women who transgressed needed to be physically controlled and separated from society, and contributed to the incarceration of women in the Magdalene institutions. While they were in the institutions, the 'shameful' nature of their identity was reinforced by the nuns, who frequently told those in their care that they were no one, or that they deserved to be incarcerated because of what they had done – or more likely, had had done to them:

> **SP** Did you tell anyone about your time, before you went through the redress board?
>
> **Jane** Oh no, I was ashamed to tell anyone where I was from, I thought I was no- one, absolutely no-one, which I know now, totally different ... cos the nuns told me I was no-one ... they always kept me down because of what happened with my uncles when I went in there. (MAGOHP/16/ANON, Jane: 27:44)

When they left the institutions, they were returning to a social environment in which this system of morality very much still existed and continued to impact on the ways in which they could express and understand their experiences as they navigated their lives post-incarceration. It is important to highlight the extent to which this anxiety around their identities was not an empty fear for these women – the stigma of having been in a Magdalene institution was real and significant.

Goffman describes stigma as a socially constructed attribute which has the potential to reduce those it attaches itself to from 'a whole and usual person to a tainted and discarded one' (1990: 12). It is the situation of someone who is disqualified from full social acceptance, a spoiled identity. Stigma marks a person out as different, and induces strong negative reactions in those around them, which frequently translate into harmful material and social consequences. However, moving beyond stigma to consider the specific instance of shame, it is important to think about how shame is constructed. In order to be shamed, you must have your shameful identity made visible. Lisa Guenther demonstrates how 'shame intersubjectifies; it attests to an irreducible relation to others in the midst of one's own self-relation. However painful shame may be, it confirms this relationality of the subject, and could not arise without it' (2012: 61–2). This focus on the *intersubjective* nature of shame suggests how the experiences of the Magdalene women can be thought of not only as shame but also as shame characterized by terror and fear. It is not simply the feelings of shame which prevent them from speaking out but the fear of shame before others, of making visible this highly stigmatized identity. This is, of course, deeply gendered, both shame and fear bound up in the stigmatized idea of being a 'Magdalene woman', shaped by ideas of 'good' Catholic womanhood. The Magdalene survivors have been, until recently, a group whose 'spoiled' identity was largely hidden from view. As the earlier extracts demonstrate, they often would not tell people about their past; society was not seeing them; they were not a group held *in view* as stigmatized. While the identity of Magdalene was a stigmatized one, unless you made this identity visible, you could avoid the shame associated with it. Therefore, what they experience is not simply shame, but terror at the potential visibility of this shamed identity.

The fear of others' reactions to revealing this identity was not unfounded, and several interviewees speak about receiving negative responses from those they did speak to. The previous chapter discussed the many ways in which women in the Magdalene institutions underwent a process of identity erosion, one of which was the repetition that they were nothing, nobody – worthless. Dr M, who worked as a doctor in the Galway laundry between 1979, and then after it closed, until 1997, speaks about his experiences of the women, saying:

> They were isolated . . . marginalized . . . and that stigma would have lasted. And when I think back, I suppose society should have made more of an effort to connect with them, and that stigma prevented society, because people had the

idea that, 'oh, once you go to the Magdalene that's it, you're nobody', which is a pity.
(O'Donnell, K., Pembroke, S. and McGettrick, C., 'An Oral History of Dr M', MAGOHP/1/ANON, 2013: 50:01 [hereafter MAGOHP/1/ANON, Dr M])

His reference to the idea that 'once you go to a Magdalene . . . you're a nobody' demonstrates that this process was not limited to the institutions. It followed the women as they left, supported by a society which upheld the stigma inscribed on them during their incarceration. Lucy describes the negative reaction she encountered when speaking about her experience:

I often wish, I'd say, 'God I wish I was different, I wish I could kind of know what they talk about', because I don't know what to talk about because for me my life is just, full of pain and full of hurt and I feel if I start talking to somebody that I'm going to tell them and I don't want to tell them because when you tell people how you are or what you're feeling and what you've been through they actually don't want to know you anymore. They have this kind of like . . . oh . . . the . . . it's kind of like they stand back from you as if you were kind of a leper or. . . . And it's not that, it's because they're scared, they don't know how to handle it; they don't know what to say to you. So, I've never even created a bond with anybody . . . (MAGOHP/07/ANON, Lucy: 55)

Lucy's use of a disease metaphor demonstrates the very physical way in which she experiences this stigma – it impacts not only on her sense of self but also on the bodily way in which she interacts with people. Upon making her identity visible, they react by attempting to remove themselves from her presence, as if the experience of being in a Magdalene laundry is catching.

Sadie O'Meara states that she didn't speak about the laundries after she left:

Because I was too nervous, I was too ashamed, I was ashamed . . . my marriage broke up over it, because I told him, told my husband, thinking I was doing right, and it was all thrown into my face, so we broke up. (MAGOHP/80/ANON, Sadie O'Meara: 47.47)

Sadie's experience shows the way in which 'speaking out' had the potential for real and damaging consequences for these women. It is interesting to consider what she means when she says that, in telling her husband, she thought she 'was doing right'. In chapter three, I considered the ways in which 'speaking out' can be conceptualized as a universal good; survivors are often encouraged to do this, but in this instance, the very real risks are made evident. An extract from the interview with Phyllis Morgan, an activist who was born in a Mother and Baby home, and raised by nuns, shows that it wasn't even necessary to have spent time in a Magdalene institution, or to have yourself transgressed these strict gendered moral codes to be marked as 'other' – mere proximity to women who might have done so was enough:

> **SP** And did you ever tell . . . or . . . your husband like, about like . . . your past?
>
> **PM** I never . . . I never sort of told him, I . . . no I never really used to talk, I didn't . . . never really wanted to talk about it because I always had that feeling because I know when I was in Ireland that you know, a few times a couple of the older girls that worked around the corner from me, took me to Barry's Dance Hall for dancing. And I remember men [would] get you up to dance you know . . . I found that when men used to say to me, 'what? You're from Dublin? No you definitely aren't, you're a fecking culchie!'[1] And I used to say, 'I'm not a culchie, I'm from Dublin', you know. And then they would say, 'well how have you got an accent like that?' And I used to say, 'well I suppose I was brought up in the nuns', and straight away you would see, 'what? Oh you're one of them!' And they would say that to you, 'oh you're one . . .' and the look on their face of horror, 'you're one of them!' And they . . . they would just walk off and leave you on the dance floor. Yeah, just walk off and leave you and you'd be there like a . . . you know, sidle back to where your friends were and like . . . oh didn't . . . you know, and, 'he says to me, "you're one of them" – what does he mean by that?' Yeah. (MAGOHP/27, Phyllis Morgan: 21)

Earlier in her interview, Phyllis describes a similar encounter with her employer:

> And then the . . . the woman who ran the business called me into her office one day and said to me, you know, something she was saying about, 'where . . . where were you brought up?' And she says, 'you . . . that's not really a Dublin accent you have'. And I said, 'oh . . . oh yes Miss,' – I can't remember what her name was – 'Miss . . . oh yes Miss, I was brought up in Dublin'. And she says, 'with an accent like that of course you couldn't have been brought up in Dublin!' And I said, 'of course I was in Dublin!' I said, 'I was brought up in . . . in Stillorgan'. She said, 'whereabouts in Stillorgan?' I said, 'oh St Philomena's Convent'. And then she . . . she sort of like, gasped, 'oh my God!' she says, 'we can't have your sort working here . . . oh, oh!' This was the way she was, and she had this – which is your P45 as we call it today – and she sort of just threw it over the desk at me and says, 'oh! We can't have your sort here! Do you realise the type of people I'm dressing here! Oh! We can't have your sort!' – even though I never saw these people! But anyway she just said to me, you know, 'there's your cards and get out!' (MAGOHP/27, Phyllis Morgan: 14)

Phyllis Morgan was born in the St Patrick's Mother and Baby home on the Navan Road, to a mother who was not married. She was later sent to St Philomena's convent in Stillorgan, before being moved to Lakelands Convent in Sandymount in Dublin. Because of this, she held a stigmatized identity of the sort described by other women who had spent time in a Magdalene institution. She is 'one of them', 'your sort' – these veiled references to her identity speak to a system of widely understood moral boundaries, which do not even need to be articulated to be enforced. It is important then to stress that this stigma was not based on actuality of experience. Many women had not had a child outside of marriage, or sold sex, two of the key ways in which women's sexuality was seen to need regulating. Indeed, Phyllis Morgan's experience shows the extent of the 'sticky' nature of the stigma in question here. It is not bound up in the material reality of the women's lives, but in the way in which they are perceived – regardless of whether they had spent time in a Magdalene institution, if they came in close enough contact with the idea of bad womanhood that represented, it was enough to tarnish them.

As well as feeling shame around their identities, and a fear at making this identity visible in any way, some survivors discuss feeling unable to speak about their experiences out of a desire to protect their families. Survivors frequently made reference to the difficulty they had in communicating their experiences to their children. Specifically, many of them mention that they did not wish to speak to this because they did not wish to hurt them; they wished to shield them from the reality of their early life. Doris speaks about talking to her children and grandchildren about her past experiences, saying:

> I couldn't sit and talk about High Park to them. . . . I haven't got a clue why. I really haven't. . . . I could see how upset Gerrard was when he read that [news about the Magdalene laundries] and then Noel, he said Gerrard was telling him, he said 'I find that very hard to listen to', so I haven't said anything. (MAGOHP/37/ANON, Doris: tape 2, 23:24)

Doris does not have the language to speak about her experiences to her children. Although she initially says she doesn't know why she wasn't able to discuss this with them, the reactions of discomfort and sadness her children and grandchildren exhibit when they read about the Magdalene institutions appear to prevent her from sharing that part of herself with them. She continues, referring to her husband:

> He knew about Sacred Heart home and he knew about Baggott Street but I'd never told him about High Park . . . the same reason. I just didn't want . . . I just wanted to forget about there. (MAGOHP/37/ANON, Doris: tape 2, 23:57)

It is interesting that she felt able to speak to her husband about the time she spent in a home before and after being in High Park, but not her time at High Park itself, suggesting there is something specific to the experience of being in the Magdalene laundry which is uniquely distressing for others to hear. Lucy also expresses similar ideas when speaking about her decision not to tell her son about her past:

> **L** My son knows nothing about my past, absolutely nothing. He knows that my father beat me but that's about it. He knows nothing else. My daughter knows everything about me but he doesn't know anything.
>
> **SP** Why didn't you tell him?
>
> **L** (Pause) Why didn't I tell him? I think I wanted to kind of protect him because he... he is very protective over me. (MAGOHP/07/ANON, Lucy: 67)

The trauma of the laundries is presented as something with the capacity to harm not only Lucy but also her son. It is something she needs to protect him from – but what exactly is the harm she is sheltering him from? Is the identity of 'Magdalene woman' so dangerous that it could transcend generations, the stigma sticking not only to the women who were incarcerated in the institutions but also to their families? This example, and the previous quotes, demonstrate the deep level at which this stigmatized identity impacted on the Magdalene survivors. They undoubtedly experienced significant levels of shame around this identity which shaped their later lives. However, they also experienced a deep sense of fear and abjection as a result of their institutionalization, particularly evident in their fear of being brought back into the institution, of returning to that system of control. An example of this is given by Patricia Dervan, who when speaking about her sister-in-law describes a time when this fear became sharply apparent:

> She is now in a nursing home, aged 89, and interesting, my husband was there recently, and she had been unwell, she had a fever, and she was just recovered, and my husband remarked to her, 'aren't you lucky that you're in such a nice place' because apparently, she's in a nursing home where they're extremely kind, and it's a very nice place, and he remarked very casually to her, 'you're lucky these people are so kind to you, the atmosphere is so nice', and she immediately said back to him, practically screamed back to him, 'oh, don't put me back in that place!' Now, she didn't say where, but we know perfectly well where she means and he said to me, it was so frightening to hear after all these years, that because she was a little bit unwell, and perhaps her fever wasn't gone or something, that

she still had that fear, that because he'd remarked that she was in one place, it meant to her that he was threatening to put her back in the laundry. I found that quite upsetting. (MAGOHP/06, Patricia Dervan: tape 2, 16:00)

Phyllis Morgan also describes hearing similar experiences from survivors:

> They, you know, they would say to me, often they'd wake up sweating thinking they was . . . they were back in there you know, and realise it's only a dream. You know, but you know, even after they left they said they . . . God, for years, they'd wake up sweating like they'd been arrested and they're back in there and be so upset and wake up crying think[ing], 'oh my God' and then realise that they're not there. Some of them did marry and their husbands would say, 'God I can remember you know, when we got married first, oh, she'd wake up screaming and screaming, let me out, let me out, let me out!' (MAGOHP/27, Phyllis Morgan: 58–9)

This deep terror which manifests in the idea of returning to the institutions demonstrates how pervasive and effective the processes of identity erosion and removal of agency which the women underwent in the laundries were. They contributed to the formation of a shameful subjectivity for survivors, as well as a significant sense of fear about making this visible, which, in turn, meant that the women felt almost incapable of speaking about their experiences. These interviews then represent for many women, the first instance in which they felt able to speak openly about their time in Magdalene institutions, due not only to the internalized shame and fear they felt about their stigmatized identity but also to the material consequences they would have faced if they had spoken out.

Altered religious relationships: Renegotiating identity within the Catholic nation state

One of the reasons that these experiences of shame, stigma, fear and silence were so prevalent in women's narratives of their lives after leaving the institutions is the specific social context in which they existed. In particular, the sense of ongoing shame experienced by the women was borne out by a cultural system of purity and impurity structured around specifically religious relationships, beliefs and practices, which significantly impacted upon gendered experiences of subjectivity. The women's experiences of trauma frequently left them unable to continue to live in that system of meaning without some sense of alienation or distance, through either rejecting God or rejecting the Church but not God or finding some way of accommodating themselves in a society that remained structured around religious relationships. In this section, I address the ways in which survivors engaged with their religious identities after leaving the laundries, the various forms this took, and how different forms of religious expression became more or less prevalent. I will also think about the wider implications of an altered religious relationship in post-Independence Ireland. Following Orsi's (2005) approach, I consider the Magdalene survivors' engagement with the Church as an exploration of religion as a set of relationships shaped by the particular time and places in which they occur.

The Magdalene institutions represented a very specific type of religious carceral environment. Not only did the women incarcerated there suffer physical and psychological abuse, they also suffered a form of spiritual abuse, a fracturing of their religious identities. In referring to this experience as spiritual abuse, I am drawing on a growing body of research which explores the nature and process of this concept. While the literature on the subject increases, defining spiritual abuse, as with many other forms of abuse, is often difficult. Building on earlier explications, Oakley and Kinmond suggest the following definition:

> SA is coercion and control of one individual by another in a spiritual context. The target experiences SA as a deeply emotional personal attack.
>
> This abuse may include: manipulation and exploitation, enforced accountability, censorship of decision making, requirements for secrecy and silence, pressure to conform, misuse of scripture or the pulpit to control behaviour, requirement of obedience to the abuser, the suggestion that the abuser has a 'divine' position and isolation from others, especially those external to the abusive context. (2013: 21–2)

Many of the traits of spiritual abuse which they list here, and which their research describes further in depth, are reflected in the experiences of the Magdalene survivors. They speak of being manipulated, of having the capacity for decision-making removed, of requirements for conformity and of enforced silence. Oakley and Kinmond highlight how 'the context of the abuse is fundamental to the misuse of power described within the narratives; it is not possible to separate the context of the abuse from the power at work in SA' (2013: 43), and with this in mind I argue that the Magdalene institutions provide a valuable case study for further work on spiritual abuse, given the context of physical incarceration in a religious institution.

Oakley and Kinmond make a compelling case for considering spiritual abuse *as* abuse, but they also point to the distinctions between spiritual and other forms of abuse, which are important to note. For example, they highlight the threat of spiritual consequences for individuals who do not conform, and the impact upon core faith beliefs following the experience of spiritual abuse (Oakley and Kinmond 2013: 73). From the interviews, the latter is particularly borne out with reference to survivors' ability to participate in a wider, socially shared system of meaning, as well as more personal relationships to God or individual spirituality. The nature of religious identity in twentieth-century Ireland was closely linked to wider social and cultural identities. Fuller notes that

> The church's control of education and the State's acceptance and support of the Church's policy on education was a crucial factor influencing Irish culture in the post-independence era. Likewise, the Church's ... involvement in social welfare services from the nineteenth century was crucial to the power it was able to wield. The areas of education and caring were key areas of potential influence over people's lives, as far as the Church was concerned, and they were guarded jealously. (2002: 4)

Having this control over the Irish educational system significantly influenced the nature of many Irish people's relationship to the Church. Orsi writes that, for those raised and educated by nuns and priests, the 'relationship with God really present had been pressed deep into [their] bones and sinews' (2016: 224). While his work is primarily focused on an American, rather than Irish context, the statement also holds true in the latter. The Church, and by extension, priests and nuns, commanded significant authority in Irish communities. As Bernadette puts it:

> So I had grown up ... you know, if a nun told you to jump, you said, 'how high'? So when the nuns told me to jump I said, 'how high'? I never queried anything. (MAGOHP/12/ANON, Bernadette: 50)

To suffer violence at the hands of an institution which occupied such an important pastoral role in Irish society is a very specific form of trauma. The violence occurs not only at a material or psychological level, but it shatters the moral system of meaning which holds such a significant place in society, which is believed to be good and productive by those around you. There is limited research on the impact of this kind of trauma on the religious subjectivity of survivors of institutional abuse. Orsi touches on this in his recent work: describing interviews with survivors of clerical abuse in America, he highlights that 'even after they had decided to stop going to Mass, they remained deeply attached to the Eucharist on some level of their being' (2016: 227). Other work has primarily focused on the impact of specifically sexual abuse committed by members of a religious community. For example, Pargament, Murray-Swank and Mahoney, in an article on the impact of clergy-perpetrated sexual abuse describe it as

> A desecration that creates spiritual havoc. The individual's entire spiritual edifice is shaken to its foundations. Some people are able to conserve the sacred in their lives through nontraditional channels . . . . But many, if not most, enter a period of spiritual struggle, one that represents a fork in the road leading either to spiritual transformation or spiritual disengagement. (2008: 404)

Throughout the interviews, it is clear that Magdalene survivors had similar experiences, and there are some overlaps with Orsi's conclusions. Almost all of the women speak about some kind of shift in the nature of their faith and there are some who have abandoned religion and spirituality completely. Others speak about a greater attachment to personal beliefs, or a desire to remain part of the religious community for the benefit of their families. However, there is a less clear division between transformation and disengagement in the narratives of the women. The testimonies speak to a complex picture of religious identity and experience, a reflection of the deep significance of Catholicism for Irish identity and the ways in which it continued to shape their experiences after leaving the laundries. It represented a system of relationships and meanings which was unavoidable for many, despite the pain it had caused.

All the women who were interviewed for the oral history project were asked a question along the lines of the following:

> Did your time in the institution affect your religious beliefs? How? Did you ever feel that you had a vocation? What impact did the experience have on your own religious beliefs? (O'Donnell et al. 2013)

The responses to this are incredibly varied and demonstrate the multiplicity of ways Magdalene survivors engaged with their personal faith, as well as the wider Catholic Church, after leaving the institutions. These can roughly be grouped into three approaches, although they are by no means distinct and many survivors' experiences overlap. For some, we see a near total rejection of religion. There are others who appear to have separated out their engagement with the Catholic Church and organized religious orders from a more personal belief in God. Finally, some women still emphasize the importance of a specifically Catholic identity, although this is often distinguished from an ability to engage with the wider Catholic community as it exists in Ireland.

Firstly, I will look at those who seem to reject their religious belief altogether, who seem to have disengaged completely from religion. Pippa Flanagan is asked:

CMcG Right. Right. A . . . and . . . how do you . . . how do you feel about the church after all this?

PF Well, I'm a heathen, I can't go to anywhere, I never go anywhere. Only when the girls got confirmed and when they went to make their Holy Communion, I would have went then, after that, no. I just call mesel' a heathen, I've no faith. When I was brought up, they turned me against it. And they were supposed to be held . . . you know, responsible for us, they were supposed to be doing this and doing that and they never done nothing. Just slave, slave, slave . . .

CMcG Yeah. And . . . and who do you . . . who do you see as being responsible for what happened to you?

PF The nuns. Yeah. I . . . I told Judge Quirke that, I says, 'it's them that should have said, they were sorry, not Enda Kenny', because what would that man know? What is he apologising for? It wasn't up to him, it was up to the religious order at the end of the day, it was them that done the damage. That's my outlook of it. (MAGOHP/46/ANON, Pippa Flanagan: 46)

Pippa describes herself as a 'heathen' – a very specific choice of word, with a few meanings worth exploring. The term is often defined against Abrahamic religions, to mean someone who belongs to a religion that is not Christianity, Judaism or Islam – it therefore has a deliberate association with rejection. However, she also emphasizes that she has 'no faith', and so then we can think of the other associations which 'heathen' brings up. The word is often used to describe people with poor morals, uncultured or uncivilized persons. By using this word to describe herself, Pippa is perhaps pushing back against the religious system of morality which pervaded her life in the institutions. The 'heathen' stands in direct contrast to the 'penitent'; Pippa is inscribing herself with a new religious subjectivity, one which rejects the moral constraints of that which she was previously forced to inhabit with a deliberate sense of active agency. For Pippa, responsibility for her experience lies firmly with the nuns – 'it was them that done all the damage to us'. The apology given by Taoiseach Enda Kenny in 2013 means very little to her, because she does not see the State as in any way responsible. This location of responsibility with the religious orders undoubtedly contributes to her rejection of her religious identity.

We also see this rejection of religion in the testimony of Mary Smith, who speaks about her relationship to both religion and God in her interview:

> I should say here, and I hope you put this on, I'm an atheist, I don't believe in religion after what I've gone through, I couldn't. (MAGOHP/31, Mary Smith: 22)
>
> **KOD** And how do you feel . . . I know it's very clear how you feel about the church and that you know, you've no time for it, 'there is no God'. . .
>
> **MS** I can't, I can't believe there could be a God that would let somebody suffer so much. (MAGOHP/31, Mary Smith: 62)

Mary deliberately says she wants this on the tape, she wants it to be known she is an atheist, an identity which carried a stigma of its own in twentieth-century Ireland. For example, until 2015, it was possible for atheists to be fired from teaching and nursing jobs in religious institutions. For Mary, who was not speaking under a pseudonym and agreed to have her transcript immediately released to the public, the decision to publicly identify herself as an atheist in 2013 speaks to her vehemence in this position. She also makes clear that her rejection of religion involves a complete lack of belief in God. Both references to religion make a direct link between her traumatic experiences in the laundries and her lack of belief – her own personal suffering has resulted in this disengagement with religion and belief in God.

Jane's rejection of religion focuses around the body, both the abuse she suffered and the bodily control which she experienced while in the laundry. She says:

> Oh I hate religion, absolutely do, because I think it was just the controlling way with them in there as well, I mean I used to have to get up every morning and go to mass every single morning, get up at 5 o clock and go to mass. And in that way, I still live that now, because I wake up early every morning, it's like it's a habit of something that you were reared up . . . religion would be a controlling thing with me as well, that you were made to do it and you had to do it, I mean, we were told religion was everything, we were told more times in the convent that if you'd done anything wrong that you'd be punished by God. (MAGOHP/16/ANON, Jane: 24:59)
>
> Plus the abuse, I have been abused by a priest in the Good Shepherd, so that would be another thing that I trusted, where religion came . . . so, religion and, I don't have religion, whatsoever. (MAGOHP/16/ANON, Jane: 26:14)

Despite making her rejection and hatred of religion clear on two occasions during her interview, it is interesting to consider the ways in which the impact of the religious carceral environment has left a mark on Jane, specifically on her body. The religious control and disciplining of her body while in the institutions, typified by the strict routine, the repetitive cycle of prayer and work, lingers on despite her conscious rejection of both organized religion and the belief in God. The body retains a memory of religious life, even after a person may have consciously rejected their belief or relationship with God (Orsi 2005).

The body features again in Ellen Ward's account of her altered relationship with religion. She says:

> Oh, I've got no religion in me whatsoever . . . I had no religion in me from the time I was beaten so badly, it just went out of me, and I say to myself, why would these people go to church, hurt other people that never did wrong, and then still go to communion, so to me I call them hypocrites and they've hurt so many people.
> (O'Donnell, K., Pembroke, S. and McGettrick, C., 'An Oral History of Ellen Ward', MAGOHP/26, 2013: 1:13:57 [hereafter MAGOHP/26, Ellen Ward])

The physicality of her words here is jarring – she describes religion as being beaten out of her, the violent bodily trauma she experienced manifesting itself in a significant and long-term shift in the nature of her religious subjectivity. The experience of being exposed to such violence from people who had previously embodied a role of authority and pastoral care corroded this social relationship, fracturing a system of religious meaning which was embedded in Ireland's social system. The result of experiencing abuse from institutions and figures who occupy such a powerfully symbolic position in the cultural imagination is very viscerally exposed through her words.

Secondly, there are those who have separated out their belief in the Catholic Church and organized religious orders from a more personal belief in God, as seen in Lucy's interview:

> I hate religious orders. Now I am a religious person myself personally, I have faith in God and I have faith in Jesus and I love the angels; the angels are my inspiration I talk to the angels all the time, absolutely love them. I hate religious orders because to me they're money grabbers. What do they do with their money? I would love to know what they do with their money. Every Sunday in church, why do they have a church? The Lord . . . the religious . . . like the Catholic faith always taught us that the . . . the Lord was everywhere, so why do they have to go into the church? Why do they have to give money? The Lord never asked people for money. The Lord gave to people. I don't see the church giving to anybody. I have never seen the church give to anybody . . . do you ever

see all their ... their ... all the Cardinals, all the clothes they wear? What laundry did them for them? (MAGOHP/07/ANON, Lucy: 82)

Lucy has separated faith in God, Jesus and an affiliation with angels from the religious orders; this demarcation between these particular strands of religious belief allow her to describe herself as a religious person while also expressing her hatred for the religious orders. It seems she is able to exist within the systems of religious meaning to an extent, by making a separation between the God she refers to here and the God she was exposed to while in the laundries. Her spiritual focus has shifted towards angels, supramundane beings removed from the moral transactions around sin and penance which may have characterized her earlier religious relationships. Her focus on money also evidences her discomfort, shared by others, at the ways in which the institutional church was inextricably linked with power, status and control, things which Lucy seems to feel have no place in her spiritual expression.

This separation between the spiritual and the material is found in several of the survivor narratives – the women reject the institutional nature of the Irish Catholic Church, with a particular focus on the material greed they see within the religious orders, while maintaining their own personal religious beliefs. Lucy's focus on the financial aspect of the Church is something we see repeated throughout the interviews. The women who worked in the laundries were never paid for their labour, and many continue to have difficulties accessing state pensions because of 'gaps' in their careers. The institutions took in a lot of laundry and had access to a significant labour force whom they in no way compensated. While many of the orders maintain that they made little money from the laundries, survivors and activists have pointed out that this seems unrealistic.

However, there are other women, who, while also discussing the financial issues they have with the Church, take a less hostile position than Lucy:

SP How do you feel towards the church and the religious orders?

MC I ... do ... I don't want to blame the church itself or the man above ... it's human error that our lives were mapped out as they were. The ... the convent started off on a good footing but then turned bad. *Greed* turned it bad you know, and they were making *mega bucks*. So no, the church, I ... I don't blame them at all. I'm not a fully Cath ... lic ... practicing Catholic. My local parish priest, Father Scott [pseudonym] is a wonderful guy, a human being really, you know. And he would never preach or try and drill in the faith to you and whenever I see him, my friend relies on him a lot so I go over and sit down and chat with him, with my friend, you know . . . (MAGOHP/15, Mary Currington: 104)

Mary Currington's answer demonstrates how for her, responsibility for her abuse and trauma lies not with 'the church itself' or 'the man above' but with the 'human error' of the actual people involved, presumably the nuns. This responsibility does not translate to other members of the clergy, as shown by her friendship with Father Scott.

> **SP** Yeah. Did . . . did it affect your . . . your attitudes towards the church and religion?
>
> **M** Definitely, yes.
>
> **SP** Can you tell me how?
>
> **M** Well, as . . . as I am now I do not believe in the teachings of the Catholic Church. I believe there is a God but I don't believe in all the stuff they tell you. And I think that they done an awful lot of damage to a lot of people. (MAGOHP/04/ANON, Mary: 52)

Mary's statement again shows a rejection of organized religion, but she emphasizes that she does still believe in God. She rejects 'all the stuff they tell you', the authoritative side of the Church, while maintaining a faith in God.

Some of the women's accounts of the change in their religious relationships focus not only around a shift in emotional and interpretive understandings of these symbolic meanings but also in the way they experience and engage with their physical environment. This is most evident in the statements around attending Mass or going to Church. Kathleen says:

> I base religion on myself, I'm not going to mass because somebody says you must go, I'm going to do these things if I feel it's right at the time, I will go. So I base my religion on myself. (MAGOHP/34/ANON, Kathleen: 1:11:53)

She shifts the location of meaning from an external power to an internal one – *she* decides how to structure her relationship with religion and, specifically, the bodily control which this exerts upon her. Similarly, Celine says:

> I still go to mass, not every Sunday, but I do go to mass quite a lot, and I even support the church across the road . . . I don't know why I do it, I really and truly don't, it's this thing, I suppose here where I am as well there isn't a lot for me to do . . . I don't know . . . it's part of what I know, I suppose . . . I don't see the Church as God, I just see it as part of the community . . . but when the priests are up there, speaking on a Sunday morning, I always find myself thinking, I

wonder what you've done. I never trust any of them. (MAGOHP/22, Celine Roberts: 1:36:30)

She emphasizes that she does not go to Mass *every* Sunday, pushing back against the routine which would have characterized her time in a laundry. For her, it is the ability to take part in the community which keeps her in this system of meaning, rather than a belief in God.

However, belief in God is for others, the primary motivator for remaining in any sort of religious environment:

> I've thought about that [religion] an awful lot, and went through a stage of wanting nothing to do with it. After the redress, before the redress, I decided that it wasn't God that did it, it was tyrants and dictators, no different than Hitler was, and God didn't tell them to do these things, and they took it upon themselves, and both the nuns and the priests were hiding behind the veil and the collars, that's how I felt about it. I go to church when I want to, I don't go to communion. (O'Donnell, K., Pembroke, S. and McGettrick, C., 'An Oral History of Theresa', MAGOHP/23/ANON, 2013: 32:51 [hereafter MAGOHP/23/ANON, Theresa])

Theresa also emphasizes her own bodily autonomy within this new religious relationship. Like Kathleen and Celine, she goes to church when she wants to rather than every week, and she rejects the physical ritual of communion. She does not elaborate on why she no longer takes communion, but the bodily nature of her renegotiated religious relationship is made evident. This shift in religious practice is also found in some of Orsi's work, and it raises the question of what avoiding communion means for survivors of spiritual abuse. Is it about avoiding a sacred contact, made particularly real through the Mass which becomes difficult for these women, or is it avoiding the exposure to moral meanings around sin and penance which might be more evident in this religious ritual?

Within the laundries, religion emerges as a form of control and discipline, enacted on the bodies of the women through the insistence on constant prayer, as well as the basis for an ideology which legitimated their indefinite incarceration. It was something imposed and inflicted *upon* them, rather than being something they could choose to engage with, reflected in the ways they speak about religion during their time in the laundries. Once they have left the institutions, then, it is clear that women wish to regain control of their religious relationships, which in the context of twentieth-century Ireland are very much interlinked with the wider society in which they must exist. It is unsurprising that this frequently entails a distinctly physical reengagement with religious practices, and for some women, it remains an experience which retains some of the characteristics of physical discipline which were present within the institutions. For example, we can see the bodily religious memory spoken about by other survivors articulated in a different context by Patricia Dervan, who, speaking about her sister-in-law, says:

> I think to this day she's still religious, she went to mass frequently and she went to communion, but that was just . . . a routine part of her life. I wouldn't think she put any thought into the matter at all. I think it just became part of her everyday life, and I suppose if you've been brainwashed into repetitive religious rituals for twenty years you're not going to break away from them . . . in old fashioned parlance you'd call her religious, but I would think, there's no depth to that religion, it's merely physical ritualistic behaviour, that really, doesn't mean a thing. (MAGOHP/06, Patricia Dervan: tape 4, 40:24)

Other women specifically emphasize the Catholic nature of their faith.

> I never gave up my religion, I have no qualms about my religion. I'm a Catholic. Anything that happened was man made, it wasn't made by the lord, so I've nothing against the lord. The lord has nothing to do with this. (MAGOHP/45/ANON, Bridget O'Donnell: tape 1, 2:27:17)

However, even within this answer, we see how Bridget makes a clear distinction between things made by man, and things made by the Lord, with her experiences in the Magdalene institutions firmly falling into the former. Kate O'Sullivan also continues to identify as a Catholic, although her answer to the question of religious belief at first appears confusing.

> **CMcG** A . . . a . . . and did it affect your . . . your religious beliefs at all?
>
> **KOS** Yes it did.
>
> **CMcG** In what way?
>
> **KOS** I don't believe.
>
> **CMcG** At all?
>
> **KOS** No! No, no, no. Oh very . . . for people that took the . . . the veil and the priests that used to run the church. No . . . no. I'd say, they had a feeling . . . I knew . . . the priest that was the chaplain down below like you know . . .
>
> **CMcG** Yeah.
>
> **KOS** . . . I'd say they had a feeling where I came from. I never had any time for them. No.
>
> **CMcG** And . . . so, it's . . . it's . . . it's . . . it's coloured how you view . . .
>
> **KOS** Yes.

CMcG ... the clergy and the religious and ... but your own beliefs in ... do you believe in God and that sort of thing yourself?

KOS Oh yeah, yeah, yeah.

CMcG You do, okay, okay.

KOS Yeah.

CMcG And ... and, so it hasn't affected you that way?

KOS No, no, no, no.

CMcG And would you still be like ... would you still consider yourself Catholic?

KOS Oh yeah.

CMcG Right, right, right.

(O'Donnell, K., Pembroke, S. and McGettrick, C., 'An Oral History of Kate O'Sullivan', MAGOHP/50/ANON, 2013: 33–4 [hereafter MAGOHP/50/ANON, Kate O'Sullivan])

She initially states she 'doesn't believe', although she does not say what she no longer believes in. It is a very blunt and immediate response, and is then qualified when the interviewer asks, 'At all?' However, she then goes on to state that this is referring to her views on the clergy, but she still believes in God. She also says she would still consider herself a Catholic. After her initial vehement denial of belief, this assertion sounds a little jarring, but it demonstrates the complex and fluid ways in which survivors of this religiously saturated abuse must negotiate their experiences. While for ease of analysis, I have divided their responses into three broad themes, it is evident that there is much overlap – and it should be expected that people's engagement with their faith will shift and change as their experience of their trauma does. Religious belief – whether that is a belief in God, an engagement with a Catholic identity or a desire to be part of a religious community – is entwined with a number of internal and external factors, which themselves will fluctuate.

For many people, particularly those who exist in a more secular social environment, a disengagement from religion entirely might seem like the 'logical' reaction to trauma of this nature. However, when placed in the context of twentieth-century Ireland, this decision to reject religion and faith, as well as the Catholic Church, represents not only a rejection of religious meanings but a disconnect from wider social ones as well. There were few spaces in twentieth-century Ireland for women to occupy which were not in some way overlaid with religious meanings, and therefore to abandon religion altogether was not only spiritually painful but also had the potential to cut them off from other forms of cultural meaning, or community support. It is clear that for many of the survivors, there is no strong desire to abandon their religious beliefs, despite the religious nature of the abuse they have suffered. Through an understanding of survivors' experiences as a renegotiation of relationships – with God, with the Catholic Church, with the wider Catholic community or with their own sense of spirituality – we can read into these discussions a desire to regain control of religious subjectivity, pushing back against the religiously saturated processes of control and discipline which were explored in the previous chapter. It is also useful to consider how these altered relationships represent a desire to reclaim a sense of meaning in the lives of survivors. It is evident that many of these women find it difficult to remain in this religious system of meaning because it is within this that they are formed as shamed subjects. The hermeneutical resources provided by the Catholic Church do not allow for an understanding of their time in the laundries as anything but shameful and sinful, an experience which marks them out as other. By rejecting or reimagining their religious relationships, in both the personal and public sphere, they create space for their identities which perhaps begins to resist this inscription, drawing on new hermeneutical tools to express their experiences. However, it is evident from my earlier discussions of silence that these new forms of expression were not always possible, and the pervasive nature of the stigma which was a constant threat in their later lives demonstrates the significant symbolic power exerted by the Catholic Church in the Irish social consciousness.

Making new forms of moral meaning: From respectability to ordinary acts

Religious relationships emerge as being fraught with tension for survivors of the Magdalene institutions. Women often describe a sense of alienation from the wider religious community, an inability to mend the fracture caused by their incarceration within carceral religious environments. However, within the context of twentieth-century Ireland it would have been very difficult to completely extricate oneself from these religious relationships, due to the centrality of Catholicism to Irish identity. Therefore, in this section I consider the impact of these altered religious relationships on women's subjectivities, focusing particularly on the ways in which they renegotiated their identities through finding routes to respectability and credibility. I focus on two broad themes within this. Firstly, I think about the role of motherhood and respectability through family life, exploring how the identity of 'mother' had the capacity to give women access to social capital of a sort. This was to a great extent due to the significance and importance given to 'motherhood' as a vocation, and the symbolic religious and cultural meanings held within this identity. In doing so, I demonstrate how rejection of religion, or a shift in the nature of one's religious identity, was not just about a relationship to spirituality, but something which impacted on a whole range of social structures. Secondly, I engage with the process of finding relief and a recovery of agency in the mundane acts of everyday life, what Veena Das calls, 'the work of the everyday' (2007). Often this manifested itself in a focus on caring, and on family life. This echoes the previous discussion on motherhood, and the ways women found credibility and power through inhabiting respectable identities.

'Becoming respectable': Meaning through motherhood

The 'Irish mother' as a figure holds a significant and powerful symbolic position in post-independence Ireland. As previously discussed, Inglis (1998: 179) uses the figure of the 'Irish mother' as a case study in Church and gender relations, arguing that it was the mother who often functioned as an intermediary between the Catholic Church and the family, acting as a conduit for moral codes, to produce the Catholics of modern Ireland. This was, in part, because religion and morality were some of the only areas in which women could find any authority. With little or no power in the public or political field, and largely unable to contribute to the income of the household, women were able to wield power solely in terms of morality. Drawing on Bourdieu's ideas around capital (1986), Inglis suggests that attaining religious capital was possible for women through adherence to spiritual and moral guidelines. This became an important source of power for women who did not have access to other forms of capital, such as economic, social, political or cultural capital. Religious capital, Inglis states, 'enabled them to attain honour and respect – symbolic capital – which legitimated their position within the family and community' (2005: 66). However, it is important to note that in order to access this capital, it was not simply enough to be a mother, in the sense of having a child – it was necessary to be the *right* sort of mother. The family was the only acceptable social unit in which to have a child, and the only way of providing legitimacy for mothers. The social role of 'mother' was legitimated by marriage, which reflected an understanding of the family as valid only when positioned within the specific contexts of the heterosexual relationship. The previous chapter has demonstrated the extent to which this conception of women's social role in Ireland contributed to the ways in which Magdalene survivors were silenced both before and during their time in the laundries. However, the interviews also show how women inhabit the social role of mother in their lives after leaving the institutions to gain respectability, as well as the importance of this identity for their sense of self.

Towards the end of most of the survivor interviews, women were asked the question:

> Of all of your accomplishments, what are you the most proud of? (O'Donnell et al. 2013)

This question was added to the interview guide early in the pilot stage, as a way of ending the interview with a recollection of positive achievements (O'Donnell 2018: 89). Throughout the process of listening to and reading the interviews, it became increasingly apparent that more and more women answered this question with reference to their families, specifically their children. This is perhaps not unusual – many parents are proud of their children. However, given the significance of motherhood in post-independence Ireland, and the ways in which this identity was informed by Catholic morality and social respectability, the repeated emphasis on motherhood as a source of pride is worth exploring further.

> **SP** And of all your accomplishments what are the ... what are you most proud of?
>
> **M** Being a mother and grandmother. (MAGOHP/04/ANON, Mary: 54)
>
> **SP** And of all your accomplishments, what are you most proud of?
>
> **BM** My family. (MAGOHP/13/ANON, Bernadette and Francis Murphy: 116)
>
> **SP** Yeah. And I want to ask something a bit more positive I guess is ... of all your accomplishments what are you most proud of?
>
> **L** My children. Absolutely, I'm ... I'm proud that I brought them to the age they are without any bad memories and if you met my children now and you asked them have they any bad memories in their lives and they'd say, 'no' and they could say it with conviction because they are so happy. (MAGOHP/07/ANON, Lucy: 77)

Mary, Bernadette and Lucy all answer this question instantly and directly – unlike many of the other interview questions which prompt confusion or drawn-out answers, in this instance we see a very clear and immediate focus.

SP I just want to ask, of all your accomplishments, of all your achievements, what are you most proud of?

MS [pause] I'd say I'd have three things I'd be most proud of – I didn't hold any animosity towards my mother . . . I am proud that I did tell . . . that I can tell my story now of what they did to me and the cover up, and I think the third thing would be of my children, and that I achieved getting my own home. (MAGOHP/38, Maureen Sullivan: 1:07:25)

Maureen's answer is not quite so immediate, and is bound up with other experiences in her life. In her list of three things, she groups her children with another traditional marker of respectability – home ownership.

Pippa Flanagan's answer to the question is also fairly instant – and is accompanied by a clear physical manifestation of her pride and happiness, significant enough to not only be commented upon by the interviewer but also noted in the transcript.

CMcG And, of all your accomplishments in life, what are you most proud of?

PF My two daughters.

CMcG Hmm.

PF Yes, my two daughters, very proud of them, at the end of the day, that's . . . that's my living now, with them . . . that's . . . (Smiling)

CMcG I think that's the first time you've smiled since we started this!

PF Yeah, yes, yes, it's me two daughters, thank God for them . . .
(MAGOHP/46/ANON, Pippa Flanagan: 6)

Bernadette also speaks about her child as her proudest accomplishment.

SP And of all your accomplishments what are you most proud of?

B My son! My . . .

SP I just had a feeling!

B . . . son, that I've got . . . my Down Syndrome son (MAGOHP/12/ANON, Bernadette: 95)

She mentions her son earlier in her interview:

B When we split up, my son was a year old . . . our son was a year old . . .

SP Yeah.

B . . . as I said he's Down Syndrome, I had to grow up again. And this little thing – oh, the tears – (voice cracking) this little thing was [number of years removed] years ago now . . . who gave me unconditional love, a love I couldn't love myself.

SP Yeah.

B Which, I had never done. (Crying)

SP Oh.

B And as I say he's . . . he's great. My marriage lasted two years, my son was a year old when . . . when we split and I came back to Aislingstown because I needed the security of the family, and stayed there ever since. And . . . my husband died fifteen years ago . . .

SP Okay.

B . . . and I became a terribly respectable widow, mother of a mentally handicapped son whom everybody adores and I'm known as his mother (laughs) . . . (MAGOHP/12/ANON, Bernadette: 72)

Bernadette's choice of wording here, in describing herself as a 'respectable widow', is particularly interesting. Not only is she asserting her identity as a mother, through the mention of her son, but she also uses her identity as widow to provide respectability, placing herself within the legitimate context of a previous heterosexual marriage. Bernadette's tone is somewhat tongue in cheek – we sense that she knows her new-found respectability is wholly based on her son and deceased husband. Even her choice of verb – 'I *became* a terribly respectable widow' – indicates she is aware of the transitory nature of this. One can become respectable not only through one's actions, but also through associations and relationships with others, suggesting an intersubjective nature to this identity. In thinking through this focus on domesticity, family and, above all, respectability, I turn to work done by Bev Skeggs, specifically her ethnography of working-class women in North East England, the title of which echoes Bernadette's words earlier – *Formations of Class & Gender: Becoming Respectable* (1997). Skeggs emphasizes how 'respectability, domestic ideals and caring all establish constraints on women's lives, yet they can also be experienced positively' (1997: 41). It is through this lens that I explore respectability as a concept, thinking through the ways in which it constrained the lives and experiences of Magdalene survivors, as well as providing them with a structure through which they could gain some degree of social capital. Skeggs goes on to highlight the way in which, due to the importance placed on moral responsibility by middle-class women, working-class women were able to gain positions of respect and responsibility 'from being seen to care' (1997: 54).

There is an enduring and widely believed narrative that women were sent to Magdalene institutions after having a child outside of marriage. Whether this reflects the reality of the women's experiences or not, it is unsurprising that for many of the women interviewed, reclaiming their position as legitimate mother, either through marriage or the building of a respectable community identity, was a significant thing to do. These women were forcibly prevented form inhabiting the identity of 'mother' during their early lives, either by having their children removed from their care, or simply by being denied the opportunity of meeting partners because they were incarcerated. By choosing to actively and demonstratively inhabit this identity of *respectable* mother and wife, survivors are pushing back against the identities inscribed on their bodies while inside the institutions. Inevitably, by doing this some of the women fall into the trap of respectability politics, defining themselves against the *actual* 'bad women', those who have not managed to claw back some social capital through engagement with familial life or respectable motherhood. However, it is important to think through the power structures at work here before critiquing respectability as resistance too severely. As Sara Ahmed (2014) writes:

> Sometimes, 'coping with' or 'getting by' or 'making do' might appear as a way of not attending to structural inequalities, as benefiting from a system by adapting to it, even if you are not privileged by that system, even if you are damaged by that system. Perhaps we need to ask: who has enough resources not to have to become resourceful? When you have less resources you might have to become more resourceful. Of course: the requirement to become more resourceful is part of the injustice of a system that distributes resources unequally. Of course: becoming resourceful is not system changing even if it can be life changing (although maybe, just maybe, a collective refusal not to not exist can be system changing). But to assume people's ordinary ways of coping with injustices implies some sort of failure on their part – or even an identification with the system – is another injustice they have to cope with. The more resources you have the easier it is to make such a critique of those whose response to injustice is to become more resourceful. You might not be trying to move up, to project yourself forward; you might simply be trying not to be brought down.

Twentieth-century Ireland offered very few opportunities for women to access positions of social responsibility or power, particularly for working-class women. As highlighted earlier, respectable motherhood was one of the few avenues through which women could gain social power, even if in some cases this meant weaponizing respectability to distance themselves from others.

Making everyday life inhabitable: Survival as resistance

Returning to the quotation from Ahmed mentioned earlier, I end this chapter by thinking about what it means to survive, to get by. Ahmed writes that in coping with injustice, 'you might simply be trying not to be brought down' (2014). What does it mean for a survivor of trauma to conceptualize survival as simply a continued existence? In thinking through this focus on family respectability as a way for women to gain a degree of agency and social capital, I also draw on work done by Veena Das in her ethnography of women in post-partition India, to explore the many ways in which survivors of violence renegotiate their subjectivity after trauma. I wish to highlight her assertion that for some survivors of the riots, 'life was recovered not through some grand gestures in the realm of the transcendent but through a descent into the ordinary' (Das 2007:7). While the contexts are very different, conceptualizing resistance and survival through a focus on familial life as a 'descent into the ordinary' provides a valuable framework for understanding some of the issues at play here. Das writes that

> There is no pretence here at some grand project of recovery but simply the question of how everyday tasks of surviving – having a roof over your head, being able to send your children to school, being able to do the work of the everyday without constant fear of being attacked – could be accomplished. I found that the making of the self was located, not in the shadow of some ghostly past, but in the context of making the everyday inhabitable. (2007: 216)

For many of the women interviewed in the oral history project, everyday survival *was* the strongest form of resistance available to them, because of the continual and enduring nature of their traumatic experiences. The lack of government assistance, the continued stigmatization of their lives and the real fear involved in speaking about their experiences meant that 'moving on', or 'working through' their pain was not frequently an option. When the attitudes and underlying religiously sanctioned ideology which led to your incarceration has not been strongly challenged, and when the stigma against 'people like you' remains, how can we expect people to 'resist' in a more active way? Do we need them to, in order to recognize their agency?

I wish to think about the 'work of the everyday' in the context of Magdalene laundry survivors, the (re)making of the self, through the exertion of a new form of agency and resistance. When considering the ways in which survivors of the Magdalene laundries renegotiate their subjectivities, working within a context which is heavy with stigma and cultural meanings they may no longer be able to access, how does a framework of 'survival as resistance' help to make clear the processes they use to do this? Survival, the act of simply getting by, carrying on, is something spoken about in some of the interviews as being ingrained in their experiences:

AM Because from start to finish in those places you are surviving every single day. You're not living. And how it's affected me now is I've n ... don't know how to live, I just know how to survive. And I seem to never stop surviving, I really wish I could live and have peace and ... but it seems to be that all I ever do is survive.

KOD And what's the difference between surviving and living, what would living be like?

AM Living would be ... you'd have peace I think, and you wouldn't be always having to fight something or fight for something or ... surviving is you're continuously, daily having to just get through that day or get through that fight or get through this ... you know, I'd like ... love to be able to just live. I guess that doesn't make sense to you does it?

> (O'Donnell, K., Pembroke, S. and McGettrick, C., 'An Oral History of Angelina Mayfield', MAGOHP/49/ANON, 2013: 159 [hereafter MAGOHP/49/ANON, Angelina Mayfield])

Angelina's description of her life after the laundries, one in which she is just trying to get through each day, echoes the framework of survival articulated by Ahmed and Das. In her framing of this, it is a constant struggle, one she wishes she did not have to do, but crucially *she does*. She is, as Ahmed says, 'getting by'.

However, for other women this 'work of the everyday' is work to be proud of, an achievement. Ellen Ward, when asked what she is most proud of, says:

> Getting on, after coming out of them homes, cos they told you when you, when they let me out with two half crowns, they said you're going out now, but you'll be back ... nobody will want you, you're no good for nothing. So I thought now, I've got to prove to people. (MAGOHP/26, Ellen Ward: 1:36:20)

For Ellen, surviving, 'getting on', after this trauma is an act of resistance against the coercive practice of the laundries, being repeatedly told she was nothing, a no one. Kathleen makes what is perhaps the most direct link between survival and agency. She says:

> For twenty years, I had no say in my life, and that's the way it was ... I have plenty of say now. And I'm proud that I'm able to stand up and say I'm a survivor, and that I'm getting on with my life and that I got on with my life and that I worked, I was a worker. And that's what I've achieved in life. (MAGOHP/34/ANON, Kathleen: 1:11:25)

It is by 'getting on with her life' that she demonstrates her agency, her control over the basic choices about her life which were denied to her during her time in the laundry. In starting the previous chapter, I highlighted the attritional nature of the trauma of the laundries. This particular framing of agency helps demonstrate the way in which this trauma worked. It was designed so that you would *not* survive, you would not get by – women were meant to spend their whole lives in the laundries, erasing their identity to take on the new subjectivity of the penitent. By surviving – making a 'normal' life in which they are mothers and wives, or just getting by – they resist this coercive subjectification, making space for themselves within a system which was not designed to facilitate this. This kind of agency is less visible, less understandable to those who exist outside this framework of trauma, as Angelina Mayfield worries. 'I guess that doesn't make sense to you does it?' she asks the interviewer, uncertain perhaps that her thoughts on survival will be recognizable to someone who has not experienced this. There is so often an expectation from survivors to perform a very particular type of resistance, one in which healing becomes a performative project for the State, to alleviate lingering guilt around complicity. When this is not present, when recovery becomes survival and getting on with your life, it is harder to pinpoint when it takes place. It does not fit neatly into how recovery is frequently conceptualized. This framework therefore allows for a broader definition of recovery, and one which is less prescriptive and more focused on the realities of survivors' lives.

Conclusion

This chapter has explored the experiences of Magdalene survivors after leaving the institutions, as well as demonstrating the processes by which Magdalene survivors (re)negotiated their sense of self. Specifically, I have focused on the ways in which the disciplinary processes they experienced while in the institutions *continued* in their lives long after they had departed from the physical confines of the laundry, contributing to continued and consistent instances of epistemic injustice. This started with the manner of their departure, described by many of the survivors as abrupt, happening without warning. They had no opportunity to say goodbye to their friends or plan for the future, reinforcing the idea that they were subjects unable of being trusted with information about their own lives. They were denied agency even in leaving the institutions. This meant that the event of leaving is described by many of the women in conflicting terms – a day filled with both joy and sadness, fear of the unknown as well as relief to be leaving what was a deeply traumatic context. I then considered the nature of the shame and stigma they continued to feel, and the impact this had on their ability to communicate their experiences to others. I emphasized that often this moved beyond a sense of shame – it was a real terror of the risks inherent in making their experiences visible. I considered the intersubjective nature of shame as a way to explore why many women chose to remain silent about their earlier lives. I also highlighted the specific ways in which survivors renegotiated their religious relationships, given the heavy significance of Catholicism in twentieth-century Ireland. Finally, moving beyond their altered engagement with religious relationships, I explored the ways in which women found space to renegotiate their identities within structures of family life and respectability, reclaiming identities based around care and motherhood. I also considered a reframing of agency not as a 'grand project of recovery' (Das 2007: 216) but as simply getting by, existing in a context which may not easily make space for you.

In the previous chapter, I conceptualized the experiences of women inside the laundries as an example of epistemic injustice, primarily testimonial injustice. While entering the institutions and throughout their time there, women were denied credibility due to their social identity, as shamed women within the social and religious context of post-Independence Ireland. This chapter has demonstrated the continual nature of this form of epistemic injustice, particularly in the manner in which they left the institutions. They were not trusted as subjects worthy of knowledge of their own experiences, resulting in painful and fractured endings. This chapter has also demonstrated the extent to which we can see clear instances of hermeneutical injustice in the experiences of survivors after leaving the laundries. They found themselves caught up in religious and social systems of meaning within which they were not able to access the hermeneutic resources necessary to effectively communicate their experiences. There were few ways for them to understand their identity as someone who had been in a Magdalene institution which were not bound up in Catholic notions of purity, and therefore most women found it very difficult to speak about these experiences, resulting in painful and long-lasting instances of silence. However, there are examples of individual resistance to these processes of epistemic injustice throughout this chapter. Through accessing new forms of religious and moral meaning, through either altered relationships to religion and spirituality or a renewed focus on family life and 'respectable' femininity, women found space in which to develop an identity as credible subjects, worthy of respect. They found new ways to speak about their experiences, pushing back against the inscription of shame on their bodies and finding ways in which to renegotiate their subjectivity as both gendered and religious selves.

At the heart of this chapter is an emphasis on the multiplicity of ways in which survivors navigate their lives after trauma, and, indeed, the continual nature of the trauma itself. It does not end when the women have left the institutions but is woven into the nature of their departure, the social context in which they must exist, the systems of meaning they must work within, or choose to exist outside of. Just as every woman's experience of *being in* an institution will differ, the ways in which survivors negotiate their later lives will also vary hugely. Some find it easier than others to make space for themselves within the pre-existing cultural and religious milieu, working within structures of motherhood and family life to regain a sense of respectability. Others were not able or willing to do this. It is through an awareness of this multiplicity of experience, seeing the small forms of resistance which were available to these women as significant and important, that the experiences of Magdalene survivors should be understood.

6

Public silence and official voice: Inquiry, apology and redress

You can never wash away what went on.
(MAGOHP/18/ANON, Margaret Burke: 3.00:46)

Throughout this book, I have focused on the structures and processes which worked to produce particular types of religious, gendered subjectivities – both while the women were in the Magdalene institutions and after they had left. I have considered the ways in which these structures and processes were shaped by the specific carceral religious nature of the institutions, as well as how they were maintained by the social landscape of Ireland, which made it difficult for Magdalene survivors to speak authentically about their experiences, or find space for new forms of meaning. I have explored how this resulted in experiences of deep epistemic injustice for these women, who were frequently prevented from being seen as credible narrators of their own experiences. I now turn to the question of how expressions of public voice on the institutions produce and maintain particular subjectivities, and what this means for these processes of epistemic injustice. By public voice, I refer to statements on the laundries made by official and unofficial bodies, distributed in the public sphere in some way. This chapter will explore the extent to which these instances of epistemic injustice are addressed, maintained or replicated through public interventions of inquiry, apology and redress. Jeffrey Olick makes the point that 'memory is not an agency of storage but an active process of construction and reconstruction in time' (2007: 10). In this chapter, I consider how memories of the Magdalene institutions have been, and are being, constructed and reconstructed in public, focusing on three key events which have significantly impacted on how survivor experiences are presented and mediated. Firstly, the publication of the 'Report of the Inter-Departmental Committee to establish the facts of State involvement with the Magdalen Laundries', commonly known as the McAleese report, in February 2013; secondly, the apology made by Enda Kenny in February 2013 and the subsequent statements by the religious orders; and finally, the *Dublin Honours Magdalenes* event of June 2018. I explore the ways in which these processes of public voice operate, what they are intended to do and how they are experienced by those intended as the audience.

This chapter considers the extent to which each of these events seeks to create the conditions whereby the voices of survivors are better listened to, and how they do this. Throughout these processes, are survivors respected as producers of knowledge on their own experiences, or do these processes, instead, further co-opt and silence their voices? Are they given the space to narrate and interpret what has happened to them, or is this knowledge diffused and refracted through alternative narratives? In what ways are their experiences validated or discredited, and in what kind of contexts are they allowed to be heard? Throughout these processes, are they being produced as credible subjects? I consider how processes of apology and redress prioritize particular types of voice, and frame these as a new narrative. In doing this, I consider the nature of inquiries and apologies as speech acts or forms of intervention into public memory. The former typically invites the survivor to speak, with a view to this contributing in some way to public understanding of the issue. The latter involves a mode of address to survivors that, in itself, does not invite their speech. How do these interventions call forth and inscribe particular subjectivities onto the survivors as a result?

In the previous chapters, I focused on using the words of the women to explore their experiences of life both in and out of the institutions. This has been a consistent concern of the work – while there has been increasing attention paid to the Magdalene institutions in the past twenty years, the voices of the women directly affected are still lacking in most of the literature. Therefore, a prioritization of these voices remains a key focus of this project and this chapter continues to draw heavily from the oral history project. However, I will also use the content of the McAleese report itself, as well as the text of Enda Kenny's apology and statements made by the religious orders. Towards the end of the chapter, I will draw upon personal reflections of my experience as a volunteer at the *Dublin Honours Magdalenes* event. The chapter will follow a broadly chronological structure, moving away from the thematic approach adopted in previous chapters. Structuring the chapter in this way allows for an exploration of the way in which the structures and processes of power work in a cumulative fashion, building on previous events and interventions to produce instances of silencing or opportunity for voice. In doing so, I demonstrate the complex nature of these instances of public voice, and the ways in which they have the capacity to replicate existing processes of epistemic injustice. By framing the existence of the institutions and the experiences of the survivors in a particular way, by prioritizing specific voices and discounting others, the Magdalene survivors are once again produced as unreliable narrators of their own experiences. Their narratives are able to be heard only in specific contexts, and are frequently mediated through other, more 'credible' channels. However, it is important to also consider how these instances of public voice *have* made space for survivor voices, or, perhaps more specifically, how survivors have used these instances to make space and meaning for themselves.

The McAleese report: State responsibility and survivor voices

In June 2011, the Irish government announced the establishment of an Inter-Departmental Committee on the Magdalene Laundries, which would be chaired by Senator Martin McAleese. The report, titled 'Report of the Inter-Departmental Committee to establish the facts of State involvement with the Magdalen Laundries', commonly known as the McAleese report, was published on 5 February 2013. It confirmed extensive State involvement with the Magdalene Laundries, marking a significant shift from previous statements made by the Irish government. The report was the culmination of many years' work from activists, journalists and survivors, as well as pressure from the Irish Human Rights Committee. An extensive history of this campaign is available on the *Justice for Magdalenes Research* website.[1] In this section I consider the extent to which this inquiry addressed or perpetuated epistemic injustice for survivors of the Magdalene laundries. To do this, I will explore three strands of enquiry. Firstly, I will consider the extent to which an intervention of this nature is *intended* to address and alleviate epistemic injustice, drawing on the official stated aims of the report, data from the interviews and the content of the report itself. I will explore the tensions between how the Committee framed its approach to the work, and the nature of the finished document. I will then move on to an exploration of how the voices and narratives of the women are used throughout the report, and what the presentation of their voices demonstrates about their perceived epistemic value. Referring back to the question of the extent to which inquiries such as this can both address and perpetuate processes of epistemic injustice, I ask questions regarding the inclusion or exclusion of survivor testimony, and what this means for their ability to be respected as knowledge producers. Finally, I will think through the ways in which the report was experienced by survivors, through interviews with women who gave evidence to the committee as well as others who engaged with the report after it had been published. What does their experience of the document, and the process of inquiry itself, tell us about its function with regard to epistemic injustice?

A statement of aims and intentions

The McAleese report is very clear that the purpose of the Committee was strictly fact-finding – 'It was not intended as a forum for determination of individual complaints, nor was the Committee intended to make recommendations or provide redress in individual cases. This fact-finding role also meant that it was not for the Committee to recommend or issue an apology or apologies' (2013: 11). However, this stated aim of establishing a narrow range of facts is complicated by testimony from Mari Steed, a founder of *Justice for Magdalenes*. Speaking in an interview taken in advance of the report's publication, she stated that she felt the report was almost a waste of time, as there was already enough evidence of State involvement. Mari spoke to Senator McAleese before this interview, saying:

> His parting words to me yesterday were that they wanted to include not just the paperwork body of evidence, but the voices, interviewing the women, the testimonies, and to try to put a human face on it. Now, how much of that is politi-speak and just ... being a politician, I don't know.
> (O'Donnell, K., Pembroke, S. and McGettrick, C., 'An Oral History of Mari Steed', MAGOHP/02, 2013: 2:08:40 [hereafter MAGOHP/02, Mari Steed])

This quote seems to sit at odds with the stated assertion that the role of the Committee was strictly 'fact-finding'. What does it mean to 'try to put a human face' on something if the aim of the inquiry was to establish a fairly narrow range of facts – what value would be gained from doing this? It is also useful to consider this stated goal of objective fact-finding in conjunction with the content of the report. The McAleese report stresses how 'the Committee had the benefit of full access to all surviving records of the Religious Congregations which operated the Magdalen Laundries, as well as the ability to search for and access all surviving official records' (2103: 48). From these records, they examined routes of entry, duration of stay, family background, place of origin, age on entry and routes of exit for the women who had been in the laundries post-1922. After this report had been published, the Committee returned all records to the religious communities. At the time of writing, the Committee remain the only people who have had this kind of access to the records of the religious orders.

However, despite this unprecedented access, there are still large gaps in the data from which the Committee drew its conclusions. No records survive from the laundry in Dun Laoghaire, and only partial records survive from the laundry in Galway. This has significant implications for the conclusions drawn by the committee. For example, the duration of stay is listed as 'unknown' for 5,047 women (45%) (2013: 168). Therefore, when the Committee states that the average duration of stay was 3.22 years and median 27.6 weeks, they are necessarily excluding over half the women who entered the laundries. These statistics have been critiqued at length by Claire McGettrick (2015), a member of JFMR, whose work demonstrates the numerous ways in which the use of figures in the report points the reader towards misleading and unhelpful conclusions. In addition to the gaps in the records from the religious congregations, there were also issues regarding the inclusion of survivor testimony. A report from *Justice For Magdalenes Research* to the UN Committee on the Elimination of Discrimination Against Women notes that 'none of 793 pages of witness testimony which JFM transcribed and submitted to the Inter-departmental Committee (and offered to have sworn), appears in the report' (2015: 10). Again, this exclusion of data seems to sit at odds with the stated aim of fact-finding, suggesting that this body of resources was ancillary to the goal of objective truth. Maeve O'Rourke, an activist with JFMR who conducted many of the oral history interviews, as well as participating in an interview herself, spoke about the report, saying:

> I think that practically it did the job that it needed to do, in that there was an apology afterwards. But I don't think that the report will stand the test of time. The women's stories and their experiences haven't been fully recounted in that report, it's not the full truth of what people went through and that could simply be because, as was acknowledged in the report, the sample size, if you want to use that phrase, the number of women who gave testimony, doesn't reflect all of the women who are out there and the various experiences they had, so I just mean, to call it the full truth is the wrong description of what that report provides. . . . I think there are serious gaps.
> (O'Donnell, K., Pembroke, S. and McGettrick, C., 'An Oral History of Maeve O'Rourke', MAGOHP/24, 2013: 1:23:06 [hereafter MAGOHP/24, Maeve O'Rourke])

When listening to O'Rourke speak about this, her voice is measured, and it sounds like she is choosing her words carefully. This interview was taken in May 2013, just a few months after the report had been published. Her suggestion that there are gaps in the report, that it will not stand the test of time, sits at odds with the way the report was described by Taoiseach Enda Kenny a few months earlier, who spoke of the report as a 'document of truth'. She highlights the selective nature of 'truth' and 'facts' employed in the report. To return to the stated intention of the report then, to what extent can this be considered as 'fact-finding'? There are two main points to consider here. Firstly, I would argue that in a report of this nature, it is impossible to simply 'fact-find'. The ways in which the 'facts' are collected and presented, the specific methodologies chosen, the biases of the Committee – these will all impact on the findings of the report, and to ignore this is a disingenuous presentation of the data. Secondly, the serious gaps in the data, due both to the incomplete records from the religious congregations and to the decision not to include the body of resources submitted by JFM, mean that the statistical conclusions drawn by the report must be viewed through a critical lens, with an awareness of the limitations caused by this limited data, as well as the reasons for these exclusions. The stated intention of the McAleese report sets a clear limit on what it attempts to do – but facts do not exist in a vacuum. By presenting their report as an objective reality and ignoring the need for a reflexive approach to this process of inquiry, the McAleese report creates new boundaries in which accepted knowledge can exist. I now turn to the way in which these boundaries excluded the needs and voices of the Magdalene survivors themselves.

Gathering and presenting survivor narratives

In the following section, I address the ways in which the Committee went about the process of gathering and presenting survivor voices, and how this process can be considered within a framework of epistemic injustice. I begin with the process of gathering survivor voices, returning to the oral history interviews to think about how survivors experienced the process of engaging with the Committee and the final report. To what extent did this process allow them to tell their narratives in a way which made them feel valid and heard? In what way were they positioned as credible producers of knowledge? The McAleese report is mentioned less frequently than I initially thought it would be in the interviews. This is in part because many of the interviews took place before the report had been published – however, the inaccessible nature of the report, the length and the style in which it is written, meant that it may have seemed a challenging document to engage with for some survivors. In thinking about the women's experiences of the report, there are two key points which I wish to draw out of the interview data. Firstly, I focus on passages where women explicitly speak about their experiences of engaging with the Committee, and the impact this had on them emotionally and materially, as well as how they felt in terms of their value as knowledge producers. I then consider the (in)accessibility of the final report, and what this demonstrates about the intended audience.

From the interviews with survivors which do mention the report, a key feeling seems to be that the report fundamentally misrepresented and downplayed their experiences. They did not feel as if their voices were being heard, in a meaningful capacity. Indeed, Claire McGettrick, a member of JFM, states that

> Initially, the committee didn't even want to speak to the women in person, but we fought for that. The women gave their testimony verbally and then we were given very little notice of a second meeting where we were to look at the format of the initial testimony. Instead, the women were brought in one by one for a meeting with the commission where they asked repeated questions. Their overall impression was that they were being checked to ensure that their memories were correct. (O'Sullivan 2013)

Maureen Sullivan describes the process of speaking to Martin McAleese, describing how it took about an hour, and upon leaving, 'I felt awful... now you just feel, ugh, I don't know what words to put on it' (MAGOHP/38, Maureen Sullivan: 1:00:44). She describes the experience as an extremely painful one for her, because it did not feel like her testimony was believed or taken seriously. The previous chapter explored the terror many women experienced when speaking about their experiences. The risks involved of speaking out, of identifying oneself as a Magdalene survivor and making visible this stigmatized identity, were real and impacted the women's lives in significant ways. To then speak up about this, to take that risk in a formalized and unfamiliar environment and feel as if one was not being taken seriously, further compounds the instance of testimonial injustice which characterized the women's experiences both during and after the time in the institutions. As Maureen Sullivan states, 'we were treated so badly all our lives here, and then when we did get our stories out, to treat us like this' (MAGOHP/38, Maureen Sullivan: 1:00:41). Even when their physical voices were being heard, in the most direct sense, the reality of their experiences were not. Maureen goes on to describe the bodily sensation this caused – she felt she could not be in a confined space afterwards and when leaving the meeting, took the stairs rather than the lift.

Kate O'Sullivan also speaks about feeling ignored and undervalued by the process of giving testimony, saying that

McAleese . . . he just . . . I think he . . . to me, I said afterwards to Fionnuala, 'he was more on their side, the nuns' side than on Claire's and the other girls that was fighting for us'. (MAGOHP/50/ANON, Kate O'Sullivan: 53)

The way that Kate frames the process, as an event with the nuns on one side, and survivors and JFM on the other, suggests that for her this was an experience fraught with combative tension – it was evidently not a productive or validating experience for her. This experience of feeling misrepresented and disbelieved seems to coalesce for many of the survivors around the ways in which the report addressed the issue of physical abuse in the laundries. Later in her interview, Maureen Sullivan says:

> We told Martin McAleese about being thumped and beaten up in the tunnel. And I said I seen no sexual abuse, which I didn't, but I did see women getting beaten, I heard roars up along the corridor, I heard women screaming. (MAGOHP/38, Maureen Sullivan: 1:03:37)

She expresses a deep confusion that, despite this, the abuse they suffered was barely mentioned in the report. This is echoed by Martina Keogh, who speaks about the nuns hitting women with their hands or keys, going on to say:

> I don't understand how I explained that to McAleese, and how he said he never . . . I said that to him about the abuse, you know . . . (MAGOHP/44, Martina Keogh: 48:14)

Both women describe themselves as being confused by this – suggesting that they expected something different from the experience of engaging with the Committee, from the process of telling their story and being heard. Martina goes on to say that

> He [Martin McAleese] wouldn't listen. He kind of didn't . . . you know, I didn't trust him from the minute I met him . . . he left me waiting, which was also degrading, three quarters of an hour, waiting for him, which I felt was very degrading. (MAGOHP/44, Martina Keogh: 53:28)

Martha speaks at length about her experience of engaging with the report, echoing Martina and Maureen's feelings on the erasure of abuse claims. She describes how

> When he said that about no physical abuse, no sexual abuse [referring to Report of the Interdepartmental Committee aka McAleese Report], I cried for the whole week. (MAGOHP/48/ANON, Martha: 20)

Throughout her interview she stresses that the report did not accurately represent her experience, describing it as something which 'should be dumped, it's all wrong' (MAGOHP/48/ANON, Martha: 25). The pain caused by being required to speak about your experiences, reliving these deeply traumatic moments, and yet feel as if you were not being heard, is evident throughout survivors' discussions of engaging with the Committee. As the previous chapter demonstrated, survivors experienced significant shame around their identity as 'Magdalene women' and speaking out was imbued with terror for many of them. The decision to give evidence to the Committee would not have been one many of them made lightly. This process, which was meant to be a positive step forward for these women, providing them with what appeared to be a chance to have their voices heard, their stories listened to, instead brought up feelings of hurt and trauma; they felt yet again characterized as unreliable, as not worthy of respect or serious engagement as narrators of their own experiences. When considering the relationships between interventions such as the McAleese report, and processes of epistemic injustice, it is useful to ask: Did the survivors feel they were heard, and believed? Did they feel like their engagement with the process legitimated them as credible subjects? Throughout the interviews it appears that this was not the case, and therefore I suggest that this experience represented the replication of instances of testimonial injustice the women suffered while in the institutions.

As well as their experiences of engaging with the Committee, I also consider how survivors were able to engage with the final report, with a focus on how accessible this was. In her interview, Kate O'Sullivan describes how she gave testimony to the report, but when asked whether she was given a copy, she says no (MAGOHP/50/ANON, Kate O'Sullivan: 54). Maureen Sullivan also speaks about this in her interview; she was told she wouldn't be given a copy, she had to download it (MAGOHP/38, Maureen Sullivan: 1:03:19). She makes a joke about her lack of computer literacy skills – but there is a serious reality to this, and it is unlikely that she would have the capacity or motivation to download and print such a long document. The report is over 1000 pages – unless someone is able to read this online, which many women may not have been able to do, due to either a lack of computer literacy or a lack of a computer, it seems extremely unlikely that one would be able to access it. The inaccessible nature of the report for survivors means that they are functionally inhibited from engaging with this discussion of their own lives. What does the decision not to give survivors a copy of the report tell us about the intended audience, and the value ascribed to their engagement with the document? If those whose lives are materially and directly affected by the outcome are not seen as the most significant recipients of the report, then who is it being produced *for*? By choosing not to present the report in an accessible way, the Committee is contributing to a process by which these women are denied knowledge about their own experiences, kept in a state of ignorance. They are less able to challenge assertions made in the report which might make them uncomfortable, or which they believe to be inaccurate. They are denied the space to engage with and contribute to further discussions of their own experiences.

I now turn to the question of how survivor narratives were presented in the report. What does the way in which survivors' voices are used throughout the report indicate about the value attributed to them, as experts on the subject? Are they given the space to produce knowledge on their own experiences, and if not, who is? In thinking through the ways in which survivor voices are presented in the report, I focus particularly on chapter 19, which sets out to examine living and working conditions in the laundry. In this chapter, there are approximately twenty-six pages of testimony from survivors. An additional eighteen pages are given over to testimony from male doctors who visited the laundries, along with three and a half pages from John Kennedy in his role as laundry manager, and a statement from a member of the Dublin Lions Club, who reports that in his interactions with the women he found them to be 'happy and contented' (McAleese 2013: 986).

In presenting testimony from women who lived and worked in these institutions alongside that from someone who occasionally took part in entertainment sessions for the women at Sean McDermott Street, with no acknowledgement of the fundamental difference in perspective inherent here, the report elides the vastly different experiences people had of the institutions. While it is, of course, important to seek testimony from a range of resources, it is disingenuous to present the experiences of those who lived in the institutions as equally useful as those from someone who came in from time to time, when ascertaining information about the living and working conditions. There is no acknowledgement that the women who experienced this know far more than those who simply dipped into the institutions, passing by occasionally. Nor is there any acknowledgement of the impact of identity on experience – the idea that, *of course*, the perception of a male doctor, or a male manager, will be different, refracted through the lens of their gender, as well as their religious, economic and social identity. In this instance, I argue that the decision to weight the testimony in this way is a clear example of how the McAleese report downplays the importance and value of survivors' narratives. They are just one of many, to be presented without comment, their words no more or less important than anyone else's.

Chapter 19 states that 'although this Chapter identifies a number of patterns among the stories shared with it, the Committee did not make specific findings in relation to this issue, in light of the small sample of women available' (2013: 925). As mentioned earlier, none of the 793 pages of witness testimony which JFM transcribed and submitted to the IDC appears in the report. If the Committee had included these testimonies, would it have felt able to make specific findings with regard to this issue? Where does the threshold lie in order for them to make specific findings? The question of living and working conditions, including the question of whether physical abuse took place in the institutions, is arguably an important one for the report to engage with. By excluding this large body of survivor narratives on offer, while including the testimony of male managers and doctors, the Committee are making it clear that survivor voices are not central in their approach to this issue, and indeed, the issue itself is not a primary concern for them.

Truth for whom?

The McAleese report self-describes using the language of 'facts'. It is presented as representing an objective account of what took place in these institutions, with no acknowledgement that this might appear differently depending on one's positionality – inside or outside the institution, man or woman, survivor or manager. The voices of the women are presented alongside those of nuns, doctors, infrequent passersby – all afforded the same objective value. By framing the report in this way, as a document which provided a balanced and fair summary of the institutions, getting to the heart of what *really* happened, it is presented as the truth. However, this document does not reflect the experiences of many of the survivors interviewed by the oral history project, and those who did engage with the process of giving testimony to the Committee describe feeling disbelieved and devalued. Furthermore, it is much easier to refer to an official document such as this, than the voices of survivors, which are scattered and hard to access, less coherent and polished. While some inquiries into cases of institutional abuse have encouraged the creation of an oral history archive as a specific form of redress, the McAleese report benefited from the existence of a large body of survivor testimony which had already been collected by JFM – however, a decision was made not to include this in the final report, demonstrating the lack of value afforded to survivor voices by the Committee.

In his apology, discussed further in the next section, Enda Kenny describes the McAleese report as a 'document of truth', but what does this mean? Whose truth is represented here? The excerpts from the interviews with survivors suggest that it was not their truth, so then whose was it? Many of the women feel that the report was not an accurate representation of their experiences, downplaying the seriousness of the abuse suffered and at times ignoring their direct testimony. In some cases, the experience of giving testimony, of having one's narrative ignored or downplayed, represented an experience of retraumatization, bringing back painful memories and reinscribing the idea that they are not to be trusted to know their own lives. Despite claiming to be interested in the voices of the women involved, the Committee did not make space for those voices to be heard in a meaningful capacity. The failure to give proper attention and weight to survivor voices is a clear example of testimonial injustice within the McAleese report, reflecting wider incidences of this throughout the experiences of the Magdalene survivors' lives after the institutions. However, this particular example is compounded by the testimonial weight official reports hold, occupying a space of 'expertise' in comparison to the voices of survivors. The inaccessibility of the report for survivors also meant that they were unable to engage with the contents and respond to it, which created a one-sided narrative which elided the voices of those most affected.

According to its stated aims, the McAleese report was not aiming to address the issue of epistemic injustice as suffered by Magdalene survivors. It was not attempting to position survivors as experts on the subject of their own experiences. Rather, it presents survivor voices as one resource of many to draw upon when establishing facts. In doing so, the report replicated many of the processes which contributed to instances of epistemic injustice for women while they were in the institutions, and in their lives after they had left. O'Rourke and Smith (2016) summarize the process of inquiry represented by the McAleese report, writing that the way in which the committee chose to gather and present evidence

> Was reflected in the Taoiseach's own response on 5 February 2013. Essentially, the Committee's report and Taoiseach's statement implied that, despite the undeniable extent of State involvement with the Magdalene laundries, the girls and women were not treated as badly as children in Industrial and Reformatory Schools and, in any case, they did not stay confined for very long. (O'Rourke and Smith 2016: 119)

They highlight the unhelpful nature of both these claims, not only because of the deeply disturbing hierarchy of abuse they construct but also due to the amount of existing evidence to the contrary (2016: 120). I now turn to the question of the State apology, and the statements made by the religious orders, to further explore the extent to which structures of epistemic justice are maintained by these instances of public voice.

Public apologies and statements of regret

As expressed in the previous section, the primary stated goal of the McAleese report was to establish the facts of State involvement with the Magdalene Laundries. The report concluded that there had been direct State involvement in five key areas, namely routes by which girls and women entered the Laundries; regulation of the workplace and State inspections of the Laundries; State funding of and financial assistance to the Laundries (including contracts for laundry services); routes by which girls and women left the Laundries; and death registration, burials and exhumations. This represented a departure from the State's previous assertions that they had not been complicit in the institutions (O'Rourke 2015: 146).[2] As a result of this, the State took the decision to make a public apology to the survivors of the Magdalene laundries. This was the first time an apology of any sort had been given, and therefore it is a significant event in the timeline of public discourse on the institutions. However, many of the women in the interviews also discuss the nuns and the religious orders as holding responsibility for their incarceration and express a strong desire for an apology from them as well. At the time of writing, none of the religious orders have made such an apology, but they have released statements regarding their involvement in the institutions. The State apology and the responses from the religious orders are key examples of public voice on the institutions; in this section I will explore how they function in shaping the contemporary narrative of the laundries. Unlike the McAleese report, the apology given by Enda Kenny was addressed directly to survivors, but it did not specifically draw on their voices. However, in addressing survivors, Kenny was necessarily presenting their experiences in a particular way, framing and mediating their narratives through a specific focus. To what extent should we consider this apology, and the statements of the religious orders, as instances of public voice intended to address and alleviate epistemic injustice experienced by Magdalene survivors, and in what ways do they do this?

What is an apology?

Apologies are a central feature of moral lives, both in public and in private. They can take many forms, performing a range of social functions. In his work *Relations in Public*, Goffman (2009) defines an apology as, on one hand, an admission of guilt, but it is, on the other hand, also an affirmation of the social rules which caused the guilt in the first place. In an article on political apologies, drawing on analysis of the speech act tradition (Austin 1962), Winter suggests

> A minimal account of an apology's 'existence conditions' that must be present in any apology. These 'existence' conditions differ from 'qualitative' conditions. Qualitative conditions affect how an apology can be better or worse, but are not necessary to an apology. (2015: 263)

However, in the context of this book I am more interested in what an apology *does*, rather than what it *is*, specifically, what public apologies made by States, or other large, 'well-respected' institutions do for those to whom they are apologising. Ahmed (2004: 102) explores the function of shame before others, such as a public State apology, as a form of nation building, thinking about how these declarative events have the capacity to bring nations into being as a community. Shame, she writes, '"makes" the nation in the witnessing of past injustice' (2004: 109). By exposing these injustices, these national failings, the ground is laid for a narrative of national recovery:

> By witnessing what is shameful about the past, the nation can 'live up to' the ideals that secure its identity or being in the present. In other words, our shame means that we mean well, and can work to produce the nation as an ideal. (Ahmed 2004: 109)

Similarly, Winter also considers the ways in which apologies work to build national identities, from the perspective of those who receive them. He describes how apologies work by forming survivors as legitimate citizens. Apologies do the work of nation building in that they publicly recognize survivors as 'having the standing to demand accountability from the state. In other words, political apologies treat survivors as citizens' (Winter 2015: 275). If we consider public apologies within this framework of subjectivity formation, both for the nation and for those who have previously been excluded from the nation, it is useful to consider the type of subjectivity that they call forth. Does the nature of the apology, the wording and the context in which it is given, alter this? If it is not experienced as legitimate and valid by those to whom it is given, is the nation still produced as ideal in the same way? Is the citizenship of the survivors still legitimated? By looking at the specific wording of the State apology and the responses from the religious orders, as well as how survivors experienced them, I consider how these statements call forth a particular narrative and subjectivity, and the ways in which this can contribute to wider processes of epistemic injustice at work in the lives of Magdalene survivors.

Before moving on to a more detailed analysis of the State apology and the statements from the religious orders, I want to consider what it was hoped an apology would do, drawing on the oral history interviews. Approximately half the interviews in the archive were taken before the apology had been given. In these interviews, the focus is on the way in which a public apology would work towards removing the stigma of having been in a Magdalene laundry. For example, Patricia Dervan, when asked what she thinks is important with regard to redress, says:

> Absolutely number one, an apology from the State, because I believe in giving that apology, they might de-stigmatise the whole situation and thereby make the women, I want someone to state, quite clearly and categorically, you, the victims of these institutions, were not to blame. And nothing short of an apology from our government will cover that, but I would like them in making that apology... I want them to, I would hope that they might use those words, because that is what is called for. (MAGOHP/06, Patricia Dervan: tape 6, 00:09)

She stresses the importance not only of an apology but also of an apology which clearly labels survivors as not responsible for their incarceration. In doing so, she links an apology with the removal of stigma, something echoed by survivors in other interviews. This connection implies that the stigma currently attached to the identity of the Magdalene laundry is in part due to the belief by some that the women *deserved* to be in these institutions, that either their behaviour or their innate identity meant that institutionalization was the best option for them. The apology, then, functions as a very public rejection of this, a way of shifting the locus of responsibility. The desired outcome of the apology is a legitimation of the survivors' subjectivity as just that: survivors, rather than sinful women, who deserved their incarceration. This is echoed by others, such as Nuala, who says:

> I feel the apology would go some way towards relieving this feeling of shame, because if somebody apologized for the fact that you were in this ghastly place, then you'd realize there's no need to be feeling ashamed ... and that's so unfair. (MAGOHP/19/ANON, Pearl: 1:27:31, Nuala speaking)

When discussing the content of the apology and statements made by religious orders, and the ways in which they were experienced by survivors, these questions of how they work to remove shame and stigma should be kept in mind.

The State apology

On the evening of 19 February 2013, Enda Kenny addressed the Dáil as part of the discussion on the McAleese report, which had been published two weeks earlier. During his speech, he made the first public State apology to the women who had been in Magdalene laundries, apologizing 'as Taoiseach, on behalf of the State, the Government and our citizens' (Kenny 2013). The Irish State was, for the first time not only admitting involvement in the Magdalene institutions but also making a formal and public apology. However, it is important to highlight that Kenny 'refused to apologise to survivors on the day the [McAleese] report was released' (Fischer 2017: 755). It was only after two weeks of sustained negative commentary on his inaction that he gave the apology in the Dáil.

Words and tone: Forming the traumatic past

In order to think about the ways in which the apology functioned, I first turn to the specific words and imagery used by Kenny in this speech. What particular narratives do these create, and how do these narratives operate? What particular subjectivities do they privilege? Kenny begins his speech by thanking, in turn, the Committee who produced the McAleese report, 'all the women who met with them to assist in its compilation' and the religious orders, 'who cooperated fully with Dr McAleese'. Of course, he has to thank the religious orders – they still occupy a significant position of authority and power. But reading and listening to the apology, it feels jarring to thank them for their cooperation before then proceeding to explicitly condemn the institutions they ran. In doing this, Kenny makes clear the separation between 'then' and 'now' which runs throughout the speech. The religious orders of today are demarcated from those of the past: the former to be thanked while the latter relegated to dark, shadowy history.

Throughout the speech, Kenny constantly refers to the Magdalene laundries as 'the nation's shame', 'a national shame', and I wish to turn to Ahmed's work on shame before others to further explore this. She writes about the construction of shame as belonging to the nation, arguing that

The detachment of shame from individual bodies does a certain kind of work within the narrative. Individuals become implicated in national shame insofar as they already belong to the nation, insofar as their allegiance has already been given to the nation, and they can be subject to its address. Our shame is 'my shame' insofar as I am already 'with' them, insofar as the 'our' can be uttered by me. **The projection of what is unjust onto the past allows shame to be represented here as a collective shame that does not affect individuals in the present,** even as it surrounds and covers them ... despite its recognition of past wrongdoings, shame can still conceal how such wrongdoings shape lives in the present. The work of shame troubles and is troubling, exposing some wounds, at the same time as it conceals others. (2004: 102)

This detachment is evident throughout Kenny's speech, demonstrated through the use of particular language and imagery, invoking an example of what Pine has termed 'anti-nostalgia' (2011), which she posits as the dominant form of contemporary Irish remembrance culture. This is a way of performing the past without making demands of the present – anti-nostalgia is defined against nostalgia, which, Pine argues,

> Feeds a yearning for the stability which is absent from a present that is perceived to be fast-paced and hence unstable. In contrast, anti-nostalgia's vision frames the past as inherently unstable and traumatic, encouraging audiences to be grateful that they have escaped. (2010:8)

The result of this very distinct separation of past and present is that 'the impact of past trauma on the present is lessened because it is distanced' (Pine 2011: 11). The laundries are placed in the category of 'the past', a trauma that we can now 'move on from' by focusing on the liberal, inclusive, productive present. The problems of the past are located and held there: it becomes the *site* of the trauma, something which, unlike a more nebulous iteration of trauma, one can temporally distance oneself from. This form of memory culture risks erasing the continual nature of the trauma, as explored in the previous chapter. It makes no space for narratives in which the women's pain is not simply caused by the events of the past, but maintained and replicated by the structures still evident in the present.

In opening and closing his speech, Kenny also employs imagery of darkness and light, dividing Ireland's history into the past, shadowy and full of trauma, and the future, filled with light. He tells us that 'The Magdalene laundries have cast a long shadow over Irish life, over our sense of who we are', a metaphor which has been repeated frequently in discussion on the institutions. Just one sentence later, he refers to the McAleese report as a document which 'shines a bright and necessary light on a dark chapter of Ireland's history', explicitly positioning the State as the vehicle by which this shadow is removed. He ends the speech by repeating this metaphor:

> I am also conscious that many of the women I met last week want to see a permanent memorial established to remind us all of this darkpart of our history. ... At the conclusion of my discussions with one group of the Magdalene Women one of those present sang 'Whispering Hope'. A line from that song stays in my mind – 'when the dark midnight is over, watch for the breaking of day'.
>
> Let me hope that this day and this debate – excuse me – heralds a new dawn for all those who feared that the dark midnight might never end.

At other times throughout the speech, this separation of past and present is made more evident. For example, Kenny tells us that

> Today we live in a very different country, with a very different consciousness awareness – an Ireland where we have more compassion, more empathy, more insight, more heart.
>
> We do because at last we are learning those terrible lessons. We do because at last we are giving up our secrets.
>
> We do because in naming and addressing the wrong, as is happening here today, we are trying to make sure we quarantine such abject behaviour in our past and eradicate it from Ireland's present and Ireland's future.

While there is nothing wrong with the desire to move on from traumatic events, the repeated use of imagery of darkness and light, and of the word 'quarantine', suggests an inability, or a disinclination, to fully acknowledge the continuing impact these events have had, are still having, on the women involved. They are kept separate in the past; Kenny has drawn a hard and impermeable boundary. The Ireland of 'today', which Kenny refers to, is undeniably different from the Ireland of the 1950s – but there are similarities and enduring attitudes which, if consigned to the past and 'quarantined' there, it is impossible to fully acknowledge. The narratives of the survivors clearly show the enduring nature of the trauma they suffered – they do not have the luxury of being able to enforce this quarantine. By consigning the Magdalene laundries to the past, Kenny is creating the boundaries of a new narrative, one which privileges a particular type of forward-looking subjectivity. The trauma of the laundries is also consigned to the past, and the apology marks a break from this – Ireland can now move forward. This approach risks further marginalizing the voices of survivors who, for whatever reason, do not wish to 'move forward' in quite such a distinct way. It also ignores the reality that many women still live in institutions run by religious orders and cannot move forward, constrained as much by physical illness as by their material circumstances. As Lynch highlights in reference to the treatment of children in Irish industrial schools, this practice of keeping the 'moral contamination' of abuse and neglect quarantined in the past fails to do justice to a more complex historical picture (2012: 65).

Experiencing the apology: Ambivalence to elation

I now turn to the question of how the State apology was experienced by survivors. Just under half of the interviews were taken with women before the apology was given, and most of the rest in the following months. Therefore it is not just the women's reactions to and thoughts on the speech which vary across the interviews, it is also the way they experience it as a temporal event – that is yet to happen, or that has already happened. In thinking through the ways in which the apology was experienced by the women, I draw primarily on interviews taken after the apology, but I also consider the impact of this temporality on their experiences, focusing on how they experienced it both in the immediate and in the long term. Do they speak about their experience of hearing it, or do their interviews rest more on the way in which it impacted the future?

The questions asked about the apology in interviews taken after it had occurred were fairly focused, directly asking what people thought about it. Some survivors take a fairly ambivalent attitude – for example, Margaret Burke says:

> The first time I watched it on the telly, I thought it was sheepish, I didn't think it was strong enough. (MAGOHP/18/ANON, Margaret Burke: 3.01.32)

Kate O'Sullivan's interview echoes this ambivalence – when asked what the apology meant to her, she says that it

> Was alright, you know, you know. He [Enda Kenny] did do what he had to do like, in all fairness to him. And the nuns should have [telephone ringing in background] come up with him then and apologised, do you know what I mean? But he did do his best ... Hmm. I thought it was genuine now you know, maybe it wasn't genuine, maybe ye didn't think it was genuine but ... (MAGOHP/50/ANON, Kate O'Sullivan: 53)

She sounds unsure about her feelings on the apology, particularly the question of its authenticity. The interviewer reassures her that it is what *she* thinks that matters. Other women also express the feeling that the apology meant very little to them, because it did not come from those they saw as responsible. Julia Brown states:

> I did say, when I seen it, that why is he apologising, because he didn't do it? . . . (MAGOHP/11, Julia Brown: 1:45)

Mary Currington describes how

> The apology meant nothing to me. All the nuns that treated me badly, most of them are dead, there's only one I know . . . And the apology should have come from the religious orders, not the government. That's how I felt about the apology. (MAGOHP/15, Mary Currington: 115)

For these women, the apology did little to alleviate feelings of shame because it did not come from those they saw as responsible. However, it is important to note that they did not feel the apology had any negative impact on their sense of identity – they describe feelings of ambivalence or confusion, rather than discomfort.

However, some women went to watch the apology in person, and in these instances, there are more extended discussions of the statement. There is a long discussion of the apology in the interview with Bernadette and Francis Murphy, including commentary from Bernadette Murphy and her friend Molly McCarthy, who was also in a Magdalene institution. Both women seem to be, to an extent, working through their thoughts on the apology and its impact during the interview. Considering this interview was taken just four days after the apology had happened, this is not surprising. This temporal closeness is important to remember when considering how these women speak about the apology – it was not something they had had time to process, and it is likely the feelings it conjured in them would still have been sharp and raw. Firstly, Bernadette Murphy describes her experience of going to the Dáil and listening to the speech in person:

> There was three . . . four of us and all we did was held hands when they . . . when he [Taoiseach Enda Kenny] was talking 'cause it was so emotional and you were thinking 'yeah, that really happened'. And to get an apology, and for all the people that condemned us, disowned us or whatever, we got an apology and we felt better. . . . We . . . well, we said it to him, he came over and shook our hands and I said to him, 'thanks, we can hold our heads up now'. And let's *hope* Ireland understands . . . (MAGOHP/13/ANON, Bernadette and Francis Murphy: 34, Bernadette speaking)

This is the first time the apology is mentioned in this interview and Bernadette makes a clear statement about the impact it had on her and the women she was with – 'we got an apology and we felt better'. She says that after the apology, they could 'hold our heads up', suggesting that this public gesture in some way removed the stigma of having been in a Magdalene institution. As Winter emphasizes, public apologies publicly recognize survivors as having the standing and credibility to demand accountability from the State – they are treated as citizens deserving of respect rather than subjects in need of discipline and control. This process seems evident in Bernadette's initial statement – however, as the interview proceeds, this sentiment is complicated by further discussion. In the second, more extended, discussion of the apology she starts by reiterating her disbelief that this had happened, describing her feelings as elation. The interviewer then echoes back her earlier statement to her, asking if Bernadette thinks that the apology has removed the shame felt by the women. This time, Bernadette is less certain with her words, saying:

> Yeah it was good, it made us feel good, but I don't think the people that looked down on us will change their views. (MAGOHP/13/ANON, Bernadette and Francis Murphy: 119)

She qualifies her use of 'people', stating she means the people of Ireland, who it seems she does not think will change their minds after hearing the apology. At this point, Molly McCarthy interjects, saying that the apology was "to the nation, really" (MAGOHP/13/ANON, Bernadette and Francis Murphy: 120). This is an interesting statement, which unfortunately does not get explored further in the interview – does she feel that the apology was being given to Ireland, rather than the Magdalene survivors? Or to the survivors from the nation as a whole? This sentiment is echoed in the interview with Mary Currington, who also says she felt that the apology was being given to the nation, rather than to the survivors:

> That apology might relieve the State of guilt and the religious orders. It's not words we need, it's action and soon. (MAGOHP/15, Mary Currington: 114)

Both of these extracts can be read with reference to Ahmed's ideas about public apologies as a method of working through national shame, building the nation through a clear rejection of this wrong, and absolving public guilt. Both Mary Currington and Molly McCarthy seem to recognize this intention, and it sits uncomfortably with them. The exchange in the interview with Bernadette Murphy ends on what sounds like a pensive note for the women – despite this public apology, they feel there is enduring disconnect, a public opinion which will 'never, never' be shifted (MAGOHP/13/ANON, Bernadette and Francis Murphy: 120).

There is another extended discussion of the apology in the interview with Martha, who also went to Dublin to hear it in person. Her experience is a deeply emotional one; her description of her immediate feelings on hearing Enda Kenny's apology speaks to the levels of pain which she had been carrying with her. When asked why she went to Dublin she says:

> I needed to hear that apology for myself, because that was a big day for me, that was ... That was the final ... it was the closure in the chapter. ... I won't say I'm going to be closed for a long time to come, but it was the closure that ... when he gave that apology, it was so heartfelt, and I mean he apologised for the families, he apologised. ... I think he went way beyond what we expected and what was meant of him [sic] but I think ... it's only my opinion ... (MAGOHP/48/ANON, Martha: 93–4)

However, as with Bernadette Murphy's interview, it is important to think about the date of this interview – it was done just a few weeks after the apology, and these emotions would have been very fresh for Martha. Would her feelings have changed if these questions had been asked months after the apology? These two extracts demonstrate the very immediate impact the apology had on some of the survivors, the sense of near-physical relief it caused, but they also show the complex range of emotions drawn out by the statement. It could not possibly be everything they wanted it to be or do what they needed it to do – a difficult realization for those who saw it as a real chance for change. In one sense, the apology gave some survivors validity as subjects able to challenge the State, worthy of this level of public engagement. However, there are real concerns expressed in the interviews that it will make no material difference in the lives of the women, which is understandably a key question for many of the survivors.

Statements of regret from the religious orders

As articulated in some of the previous statements, some survivors felt that the apology from the State, while valid, was insufficient. For those who saw the religious orders as bearing more of the responsibility for their experience in the institutions, apologies from these groups were spoken about as desirable. However, at the time of writing, none of the four religious orders have made an apology. A continuing feature of discourse around the laundries is silence on behalf of the religious orders, and this is particularly evident in the lack of response or financial contribution to the contemporary redress process.

However, after the publication of the McAleese report, all four religious orders who were involved in running the Magdalene institutions offered a statement.

The Sisters of Our Lady of Charity stated:

> With deep regret that we acknowledge that there are women who did not experience our refuge as a place of protection and care. . . . Further, it is with sorrow and sadness that we recognise that for many of those who spoke to the Inquiry that their time in a refuge is associated with anxiety, distress, loneliness, isolation, pain and confusion and much more. (Ó Fátharta 2013b)

The Good Shepherd Sisters said in a statement: 'We were part of the system and the culture of the time. . . . We acted in good faith providing a refuge and we sincerely regret that women could have experienced hurt and hardship during their time with us' (Ó Fátharta 2013b).

The Congregation of the Sisters of Mercy said it accepted the limitations of the care it provided for women:

> Their institutional setting was far removed from the response considered appropriate to such needs today. We wish that we could have done more and that it could have been different. . . . It is regrettable that the Magdalene homes had to exist at all. Our sisters worked in the laundries with the women and, while times and conditions were harsh and difficult, some very supportive, lifelong friendships emerged and were sustained for several decades. (Ó Fátharta 2013b)

The Religious Sisters of Charity write that they

> Apologise unreservedly to any woman who experienced hurt while in our care. In good faith we provided refuge for women at our Magdalen Homes in Donnybrook and Peacock Lane. Some of the women spent a short time with us; some left, returned and left again and some still live with us.
>
> We co-operated fully with Senator McAleese and his Committee in the preparation of this report and made available all of our archival material. Each individual woman, if she so requests, will be welcomed and provided with any information we have on file regarding her stay with us. (Religious Sisters of Charity: 2013)

Because of the continuing silence and lack of engagement from the religious orders when it comes to the Magdalene institutions, these statements exist in an uncertain space, lacking any other context within which to position the past or present actions of these religious groups. However, I include them in part because of this – it feels imbalanced to write so extensively about the laundries without any engagement with the words of those who operated them.

If these public, formal expressions of regret are the only words available, then it is worth considering them when thinking about the ways in which public voices on the laundries shape the narrative, the ways in which they shape the subjectivities of the nuns *and* the survivors and what this does for the relative credibility afforded to these groups.

The statements vary in their length and content, but none conform to a definition of an apology which requires the agent to accept culpability, to accept not only that harm has been caused but also that *they* caused the harm through their actions. If we cannot think of them as apologies, it is still necessary to think about how they function with regard to wider ideas of public voice and processes of epistemic injustice. These four statements further demonstrate the ways in which public statements of regret can serve to rewrite the public narrative, framing both the actions of the religious orders and the experiences of the survivors, in a particular way. Both the specific wording used in these statements, and the overall tone, contribute to a very specific understanding of the ways in which the institutions operated. In this section, I address each statement in more depth, exploring the ways in which they acknowledge experiences of hurt while taking no detailed institutional responsibility for this.

The response from the Religious Sisters of Charity is the only statement which uses the word 'apologise', although this is then followed by a standard caveat of 'to any woman who experienced hurt'. This phrasing neatly elides responsibility and shifts the responsibility back onto the survivors. In this framing, survivors have 'experienced hurt', rather than an acknowledgement that they *were* hurt. The person causing the harm is absent from this framing of events. There is an acknowledgement that distress happened, but no connection is made to the behaviour that caused it. The trauma and hurt are conceptualized as an internal state, experienced by the survivor, rather than something connected to external structures. This is echoed in the response by the Sisters of our Lady of Charity, who state that they regret that there were women 'who did not experience our refuge as a place of protection and care'. The responsibility for this experience is either absent or shifted onto the survivor – what seems clear is that the order accepts no responsibility for this experience. There is regret, but no acknowledgement of culpability.

The Good Shepherd Sisters also use this framing in their response, stating that they regret the women *could* have experienced hurt in their care. This places doubt on the reality of the survivors' experiences – they do not necessarily admit that people *did* experience hurt, just that it may have been possible. The repeated framing of this trauma as a subjective experience, something which could be interpreted in a number of ways, works to further discredit the voices of the survivors who repeatedly claim that harm did occur. The Congregation of the Sisters of Mercy express regret that 'the Magdalene homes had to exist at all'. This statement suggests that these institutions played an essential, if sadly unavoidable, role in Irish society, that their existence was due to some undeniable social need. In doing so they position themselves as compassionate actors within a flawed system, rather than a deliberate part of the 'architecture of containment' (Smith 2007) which helped manage subjects who threatened the social fabric of Ireland. The reason that the Magdalene laundries *had* to exist is not expanded upon, but the statement sweeps away any agency or responsibility on behalf of the religious orders.

The phrase 'in good faith' is used by both the Good Shepherd Sisters and the Religious Sisters of Charity to describe the nature of their action. This makes a very clear statement about how they wish to define their intentions. It projects a positive moral intention into the past – however, there is then no attempt to engage with the question of how an institution acting with such good intentions could have produced so many women who experienced this level of hurt. In order to enact accountability, it is necessary for agents to acknowledge not only that hurt has occurred but also specifically what this hurt was, their role in it and why it occurred. Without this, any processes of transitional justice or accountability are impossible – survivors have no routes with which to engage their perpetrators in meaningful dialogue, no way to make sense of their experiences in a new framework through discussion and understanding. None of the religious orders accept responsibility in a meaningful capacity for the harm caused by the Magdalene institutions, and therefore survivors are prevented from engaging with them, prevented from forming themselves as subjects deserving of respect in this manner. The narratives employed by the religious orders echo those highlighted by Lynch in his work on the neglect of children in Irish industrial schools – that abuse was not widespread, practised only by a few staff in an otherwise compassionate system, that these institutions were a product of their time, not to be judged by modern standards (Lynch 2012:64). This type of 'episodic narrative', as Lynch describes it, elides the structural and enduring nature of this type of abuse.

The McAleese report repeatedly emphasizes the extent to which the religious orders cooperated and how helpful they were in producing records – but this cooperation does not extend to making their archives available to anyone except the committee. In March 2016, Claire McGettrick sent a Freedom of Information request to Taoiseach Leo Varadkar on behalf of *Justice for Magdalenes Research*, asking for access to the McAleese Commission documents held by his ministry. Her request was refused twice (Justice for Magdalenes Research 2017: 6). The United Nations Committee Against Torture have also advised the Irish government to facilitate access to Magdalene laundries archives for survivors and their representatives, suggesting that the State should 'promote greater access of victims and their representatives to relevant information concerning the Magdalene laundries held in private and public archives' (2017). However, this recommendation has still not been implemented. The continuing silence of the religious orders in the years after the closure of the institutions, and their refusal to provide survivors with information and records, despite repeated recommendations from UNCAT, mirrors their silence towards the women during their time in the laundries. In that context, this silence took the form of a complete lack of information given to the women about their experiences – why they were there, how long they had to stay, what was happening to them. In the previous chapters I have explored how this silence was extremely traumatic for the women who experienced it, enacting a form of epistemic violence by denying them information about their own lives. The continued absence of the voices of those who ran the orders, along with a consistent lack of access to records for survivors and their families, means that this silence is maintained, and the pain caused by 'not knowing' continues and is replicated. The responses given by the religious orders represent almost the entirety of their engagement with the issue, and survivors are left once again without access to knowledge of their own experiences. They are denied the credibility that a more detailed, engaged response would give them.

The absence of the voices of the nuns in any other capacity, and as a consequence their continued refusal to engage with processes of redress, is another example of the ways in which public statements, or the lack thereof, continue to shape the experiences of survivors of trauma. Through these responses, the religious orders are creating a new narrative, and it is one which survivors cannot engage with, in any meaningful way. These statements are not designed to open up dialogue; rather, they present a particular understanding of the actions of the nuns as a new reality. The statements from the religious orders occupy a position of privileged voice – they are given in a formal capacity and context, with the weight of the Catholic Church behind them. Their statements were reported in the press, giving the religious orders an official platform through which they could communicate to the Irish public. In contrast, until the oral history project, there had been no large-scale collation of the voices of survivors – they existed in relative isolation, as the voices of individuals with no institutional backing. Even now, very few people will have listened to the audio files of the women's stories or read the interview transcripts. This inequality in both distribution and institutional weight means that the responses from religious orders have the capacity to shape the narrative in a way the survivors' voices do not. These responses therefore represent a replication of the processes of testimonial injustice which the women experienced while in the institutions. They present the religious orders as agents abstracted from any responsibility, and the survivors as unreliable subjects, women who *could* have experienced harm, although that is by no means a given.

Reframing the narrative?

The State apology and the responses from the religious orders represent a mode of address to survivors that, in itself, does not invite their speech. However, it is evident that the former in particular was felt by some of the survivors to be a positive instance of public voice, in that it sought to create the conditions in which their voices were better listened to, their experiences seen as credible, and survivors themselves produced as subjects worthy of engagement. By making a clear statement that the survivors themselves were not responsible for their incarceration, the State apology formed the survivors as victims, rather than actors complicit in their own trauma. Their experiences are, to an extent, validated.

We have no interview data which discusses the statements from the religious orders, and therefore no way of knowing specifically how these responses were experienced by survivors. However, the responses present the actions of the religious orders in a very particular way – sad yet unavoidable; a product of a different time. The religious orders are never framed as responsible for the trauma and hurt caused, and no meaningful apology is offered. This stands in marked contrast to the ways in which survivors speak about their experiences throughout the body of the oral history project, as evidenced in the previous two chapters of this book. The statements of the religious orders therefore cut across survivors' understanding of their own history. By publicly eliding responsibility and positioning themselves as compassionate actors within a flawed system, the religious orders are reinforcing a particular narrative regarding their involvement in the traumas of the Magdalene laundries. This narrative does not centre on the needs or voices of survivors; nor does it give credibility to their voices. Instead, it reproduces instances of testimonial injustice by once again forming survivors as unreliable narrators.

Dublin Honours Magdalenes

Finally, I consider the impact made by the most recent large-scale event focusing on the Magdalene survivors. When I started my research in 2015, the apology given by Kenny in 2013 was the only public apology made by the State regarding the Magdalene institutions. However, in the years following this, there has been a significant increase in public discussion around the laundries, with mounting pressure on the government from activist groups such as JFMR to implement processes of redress, as well as from journalists and academics. In November 2017, a report by the Ombudsman Peter Tyndall into the administration of the *Magdalen Restorative Justice Scheme* was published, criticizing the Department of Justice for its administration of the scheme and recommending that the cases of women omitted from it be reexamined. He also critiques some of the wording used, stating that '"admitted to and worked in" is the most problematic of the phraseology used' (Tyndall 2017: 7).[3]

In January 2018, following the publication of this report, JFMR wrote to Minister for Justice Charlie Flanagan requesting his Department's assistance in arranging a meeting and consultation of Magdalene survivors. They later wrote to Taoiseach Leo Varadkar requesting his intervention to ensure that the Magdalene restorative justice scheme was implemented as promised, including facilitating a meeting of Magdalene survivors and consultation on memorialization. On 9 March 2018, Flanagan and the Ministry of Justice agreed to facilitate the event as planned by JFMR, to honour survivors of the Magdalene Laundries at a two-day event in Dublin in June. In a press release published on 6 March 2018, O'Donnell highlights the importance of the event, stating that

> The Department of Justice is the only organisation which has the details of the women, but to date they have ignored our pleas to help bring them together by contacting them on our behalf. Time is of the essence here as these women are getting older. In his redress report in 2013 Mr Justice Quirke recommended that a gathering takes place before more of the women die. We are simply asking the Department, which holds all of the contact details, to invite them on our behalf. We are not asking them to hand over their contact details to us directly. When these women were in Magdalenes their names were changed and they weren't allowed to speak to each other. Bringing them together for the first time is a major step forward in redress for the huge wrong that was done to them. (Justice for Magdalenes Research 2018)

The *Dublin Honours Magdalenes* event represents the first large-scale public commemoration of the experiences of the survivors. Over 200 women travelled to Dublin for the two-day event which included a visit to *Áras an Uachtaráin* (the official residence and principal workplace of the President of Ireland); a reception and speech by Michael D. Higgins; a formal dinner at Mansion House in Dublin; and a listening exercise, designed to give women the space to talk about their experiences. This event was also a way to fulfil two of the key recommendations of Mr Justice Quirke's Magdalene Redress Scheme – that the women be supported to meet and get to know each other, and that they discuss how they would like their experiences to be officially remembered. The event represented a significant and authentic engagement with the voices and needs of survivors, particularly in comparison to the previous two instances discussed in the chapter. In particular, the listening exercise which took place on the second day demonstrated an understanding of the value in providing a space, both literally and metaphorically, where the survivors could speak about their experiences with each other, and have those experiences recorded and presented with minimal alteration.

However, there are still questions to be asked about the ways in which this engagement with survivor narratives is mediated through a public facing event. By addressing four specific parts of the event, I consider the ways in which it demonstrates both a significant shift in the narrative around the institutions and an enduring way of thinking about the nature of the laundries and the role of the State which seems hard to alter. In this instance, I do not have access to interviews with women where they speak about how they experienced this event, as with the McAleese report and the State apology. The only resources I can draw from are my own personal interactions with the women over the two days, media surrounding the event and my experience of participating in the listening exercise as a note-taker.

The Gardaí

On the first day of the event, the women were transported from the hotel in west Dublin to *Áras an Uachtaráin* by coach. In total, twelve large coaches made the journey across Dublin, and the procession was escorted by Gardaí on motorcycles, closing roads, holding traffic and providing a very public demonstration of State support. The Gardaí escort proved popular with many of the women, and several of them remarked on how important it made them feel – they're closing roads for us! As the coaches passed by, the public waved and cheered. The Gardaí motorcade flanked the twelve coaches, ensuring they safely reached the President's mansion. As I sat in one of these coaches with another volunteer, I could not help but think of the interviews in which women described other instances of being escorted by the Gardaí – women forcibly returned to the laundries after escaping, or being taken there by the police after summoning the courage to report abuse by their fathers. I wondered how a woman who had experienced this be feeling as she sat in the coach speeding towards Phoenix Park. To me, it felt like a near grotesque erasure of the role played by the Gardaí in maintaining the existence and power of the laundries. In her interview, Mary describes her engagement with the police.

> They had a policeman sitting in the parlour waiting for me and they took me off to a place, the most awful place called Gloucester Street [Sisters of Our Lady of Charity Magdalene Laundry] there on Sean McDermott Street absolutely [sic] hell hole. They took me there, I protested, I screamed, I shouted but it didn't make any difference. I wouldn't change my clothes, I wouldn't wear their clothes. So I ran away out of there. After I think about two or three maybe five weeks, I ran away from there with another lady and then I was brought back by the police. (MAGOHP/04/ANON, Mary: 2)

Was Mary one of the survivors sitting in the coaches as they sailed through the streets of Dublin? How did she feel, now that the police were attending in this new capacity? However, when I voiced this out loud to the younger volunteer I was sitting next to, she seemed confused. Why would having a Gardaí escort be a bad thing? I was keenly aware that my own personal politics around the police and their role in maintaining carceral State institutions were also impacting my feelings on this. I felt guilty at criticizing something which clearly was important to many of the survivors – having the Gardaí escort made them feel important (which, of course, they are!) However, it also appeared to demonstrate a desire to reframe the involvement of the Gardaí as positive – they are now agents of protection for the women, escorting them to the President's mansion, rather than back to the institution. Chapter 9 of the McAleese report acknowledges that the Gardaí were involved in returning women to the institutions, but beyond this there has been little engagement with this particular facet of State involvement. The fact that the Gardaí were actively involved in maintaining the physical boundaries of the institutions is significant, and involving them in the commemorative events without any kind of acknowledgement of this history felt like a glossing over of this, smoothing out the reality of their complicity.

The presidential booklet

Once the coaches had arrived at *Áras an Uachtaráin*, we were escorted through the house and towards a large, grand marquee in the garden. I picked up the programme for this part of the event and as I read it, I hesitated over the wording chosen to introduce the event.

> President Michael D. Higgins and his wife Sabina Higgins welcome former workers of the Magdalene laundries to a reception in Áras an Uachtaráin, Tuesday 5th June 2018.

The booklet was a beautiful object and gave the women something to take home from the event, to remember the experience. It also gave the event a sense of importance – the heavy white card and detailed programme imbuing the proceedings with ceremony. Several women I spoke to made efforts to ensure they had one before leaving; I gave mine away to someone who had misplaced hers and did not want to leave without one.

It is clear, then, that for many women the booklet was a valuable and positive object. It made them feel valued and important. However, the description of the survivors as 'former workers' frames the Magdalene institutions in a very particular way, namely as places of *work*. This heavy emphasis on the labour performed by the women during their time in the laundries, with no acknowledgement of the non-consensual conditions in which this labour was done, obscures the reality of the institutions. It frames the women as workers, as productive members of the nation's past, rather than survivors of state-sanctioned institutional abuse. Referring to victims of institutional trauma as 'former workers' is rewriting the narrative around what the Magdalene laundries were – here they exist as sites of labour, rather than of trauma.

However, it is also important to think about the potential positive value of this reframing, in this particular context. The event was already a difficult time for many of the survivors. For several of them, it was the first time they had publicly acknowledged their identity as 'Magdalene survivors'. By using more 'respectable' language to describe their experiences, did the event allow the women to feel less like victims? Is a commemorative event such as *Dublin Honours Magdalenes* even the right place to make evident the trauma of the laundries, or is this euphemistic terminology a deliberate choice to avoid painting the women as victims at a formal celebratory event? To what extent did the desire to imbue the event with ceremony and celebration involve a necessary erasure of the realities of the institutions? Can an event whose primary purpose is to celebrate and honour survivors of institutional abuse be expected to address this trauma? Because of the recent nature of the event, and the lack of more resources, such as in-depth interviews with the attendees, it is difficult to answer these questions. It would have been deeply inappropriate of me to have approached the women at the event, in my capacity as a volunteer, to ask them what they thought of this wording. However, thinking through the ways in which this tension between celebration and acknowledgement of trauma manifests itself demonstrates that there is still an uneasiness with acknowledging certain aspects of State involvement with the Magdalene laundries, in a similar way that the involvement of the Gardaí suggests an unwillingness to fully address the role they played in maintaining these institutions.

The listening exercise

On the second day of the event, most of the women returned to Mansion House, where they had enjoyed a formal dinner the night before. They took their seats for the listening exercise, which was structured around three questions: 'What should we know about the Magdalene Laundries?'; 'What lessons should we learn from what happened there?'; and finally, 'How should we remember what happened?' The bringing together of survivors in this way, and the facilitation of this exercise, was designed to fulfil two key parts of the Magdalene Restorative Justice Scheme as outlined by Justice John Quirke: to bring together those women who wish to meet others who also spent time in the Magdalene laundries, and to provide an opportunity for a listening exercise to gather views on how the Magdalene laundries should be remembered by future generations (O'Fátharta 2018). In this exercise, women were seated at tables in groups of about eight or nine, along with a facilitator and a note-taker. The women were asked the aforementioned questions, but the discussions rapidly dissolved into a broad discussion of their experiences, moving from commiseration to solidarity. I took notes for one of the groups, and so while I can only speak to that experience, the reactions from the women were overwhelmingly positive. In both the recorded discussion and informal interactions with the participants afterwards, they expressed how valuable they felt this to be, that it made them feel heard and listened to.

I argue that this process represents a significant attempt to address instances of both testimonial and hermeneutic injustice in the lives of Magdalene survivors. Firstly, they were given a space in which their voices were prioritized as experts on their own experiences. This is evident in terms of both physical space – the facilitated space of a circle, where each woman's voice was afforded equal and significant credibility, and temporal space – the event itself was one dedicated to them, where they were visibly positioned as reliable narrators. They were being encouraged to tell their stories in a context which aimed to create the conditions in which they could do this. In the final chapter of this book, I argue that we cannot simply call for equality of testimonial opportunities, but we must also work for equity, identifying the barriers particular subjects have in speaking on their experiences, and actively addressing them. The listening exercise is a clear example of this. By bringing survivors together and encouraging them to talk openly about their experiences, this exercise also worked to address hermeneutical injustice suffered by the women, the gap in the collective understanding. In the discussions which took place both during and as a result of the listening exercise, and the DHM event as a whole, women were able to make connections with others who had had similar experiences, talking about their histories in a way which allowed for a more coherent and cohesive understanding of what had happened to them. This exercise is part of a process of collective understanding among Magdalene survivors, one which is significant in creating better epistemic conditions in which they can speak about their experiences.

The Tablet

Finally, I consider the wording chosen in one of the many articles which reported the event. There was considerable media attention given to the two days, and news outlets in both Ireland and the United Kingdom featured stories on the proceedings. These were largely positive, choosing to focus on the opportunities given for survivors to have their stories heard, and the support given by the people of Ireland. However, the wording used in one of the articles stood out as interesting, because of the very specific way in which it presented the experiences of the women while they were in the institutions.

The Tablet is a liberal Catholic magazine that has been published continually since 1840. The article, published on 6 June, gives an overview of the two-day event, and includes a brief summary of what the laundries were. The author writes:

> The women sent to work in the laundries, the last of which closed in 1996, and to live in the convents attached to them were given the work of washing laundry as a penance for sins, real and imagined. (Catholic News Service 2018)

Obviously, this is just one article, and without a more thorough analysis of media coverage it is not possible to draw wider conclusions about the ways in which the event was reported, and what this can tell us about public voice on the Magdalene institutions. However, the choice of wording used is unusual enough to merit further analysis, as an example of how lingering ideas about the nature of the Magdalene women are still circulated in contemporary culture. What does this choice of words used by *The Tablet*, in 2018, tell us about the enduring underlying social narratives surrounding the women who were incarcerated in the laundries? What does describing women who were sent to laundries as having committed 'sins, real and imagined' mean? Firstly, we can ask what is meant in this context by a 'real' sin, and what this implies about how the (unnamed) author wishes to present the women who were sent to the laundries. By demarcating the sins into 'real and imagined', the suggestion is that there were certain women who had committed real sins. If a woman had committed a real sin, is there an implication that her incarceration in the institution was in some way more legitimate than that of a woman who had committed an imagined sin? The *Dublin Honours Magdalenes* event was intended to honour survivors of the Magdalene laundries, recognizing the trauma of their experiences and making good on State promises of commemoration and redress. The fact that, in 2018, a self-described liberal Catholic magazine would choose to describe women incarcerated in the Magdalene institutions as having committed 'real and imagined' sins demonstrates the lingering associations which persist in discussion of the Magdalene survivors. This is not to imply that I think *The Tablet* believes some of the Magdalene survivors to be truly sinful – rather, I think that the casual nature of this phrasing gives an interesting example of the ways in which the pervasive narrative around the laundries as sites of penance still lingers.

To what extent can we see this phrasing as informed by previous instances of public voice such as the McAleese report, the State apology and the responses from the religious orders? This chapter has explored the ways in which statements of public apology and redress have the potential to contribute to instances of epistemic injustice, reshaping the narrative in a way which continues to marginalize and devalue the voices of survivors. I argue that this line in *The Tablet*, although representing just one small instance of public voice, is a useful example of the outcome of this. Earlier in this chapter, I discussed how for many women, the desired result of the State apology, and subsequent instances of public voice, was the legitimation of the subjectivity of 'survivor', as someone who was in no way to blame for what happened to her. By presenting women who were in Magdalene institutions as women who had possibly committed 'real sins', *The Tablet* continues to uphold the narrative that, perhaps, it is possible to make a historical justification for their incarceration, that some women are to blame for what happened to them.

A special band of heroes?

As the coaches arrived at Mansion House after the visit to *Áras an Uachtaráin*, they were met by a cheering crowd of over 200 people. Many people held homemade placards, reading 'Welcome Home', 'We Honour You' and 'The Women of Ireland Salute You'. The presence of this crowd was in part due to the work of Norah Casey, an Irish businesswoman, television personality and broadcaster, who was involved in the event. On 2 June 2018, she tweeted:

> Please RT: A special band of heroes arriving Tuesday – would be lovely to give them a big welcome and make this memorable – 430 survivors and their families in 8 buses arriving Dawson Street 6.30pm Tuesday (5th) after the Áras for a Gala Dinner at the Mansion House #SpreadTheWord. (Casey 2018)

At the time of writing, the tweet had been retweeted 551 times and has received 681 likes – it was evidently effective, as shown by the large crowd of supporters. The existence of this crowd, the largely positive media coverage and the level of ceremony afforded to the survivors throughout the whole event demonstrate the unprecedented levels of support for Magdalene survivors by the Irish public in 2018. In Norah Casey's tweet they are framed as heroes, to be honoured and welcomed, rather than problematic subjects to be hidden from view. Their narratives and experiences were being validated and believed, and during the event women expressed to me how valuable they felt this was. While I wish to acknowledge the importance of this support, I have chosen to focus on instances which trouble the categorization of the event as overwhelmingly positive. The event, as the publication of the McAleese report and the apologies had done five years previously, called forth a particular type of survivor subjectivity, one which could be said to gloss over certain realities of the trauma of the Magdalene institutions while still forming them as credible subjects to a greater extent than previous instances of public voice have done. In this way, the *Dublin Honours Magdalenes* event should be seen as one which provides a meaningful attempt to address survivors' experiences of epistemic injustice. However, it must be situated within a cultural and religious framework which cannot fully escape the influence of previous instances of public voice, and of the particular Catholic religious imaginary in which it is both possible and legitimate to inscribe some women with a sinful identity.

Conclusion

The three instances of public voice explored in this chapter – the McAleese report, the apology and the *Dublin Honours Magdalenes* event – demonstrate the ways in which public memories of the institutions and perception of the survivors has been shaped since 2013, and how this has impacted on the experiences and subjectivities of survivors. The two previous chapters explored the ways in which the experience of being in a Magdalene institution involved a process of identity erosion, a gradual attrition of agency, resulting in instances of testimonial and hermeneutical injustice which continued to function in the lives of the women after they had left the laundries. This chapter has demonstrated the extent to which these instances are maintained and replicated through expressions of public voice on the institutions, specifically, processes of inquiry, apology and redress. However, I have also considered the ways in which these processes of public voice have the capacity to address instances of epistemic injustice as well, when the institution involved adopts a reflexive approach to the process of communicating with survivors.

These examples also demonstrate the importance of paying close attention to the continual and ongoing nature of trauma. Jennifer Lind writes that 'coming to terms with the past is an unpredictable process that is as likely to antagonize as soothe relations with former victims' (2008:8), and it is not something which can be easily demarcated into then and now, as Kenny's speech risks doing. The trauma of the Magdalene laundries lingers in the lives of the women, and therefore any approach that wishes to address this must be similarly long-lasting, addressing not only the past trauma but also the structures through which this trauma is upheld in the present. In order to prevent and mitigate epistemic injustice, Fricker suggests that we must cultivate virtues of both testimonial and hermeneutical justice. To do this, the hearer must 'be alert to the impact not only of the speaker's social identity but also the impact of their *own* social identity on their credibility judgment' (2007: 91). With regard to the virtue of hermeneutical injustice, Fricker argues that this takes the form of

> An alertness or sensitivity to the possibility that the difficulty one's interlocuter is having as she tries to render something communicatively intelligible is not

due to its being a nonsense or her being a fool, but rather some sort of gap in collective hermeneutical resources. (2007: 169)

The virtuous hearer must again be aware of their own social identity as well as that of the speaker, and how this impacts on the nature of their communication. She concludes that 'combatting epistemic injustice clearly calls for virtues of epistemic injustice to be possessed by institutions as well as by individuals' (2007: 176), by the judiciary, the police, local government and employers, among others. When thinking about how public interventions such as inquiries, apologies and redress impact upon processes of epistemic injustice it is therefore necessary to consider the extent to which the institution engaging in this has cultivated these virtues. This is something I discuss further in the final chapter, although it is beyond the scope of this book to engage with the question of what a 'virtuous' institution should look like as fully as is necessary. However, it is possible to make some suggestions, situating this within the context of the Irish State. I would argue that at the heart of this is a commitment to what O'Donnell describes as 'listening attentively' (2018b) to survivors, as demonstrated by the listening exercise conducted during the *Dublin Honours Magdalenes* event. This process of attentive listening is founded on an understanding that it is not enough to simply expect marginalized subjects, those who have experienced epistemic injustice, to be able to articulate and express themselves. Institutions, particularly those charged with care for societies, must actively work to create the conditions in which these subjects can speak freely and feel heard. The amount of work which goes into creating these conditions will vary for different groups, depending on the levels of credibility deficit they have experienced, their social identity in any particular context and the stigma they face. It is not enough to offer everyone an equal chance to speak – some people will need more than this, because their starting point is one of much greater disadvantages. The recent revelations[4] around the disregarding of survivor testimony in the Mother and Baby Home Commission of Investigation (Enright 2021b) suggest that the Irish State has yet to develop this virtue.

In this chapter, the Magdalene survivors have been women who shared stories and women who held Ireland's shame. They have been heroes and former workers, women who committed sins both real and imaginary. They have been women who *could* have experienced hurt and hardship and regretful victims of an unavoidable social context. This chapter has demonstrated the multiplicity of narratives and modes of engagement which are now present within discussions of the laundries; in doing so, I work towards an understanding of the varied forms of identity power at work during these instances of public voice. It is evident that since 2013 there has been a marked increase in public expressions of support for Magdalene survivors. However, these official demonstrations of support and responsibility should not be considered uncritically. Whether intentionally or not, they shape the public narrative around the laundries, and they hold a different epistemic value than survivors' narratives. Survivors' voices are pushed to the side, or simply seen as one resource upon which to draw. New narratives are constructed, and boundaries drawn regarding what is 'known' about the institutions. Particular voices and stories are called forth, and in doing so, the voices of those who do not fit these new narratives are pushed further from the public consciousness. When the survivors occupy an identity which is already attributed a certain degree of credibility deficit in contemporary society – they are women, they are older, they may not have high levels of literacy – then an institution must be attentive to the significant imbalance of epistemic power involved when engaging in processes of inquiry, apology and redress if they wish to address rather than replicate the structures which cause this.

7

Conclusion: Challenging a lingering silence

In the spring of 2019, I visited Cork with my family. I took the opportunity to try and visit the sites of the Magdalene institutions in Cork, particularly the Sundays Well location, which is described at length in great visual detail by some of the interviewees. I wanted to be able to picture the building, to ground myself in the physical reality of the institution I was writing about. So, on the last day of our trip, I persuaded my brother to accompany me on a visit to the site. As we walked up the steep hill to the gate, we could see that there were two other people there – a young man and an older woman. They were, like us, dismayed to find that the driveway was blocked, a sturdy iron gate and padlock preventing us from getting any closer to the dilapidated building. Unlike us, they were less interested in the Magdalene institution; they were Polish pilgrims attempting to visit the shrine of Little Nellie of Holy God. Little Nellie's grave is a Cork pilgrimage site – it is well cared for, despite having been largely inaccessible to the public for several years. It stands in stark contrast to the graves of the Magdalene women who lived in the institution in the grounds of which Little Nellie's grave site sits. The graves in the Sundays Well site itself are badly maintained and frequently inaccurate, and there is a large gap from 1896 to 1928, during which period there are no names recorded. At other grave sites in Cork, there are more concerns around inaccuracy. Four women are listed on headstones at mass graves in two different locations in Cork. Another woman with a distinctive first name is listed twice on the same headstone at another site but with different dates of death two months apart. The women died on dates ranging from as far back as 1882 right up until 1983. The Good Shepherd order have issued no explanation for this (Ó Fátharta 2013a).

The four of us – myself and my brother, and the two pilgrims – stood for a while, considering our options, thinking about whether we could find another way in. Eventually we gave up, and wandered around the walls, peering through the cracks in security doors and over fences in people's driveways. I felt frustrated. The site was on the brink of redevelopment, due to be turned into over 200 new apartments, and I desperately wanted to go and connect the visual dots in my brain which had heard the name 'Sunday's Well' repeated over and over in the interviews, before it was too late. There is undoubtedly a significant opportunity for work on the rich question of the psychogeography of the Magdalene institutions, which is beyond the scope of this book. However, on the six opportunities I had to visit the sites of laundries when I was writing, each time felt significant, in both a personal capacity and also as a way of improving the nature of my work. Seeing the high walls gave a solidly material reality to the descriptions of the survivors' experiences, the opportunity to see and touch the heavy doors adding a visual element to the narratives of arrival and departure.

It is hard to imagine the size of some of these buildings without seeing them. They were not small houses, tucked away on a side street, but large, imposing institutions, often right in the centre of town. They are not hidden in a physical sense. The Sundays Well site is not the only Magdalene institution at risk of being torn down, the history erased and the lives of the women who were incarcerated further forgotten. The site in Donnybrook, Dublin, is also on the brink of redevelopment. The Religious Sisters of Charity, who still own the convent beside the site, sold the laundry to a private owner years ago and in 2016 the property went up for sale, advertised as 'an exciting and rare opportunity to develop in the heart of Donnybrook' (McGrath 2016). There was no mention of what the site had been previously, and in 2020, plans by the Pembroke Partnership to construct an apartment block complex on the site were approved. The only structure guaranteed to remain is the chimney stack, pictured on the cover of this book, which has had a preservation order since 2012. The Sean McDermott Street site in Dublin also has an uncertain future, although it is slightly more promising. In September 2018, Councillor Gary Gannon successfully put forward a motion to block the sale of the site to a Japanese hotel chain. In 2020, Dublin city councillors voted in favour of progressing plans to turn the building into a centre for third-level education, including the development of social housing units for older people and a memorial in memory of victims and survivors of Ireland's institutional homes.

The uncertain future of the physical Magdalene laundry sites, with many being torn down to make way for expensive flats, tucked away behind locked gates or converted into new institutions, with barely any recognition of the buildings' history, echoes the ways in which the narratives of survivors are at risk of being slowly erased, either through deliberate action or simply as an unavoidable consequence of an ageing group. The significance of the oral history project, then, cannot be understated. As the first large-scale collection of survivor narratives, it is an invaluable resource for both researchers and the general public. This book represents the first significant secondary analysis of this project, approaching the topic of the Magdalene institutions not from a desire to construct a narrative of historical accuracy, but, rather, to learn more about the nature of women's experiences in these institutions, and the ways in which they were (un)able to communicate these experiences. Drawing extensively on the interviews taken with survivors, I have demonstrated the ways in which the trauma suffered by the women was not only physical and psychological but also distinctly *epistemic* in nature, a violence done to them in their capacity as knowers. Within the laundries, they underwent processes of bodily and spiritual discipline which prevented them from communicating their experiences to others. As well as being consistently formed as unreliable subjects, 'nobodies', they were kept in a deliberate state of 'not knowing', characterized by a lack of information about their rights, the duration of their stay and why they were there. Combined with processes of bodily discipline, such as the rule of silence and physical confinement, this had the intention of producing a particular type of religious, gendered subjectivity – a docile, productive body which no longer threatened the moral or social life of the newly formed Irish State. It was also a social identity which could be further discredited, leading to persistent instances of epistemic injustice in their lives after they left the institutions.

These instances of epistemic injustice continue to be present in their experiences after leaving the laundries, maintained and replicated by the complex social and religious structures of twentieth-century Ireland. This state of deliberate ignorance, which was so prevalent within the institutions, continued after they left, the circumstances of their departure marked by a suddenness which left them confused and unable to communicate with their friends. In their lives after the institutions, they had no access to information about their experience there and were often inhibited in communicating these experiences due to the terror of making visible a highly stigmatized identity. This prevented them from making connections with others with whom they might build a shared community around the experience of having been in a Magdalene institution, again, limiting their access to knowledge and resources which would provide clarity and support. This is further heightened by the position of their narratives and voices in contemporary Irish society – this book has engaged with the impact that processes of inquiry, apology and redress can have: by creating new forms of 'official' knowledge on the experiences of Magdalene laundry survivors, through the creation of new narratives which frequently ignored or erased the voices of survivors, the women are again denied the space to be seen as credible producers of knowledge on their own experiences.

This book has demonstrated the value of considering the experiences of Magdalene survivors within this framework of epistemic injustice, understanding the ways in which the harms inflicted upon them included harms done to their capacity to both communicate knowledge and be respected as knowledge producers. During their time in the laundries, they were consistently produced as unreliable subjects – they were 'liars', seen as too untrustworthy or stupid to be trusted with knowledge of their own experiences. Over and over again, Magdalene survivors are portrayed as unreliable narrators of their own experiences, suffering repeated and sustained instances of testimonial injustice. The Magdalene institutions occupy an uneasy descriptive position in that until very recently there has been no discursive structure in which survivors could make sense of their experiences. There was no framework to draw upon, no language structure survivors could use to describe what happened to them and, therefore, no coherent framework in which to place their experiences in a way which made sense to others. By considering this as an example of hermeneutic injustice, we are able to better understand the nature of their silences, and the impact that it had on their sense of self, and interactions with others. To speak about their experiences was risky and dangerous speech – to do so would have made visible their stigmatized identity, and as I show in Chapter 5, resulted in very real consequences for those who did.

In concluding this book, I wish to highlight two key themes which run throughout the work and consider how an understanding of the epistemic nature of the trauma of the laundries helps bring these together, as well as considering how these traumatic processes cannot be separated out but have a compound effect on the lives of the women. First, I argue that the laundries represented a specific manifestation of the powerful religious and cultural imaginary which existed in twentieth-century Ireland. They are an example of Foucault's disciplinary institutions (1977) in that they aimed to erode the identity of those incarcerated, through processes of discipline which worked to control the body and self. However, further to this, they should be seen as a very particular type of *religious carceral* environment, which relied on the sacred form of the Irish Catholic nation for legitimacy. Secondly, with this in mind I highlight what I call a rationale of vicious paternalism which has emerged throughout this book as a consistent theme. This is based in an understanding of gendered subjectivity which conceptualizes certain women – those who transgress socially and religiously constructed boundaries – as both deeply vulnerable, unable to know their own minds or make their own decisions, and highly threatening, in need of punishment and confinement for the public good. This ideology meant that the laundries could be posited as a form of social care, a way for the State to elide responsibility for vulnerable women, as well as those whom they simply saw as a problem in need of a carceral solution.

Disciplinary institutions and religious meanings

The Magdalene institutions were intended to strip away the identity of those who entered, eroding their agency and reforming them into a new desirable female subjectivity, that of the penitent and reformed woman, through processes of discipline and punishment. This book has demonstrated the various forms these processes took, and the ways in which they continued in the women's lives well after they had left the physical confines of the institution. These processes are an example of how these types of institutions operate more generally, in terms of depersonalizing individuals in order to incorporate them into a system of institutional control. However, beyond this, they are also a specific manifestation of the particular religious and cultural imaginary which existed in twentieth-century Ireland. As Gordon Lynch demonstrates in his work on the industrial school system in Ireland, 'this sacred form of the Irish Catholic nation, which shaped both imagined visions of Irish collective life as well as the sexual subjectivities of individuals, provided a central source of symbolic legitimation for the industrial and reformatory school system' (Lynch 2012: 69). Similarly, this book has demonstrated the ways in which this symbolic legitimation can also be seen in the context of the Magdalene institutions.

This specifically religious nature of the institutions, and the way in which they were firmly situated within this Irish Catholic imaginary, is evident throughout the experiences of the women, from their time in the laundries to the ways in which they navigated religious relationships upon leaving. It is present in the types of disciplinary processes by which the subjectivities of Magdalene women were shaped. The voices and bodies of the women were regulated through constant prayer, a very religious form of discipline. Upon leaving the institutions, this sacred form of the Catholic nation was so pervasive and ingrained into the dominant forms of cultural meaning that many women struggled to find a space for themselves within society. The nature of the trauma suffered at the hands of a religious institution meant that their religious relationships were fundamentally altered, and as a result of this the forms of moral meaning on which they drew inevitably impacted. As Patricia Dervan highlights,

> The moral code of the day was that which was decided by the Catholic Church. The Catholic Church had such dominance and such power over people, I think we as a society when I was growing up, I think everyone was brain washed, because you conformed, or if you didn't conform you were hidden away into what I call the hidden Ireland. And so in perpetuating this story, it allows them off the hook, it allows us to look on these women as somehow different to the rest of us, because they didn't conform. (MAGOHP/06, Patricia Dervan: 29:45)

Even now, as the institutional power of the Catholic Church in Ireland wanes (Foster 2007, Fuller 2002), the residual power of this sacred form is evident, from the unwillingness of the State to insist on a contribution from religious orders to redress schemes to the continued involvement of these same orders in the welfare sector. The religious orders who ran the Magdalene institutions continue to receive State funding to do charitable work with women, in the form of Ruhama, a Dublin-based NGO, which is in part funded by the State and works with 'women affected by prostitution, sex trafficking and other forms of commercial sexual exploitation' (Ruhama 2018). An article published in 2011 cites the Ruhama website as describing themselves as 'a joint initiative of the Good Shepherd Sisters and the Sisters of Our Lady of Charity, both of which had a long history of involvement with marginalised women, including those involved in prostitution' (McGarry 2011). However, this does not appear in the organizations' current description, and the website contains no mention at all of either the Good Shepherd Sisters or the Sisters of Our Lady of Charity, suggesting a desire to distance themselves from their history. In reframing themselves as agents of charitable action, the nuns involved in Ruhama are working within this framework of the Catholic Church's symbolic and material power to maintain their positions of pastoral power. Despite the many scandals endured by the Church in the past fifty years, both in Ireland and globally, the interaction between the Church and the State in the realm of education and welfare continues, demonstrating the power that this sacred form still holds.

'For their own good': A rationale of vicious paternalism

With the power of this sacred form in mind, I now turn to the next overarching theme which has emerged throughout the project. This book does not ask why the Magdalene laundries existed. While I have highlighted the specific social and religious context which enabled them to continue until the end of the twentieth century, the focus of this work has been primarily on the ways that this shaped the lives and identities of the women who were incarcerated within these institutions. However, in order to do this, it is useful to consider some of the ideology which underpins the function of the institutions, which is itself given legitimacy by the power of the Catholic Church, as explored in the previous section. At the heart of the Magdalene laundries lies what I refer to as a rationale of vicious paternalism – the idea that these women should be considered as both deeply vulnerable and highly threatening. They pose a risk to themselves as well as a risk to the social context in which they exist, and therefore they must be contained *for their own good*. This attitude is, of course, not unique to this context – it is a common theme in the way states choose to manage unruly women. It allows for the containment and punishment of women who are conceived of as threatening, in the name of compassion. I argue that at the root of this vicious paternalism are the complex emotions of fear and disgust caused by the figure of the prostitute. Luddy (2007) demonstrates the way in which public debates around prostitution in pre-Independence Ireland were dominated by ideas of moral and epidemiological contagion by the prostitute, resulting in attempts to both reform her and contain the spread of disease. The Magdalene institutions grew out of these ideas, and so despite the fact that it was unlikely any women were sent to Magdalene institutions for the specific reason of engaging in transactional sex in the twentieth century, this rationale of vicious paternalism is something which underpins the experiences of the women throughout their lives. In Chapter 4, it emerges in the ways in which women speak about their entrance to the institutions, often conceptualized both as a way of keeping them safe *and* as a punishment for social transgressions. It appears again in Chapter 6, when looking at the wording of the McAleese report. Over and over again, the committee emphasizes that certain things which caused survivors significant trauma were done *in the best interests* of the women – for example, changing their name, allegedly a practice which was designed to avoid causing them shame in later life. In conceptualizing women in this way, they were inscribed with a particular social identity which meant their testimony could be discredited, because they were not seen as able to make the 'correct' decision about their own lives.

By the twentieth century the Magdalene institutions were no longer being used as a method of controlling the 'scourge of prostitution', but the anxiety at the figure of the prostitute imaginary (Gira-Grant 2014) is still evident in the minds of many people, not least the women themselves. This is typified in some of the answers given during the listening exercise which took place as part of the *Dublin Honours Magdalenes* event of June 2018. One of the questions asked was: 'what do you think people should know about the Magdalene laundries?' The answers varied, and the conversation ebbed and flowed around this. However, on four occasions, different women went to great lengths to make clear that they were not prostitutes:

> People out there think when they hear of High Park or they hear laundries, that we were all prostitutes. We were not all prostitutes and we didn't all have babies.
>
> ...
>
> People just assumed because Mary Magdalene the contact name was there, they thought we were prostitutes in the street. It's so awful.
>
> ...
>
> We need to put out there that we weren't all prostitutes. We need that. We need you to do that for us.
>
> ...
>
> Speaker 2: I'd like to go to my grave with my name on it without people thinking that I was a prostitute.
>
> B: We're not prostitutes. (O'Donnell and McGettrick 2018)

Each time someone said this, the others nodded along and joined her in reiterating it emphatically. The figure of the prostitute looms large and threatening in the cultural imaginary, even when she does not appear to be physically present, and the women's insistent denial of the association is an echo of the disgust and hatred which characterizes attitudes towards prostitution (Mac and Smith 2018). This disgust, which is entangled with the fear of a visibly 'other' body, seeps into the way in which society treats not only women who sell sex, but any woman whose behaviour transgresses socially constructed gender roles, any woman who detaches herself from the context of the heterosexual family. As Pheterson (1996) demonstrates, a woman can be inscribed with 'whore stigma' merely through a transgression of these gendered boundaries – it can be used against 'women who speak out against men who abuse them, visible lesbians, demonstrators for abortion rights . . . it is likewise suited to throw suspicion upon widows, battered wives, single mothers' (Pheterson 1996: 12). It results in a desire to criminalize and ultimately incarcerate those inscribed with this identity, but often under the guise of rescue – 'for their own good'.

This attitude is starkly evident in an interview with two nuns, broadcast on RTÉ Radio 1's 'The God Slot' in March 2013. Reporter Claire McCormack interviewed the nuns for *America* magazine and was allowed to share it with The God Slot on condition that the nuns, their congregation and where they worked were not named. Their words are voiced by actors. Reporting on this for an article in *The Irish Times*, McGarry (2013) writes:

> Asked whether an apology might be in order, 'Sister A' responded: 'Apologise for what. Apologise for providing a service? We provided a free service for the country. Okay, it may have been putting away an ugly part to society, which it was in a sense, but it was the family who chose to put them there,' she said.
>
> 'Some of the orders accused educated the country, nobody is blamed for that. Society at the time had a great need to help these women and we stepped in ...'
>
> 'There was a terrible need for a lot of those women because they were on the street, with no social welfare and starving. We provided shelters for them. It was the 'no welfare' state and we are looking with today's eyes at a totally different era.'
>
> Asked why the four congregations were not speaking out more, 'Sister A' said: 'Because we would be stoned! . . . Society is more inclined to believe the bad stories and people have forgotten the good we have done through all our years.'

As highlighted earlier in this book, we have almost no access to statements from the religious orders about the Magdalene institutions. Therefore, it is impossible to draw wider conclusions from isolated statements such as these as to what either individual nuns or religious orders saw as their motivation or intention. However, this idea of the Magdalene laundries as sites of welfare is not limited to the words of individual nuns and appears in statements made by key informants throughout the interviews. For example, it is present in the words of Dr M, who worked as a doctor in the Galway laundry between 1979, and then after it closed, until 1997. He makes the following statement on the ways in which he feels we should consider the laundries, and the events which took place there:

> One would like to put a balance on the nature of things, it is very important not to criticise 1950 with 2010 life, I think that's an important . . . it's the times we live in, and the times we live in back in the 50s reflected attitudes and cultures which were already very fixed, moulded, and protected and governed by a very austere type of society and church, aided and abetted by state. When I think back to times when girls, especially girls who had become pregnant or girls who had to escape from dysfunctional families, found refuge in these kinds of places, I suppose I'm still glad some refuge was there for them, that they didn't end up

> running away and becoming street urchins or what have you, and yet, I'm cross that I'm given to believe that they were in some instances, not in all instances, treated and mistreated by individuals who perceived them as daughters of the devil, who had to be punished forever for their sins, and treated them unfairly, perhaps cruelly, because of that. I'm cross that we in society didn't detect that through the years, and do something about that (MAGOHP/1/ANON, Dr M: 1:05:57).

His particular turn of phrase – 'given to believe' – suggests that perhaps he is still not convinced, and needs more evidence from reliable sources, a category which does not seem to include the survivors themselves. Women were treated 'unfairly' – he concedes that *perhaps* there was some cruelty. He describes himself as being 'cross' – a word I associate with mild inconvenience and frustration. To hear this word being used to describe his feelings towards institutional abuse of women suggests just how little weight he gives to the trauma experienced by the women. Dr M tells us that, despite his minor misgivings, he is 'glad' that these 'refuges' existed. His words echo the statements from the religious orders analysed in Chapter 6, which lament the necessity of the existence of Magdalene institutions. It was a shame, yes, but what other options did these women have? This book has demonstrated the importance of paying close attention to the epistemic nature of the harm done by this attitude of vicious paternalism. In conceptualizing women as incapable of knowing their own minds, and furthermore as *a risk* to society because of this, they are formed as unreliable narrators of their own experiences. Their testimony is liable to be disregarded and their voices further discredited.

Enduring trauma and active epistemic harms

Throughout this project I have demonstrated the ways in which the trauma of being in a Magdalene institution did not end with exit from the laundry – both physically and psychologically, the impacts of this experience stayed with survivors for the rest of their lives. This is not to say that their lives were always defined by their trauma – to imply that would be to do a disservice to the multifaceted and nuanced experiences described by the women, the ways in which they found new forms of cultural and religious meaning after leaving the institutions. They are more than their trauma – but in this context it is important to stress the continual and enduring nature of the abuse inflicted on them by the religious orders and the Irish State. This is, of course, the case with many survivors of trauma and abuse. However, in this instance I have demonstrated that the epistemic nature of the harms inflicted on the women during their time in the laundry had such a lasting effect on survivors because of both the power of the sacred form of the Irish Catholic nation, working in conjunction with the significant cultural symbolism of 'fallen women' to create a context in which the voices of Magdalene survivors could not and would not be heard.

In highlighting these two themes, I wish to demonstrate the ways in which these symbolic forms of meaning enabled forms of epistemic violence to manifest so consistently in the lives of Magdalene survivors. The harms this caused did not end when they left the institutions but were replicated and maintained by the structures which existed, and continue to exist, in contemporary Ireland. This book therefore presents the experiences of the Magdalene survivors as more than just a linear progression, their lives categorized as in/out of the institution. The Magdalene institutions were not just a 'product of their time', but the specific result of a social, cultural and religious context in which the bodies of 'problem women' could be both physically and morally disciplined, under the guise of protecting wider society. The effects of surviving within and then existing outside of the institutions are enmeshed – *because* of the nature of the context in which they existed, which meant that survivors stayed to an extent in stasis, trapped in a system of cultural meaning which maintained the instances of epistemic injustice produced in the institutions.

My research also demonstrates that this is an active epistemic harm. While the existing literature on the Magdalene institutions does much to situate them in the historical and social context of post-Independence Ireland, it is only through an analysis of survivor narratives that we can understand their position in the current social climate. The trauma of the laundries did not end with the closure of the last institution, and it is vital to develop a strong awareness of what this means in both a sociological and material sense. By evidencing the ongoing and consistent harms of the laundries – as well as the active and ongoing resistance – my work situates the institutions not only within Ireland's architecture of containment as it was, but also demonstrates how we can understand their position in the social fabric of twenty-first century Ireland.

Communities of resistance

Fricker's work on epistemic injustice has been criticized for its focus on the individual, and in doing so erasing the agency and resistance of marginalized communities (McHugh 2017: 274). My research takes these critiques seriously, and builds on Fricker's work by paying close attention to the ways in which Magdalene survivors resisted processes of epistemic injustice in an individual sense: from the forms of resistance inside the institutions to the ways in which survivors renegotiated their religious relationships and drew on conceptions of 'respectability' after leaving. However, I also considered the extent to which official and unofficial processes of redress were able to challenge the instances of epistemic injustice in the survivors' experiences, something which is again alluded to only briefly in Fricker's original text. Chapter 6 showed how for many survivors, the official processes of redress were insufficient, and failed to make any meaningful differences in their lives. However, through events like *Dublin Honours Magdalenes*, in particular the listening exercise, survivors were able to come together to share and discuss their experiences, and many women spoke about how powerful and restorative they found this process.

I suggest that this is an example of what Nancy Arden McHugh (2017) describes as the formation of communities of epistemic resistance. McHugh details the ways in which groups can 'function as communities of epistemic resistance in spite of and frequently without the notice of dominant epistemic frameworks' (2017: 275), because oppressed epistemic groups have knowledge resources to draw upon which are outside of the mainstream hermeneutic lacuna. The value of a community is evident in the *Dublin Honours Magdalenes* event, which was the first time survivors had been brought together to such a great extent. Through this event, they were able to share experiences and develop new ways of speaking about their experiences, challenging the instances of hermeneutic injustice which characterized much of their lives. If we consider broader groups of people as oppressed epistemic communities, such as survivors of sexual abuse in carceral religious institutions, then my work demonstrates the value of creating new contexts and spaces for them to make epistemic resistance to the dominant narratives under which they suffer. It is not enough to expect groups who have suffered enduring instances of epistemic injustice to be able to create these spaces without assistance – although they may well be able to, as McHugh (2017) emphasizes. However, it should not be their responsibility to carve out space for themselves; rather, it is the responsibility of those who occupy a position of greater epistemic privilege to do this.

In accepting the value of creating these dedicated spaces for epistemically marginalized communities to be heard, it is likely that we will come up against an inevitable tension between the role played by inquiries and reports in assessing whether compensation should be paid to survivors, and the importance of making spaces and contexts in which their voices and experiences can be heard in a meaningful capacity. In practice, public inquiries into institutional abuse are often structured in a way that makes it difficult to give significant time to survivors speaking about their experiences, because of the other forms of evidence they must hear to establish cases of state (or some other official body) culpability. However, in many societies, official inquiries are presented as the most meaningful way of making amends for issues of institutional abuse. It is important to consider why this is so, and what implications this perception has for the experiences of those who are struggling to be heard. Further work on how these communities of epistemic resistance are formed, how they operate and the ways in which they have the power to challenge dominant narratives would enable a better understanding of this tension, and how best to mitigate it. In doing so, we should also ask broader questions about how societies, both at the state and social level, can publicly address histories of systematic institutional abuse, and whether official processes of inquiry are the best way of doing this. If, as Fricker suggests, we are able to counter the harms of epistemic injustice with the virtue of epistemic justice, a crucial question is whether states and institutions can possess these virtues, how they can embody them in their interactions with those who have been epistemically marginalized. Elizabeth Anderson (2012) expands on these ideas, considering the extent to which social institutions can demonstrate this virtue. She writes:

> It is not wrong to promote practices of individual testimonial and hermeneutical justice in these contexts. Such individual virtues can help correct epistemic injustices. But in the face of massive structural injustice, individual epistemic virtue plays a comparable role to the practice of individual charity in the context of massive structural poverty. Just as it would be better and more effective to redesign economic institutions so as to prevent mass poverty in the first place, it would be better to reconfigure epistemic institutions so as to prevent epistemic injustice from arising. Structural injustices call for structural remedies. (Anderson 2012: 171)

Anderson suggests that such a structural remedy for epistemic injustice would necessarily involve a virtue of large-scale systems of inquiry, requiring us to be accountable not only for how we act independently but also for our collective actions (2012: 171). She suggests that while a proper investigation of the way in which social institutions can cultivate this virtue would require considerably more development, it can begin from a place of 'epistemic democracy: universal participation on terms of equality of all inquirers' (2012: 172).

If we accept group segregation as the structural ground for epistemic injustice, then group integration is a structural remedy, and can be considered a virtue of epistemic institutions. She gives the example of segregated schooling along the lines of race and class in the United States, 'by which educational opportunities are unequally distributed, with profound effects on the ability of marginalized groups – African-Americans, immigrants, the poor – to acquire the markers of credibility' (Anderson 2012: 171). She continues:

> When social groups are educated together on terms of equality, they share equally in educational resources and thus have access to the same (legitimate) markers of credibility. . . . Shared inquiry also tends to produce a shared reality, which can help overcome hermeneutical injustice and its attendant testimonial injustices. (Anderson 2012: 171)

In this way, she begins to consider the ways in which social institutions can develop a virtue of epistemic justice, through an equal allocation of social resources and knowledge. However, I would suggest that in some instances, equality for all enquirers is not enough to combat structural issues of epistemic injustice. Equality, treating everyone in the same manner, does not take account of the various ways in which marginalized communities are not starting from the same baseline level of social credibility. Instead, we should aim to cultivate a situation of epistemic equity for all speakers, providing them with the contexts and resources in which they can be viewed as epistemically valuable, as credible producers of knowledge. In some instances, this might mean providing certain groups with more access to social resources, which a theory of equality does not allow for. However, it is in doing this that we create a situation in which we can begin to correct for ingrained structural prejudice, and ensure all voices are afforded credibility.

Glasnevin cemetery and the Magdalene gravestones

I stayed an extra day in Dublin after the *Dublin Honours Magdalenes* event, re-booking a new flight in order to visit the Glasnevin cemetery with members of *Justice for Magdalenes Research*. While I felt emotionally and physically drained by the previous two days' experiences, I also felt deeply privileged to be able to visit the cemetery with the people who had invested countless hours of their lives in making sure that these women were not forgotten. The cemetery is vast, and the graves of the Magdalene women are scattered across the site. They are not clearly identified. If you did not know what you were looking for, you would struggle to find them. JFMR provide a map and key for those who wish to explore the graveyard – not only do they attempt to guide people to the location of the graves, but they also give information about the names listed on the headstones, and whether those names correlate to the women who are buried there. In many instances, they do not. It was an incredibly powerful experience listening to Claire McGettrick speak about the inconsistencies in names on the gravestones, about the ways in which even the manner of their burial demonstrates the lack of care afforded to these women by the State and the religious orders. No one in the world has as much knowledge about the Glasnevin graves as she holds in her head, and the stream of information about these women, about how their names came to be on the headstones, was a powerful narrative of commemoration. Even in death, the disregard for these women's lives and the continual erasure of their experiences was evident. Take, for instance, the gravestone which listed the date of death of one woman as 31 April. I had to have this repeated to me a few times before it sank in, showing the complete lack of care for any kind of accuracy or dignity in recording these women's deaths. Again and again, their lives are dismissed as unimportant, undeserving of the respect afforded to others.

Another monument nearer the entrance, erected by the nuns, asks us to 'Pray for the Souls of the Magdalen Female Penitents Asylum, 73 Lower Mecklenburgh St'. The stone under the word 'penitents' is curved, dipping inwards. Apparently, someone has repeatedly crowbarred the word off – each time the nuns must have the letters re-carved into the stone, gradually wearing it down. Hearing of these wilful instances of direct action against the outdated and offensive language was uplifting. I hope whoever is responsible for it continues to remove the word – if they do, will the granite become paper thin, disintegrating as we run our fingers over it? How many times can the word be reinscribed before it vanishes?

Writing in 2016, the centenary of the Easter Rising and the Proclamation of the Republic of Ireland, O'Rourke and Smith reflect on a situation whereby 'the State, having apologised to the women in 2013, is once again distorting and refusing to acknowledge the reality of the Magdalene Laundries abuse because of the obligations which doing so would entail' (2016: 125). They point to the numerous women who still lie in unmarked or wrongly marked graves, and the continued refusal by the religious congregations to open their archives, apologize or contribute to reparation schemes. There have been 'no measures of accountability . . . no official attempt to root out and overturn the beliefs, behaviours, policies and structures which allowed the Magdalene laundries to happen and continue with impunity' (O'Rourke and Smith 2016: 125). Five years on, it is hard to say whether much has changed. While the *Dublin Honours Magdalenes* event represented a shift in the ways in which survivors' stories are engaged with, the Irish State continues to elide responsibility for the institutions. Just two months after women shared their stories as part of the DHM event, on 14 August 2018, the Irish government rejected a plea from the United Nations for a renewed investigation into allegations of abuse at the nation's Magdalene laundries. An article in *The Irish Times* reported that Felice Gaer, the committee's vice-chairwoman, described the actions of the State as 'walking back' (Coyne 2018) from the apology made by Enda Kenny in 2013, returning to a position whereby the State avoided accepting responsibility for the harms caused to the Magdalene survivors. Gaer stated that she was concerned that Ireland had repeatedly claimed to have no basis for believing that serious harm was perpetrated against women and girls who had been in the laundries. 'How can the government claim it established no systematic ill-treatment when it made no public call for evidence and had no subpoena powers?' (Coyne 2018) This is a stark reminder that the processes by which Magdalene survivors have been able to make their voices heard in a meaningful way are not part of an inevitable march of progress towards a situation of greater epistemic justice. Rather, they are part of a contested field shaped by the social and political context in which they take place, by the current configurations of power, moral meaning and shifting institutional structures.

This disinclination to fully address the issue of institutional abuse is not limited to the Magdalene laundries. For example, in February 2019, the Minister for Justice Joe McHugh introduced the Retention of Records bill, which seeks to seal, for at least seventy-five years, all documents contained in the archives of the Commission to Enquire into Child Abuse (also known as the Ryan Commission), the Residential Institutions Redress Board (also known as the Redress Board), and the Residential Institutions Redress Committee. Echoing the decision to keep the archives of the religious orders who ran the Magdalene institutions closed, this bill limits access for survivors, family members and researchers, making transparent and accessible knowledge on institutional abuse far more difficult. More recently, the publication of the Mother and Baby Homes Commission of Investigation in January 2021 demonstrates that these issues of credibility, silencing and the weight afforded to survivor testimony are as relevant as ever. The findings are an echo of issues discussed throughout this book. According to the commission, responsibility for the 'harsh' treatment women suffered in mother and baby homes rested 'with the fathers of their children and their own immediate families' although it was 'supported by, contributed to, and condoned by, the institutions of the State and the Churches' (Department of Children, Equality, Disability, Integration and Youth 2021: 1). The report states:

> However, it must be acknowledged that the institutions under investigation provided a refuge — a harsh refuge in some cases — when the families provided no refuge at all. (2021: 1)

The report also concluded that there was 'very little evidence' of 'forced adoption' (2021:9) in Ireland in the period between 1922 and 1998, another point on which there has been significant contention from adoption rights activists. Máiréad Enright highlights this as a particular example of the State's enduring failure to communicate with survivors and recognize their experience, arguing that 'this conclusion is based on an analysis that divorces law from its social and political context, assuming that if conduct was "lawful" then it cannot have been abusive' (Enright 2021a).

The report was met with widespread outcry from journalists, activists, campaigners and survivors, who pushed back against the narrative that the State and Church bore little to no responsibility for their treatment in these homes. As Claire McGettrick (2021) highlights, a comprehensive analysis of this report will take a considerable amount of time, but the initial evidence, and the most recent revelations around the disregarding of survivor testimony (Enright 2021b), suggest that the State has once again failed to take seriously the experiences of survivors of these institutions. However, she highlights that

> In 2013, once the Magdalene apology came, nobody (apart from @ococonuts @Tupp_Ed & a few others) was interested in what an insult the McAleese Report was to the women's lived experiences. This time feels different – this time we have a movement (as @Ka_ODonnell keeps saying!). (McGettrick 2021)

There is evidence, then, that the attitude towards survivors in the Irish public consciousness is significantly shifting, and regressive and stigmatizing narratives are increasingly being challenged, by the public if not by the State.

Emilie Pine writes:

> We talk so often in Ireland about a 'culture of silence' around abuse. This suggests that those who have been abused are not speaking out, not giving testimony. It is time to recognise that we don't have a culture of silence, we have a culture of not listening. (2019)

I would qualify this with an understanding that this has not always been the case – for many years Magdalene survivors *have* been silent and silenced, existing within a system of religious and cultural meaning which did not make space for their pain and their voices. However, as this silence is increasingly challenged, and survivors speak out about their experiences, it is equally important that their speech is heard in a meaningful way, and that they are recognized as credible epistemic subjects and respected as knowledge producers.

Appendix A
List of Magdalene institutions

Sisters of Our Lady of Charity of Refuge:

St Mary's Refuge, High Park, Grace Park Road, Drumcondra, Dublin; founded 1833, closed 1991

Monastery of Our Lady of Charity Sean McDermott Street (formerly Gloucester Street), Dublin 1; founded 1822, closed 1996

Congregation of the Sisters of Mercy:

Magdalen Asylum/ Magdalen Home, No. 47 Forster Street, Galway; founded 1824, closed 1984

St Patrick's Refuge, Crofton Road, Dun Laoghaire, Co. Dublin; founded 1786, closed 1963

Religious Sisters of Charity:

St Mary Magdalen's, Floraville Road, Donnybrook, Dublin; founded 1798, sold to a private company in 1992. This company continued to operate the laundry as a commercial entity until 2006

St Vincent's, St Mary's Road, Peacock Lane, Cork; founded 1809

Sisters of the Good Shepherd:

St Mary's, Cork Road, Waterford; founded 1842, closed 1994

St Mary's, New Ross, Wexford; founded 1860, closed 1967

St Mary's, Pennywell Road, Limerick; founded 1826, closed 1984

St Mary's, Sunday's Well, Cork; founded 1872, closed 1977

Appendix B

List of interviews

Interview Code	Name	Interview Date	Interview Type	Age on Entry	Religious Order	Institution	Date entered	Date left
MAGOHP/1/ANON	Dr M	29/11/2012	Key informant					
MAGOHP/02	Mari Steed	07/12/2012	Relative/ Activist					
MAGOHP/04/ANON	Mary	05/01/2013	Survivor	17	Sisters of Our Lady of Charity, Good Shepherds	Gloucester Street, Dublin; Limerick	1962	1964/5
MAGOHP/06	Patricia Dervan	25/01/2013	Relative/ Activist					
MAGOHP/07/ANON	Lucy	23/03/2013	Survivor	14/15	Sisters of Our Lady of Charity	Sean McDermott Street	1977/78	1979
MAGOHP/10/ANON	Evelyn	02/03/2013	Survivor	14	Sisters of Our Lady of Charity	High Park	1967	1968
MAGOHP/11	Julia Brown	01/03/2013	Survivor	12	Good Shepherds	Limerick	1952	1954
MAGOHP/12/ANON	Bernadette	11/02/2013	Survivor	22		[anonymous]	1966	1967
MAGOHP/13/ANON	Bernadette and Francis Murphy	23/02/2013	Survivor/ Relative	14	Good Shepherds	New Ross	1958	1964
MAGOHP/14	Rose Brien Harrington	01/03/2013	Relative					
MAGOHP/15	Mary Currington	23/02/2013	Survivor	18	Good Shepherds	New Ross	1963	1969
MAGOHP/16/ANON	Jane	04/03/2013	Key informant					
MAGOHP/17	Bridget Flynn	11/04/2013	Key informant					
MAGOHP/18/ANON	Margaret Burke	26/02/2013	Survivor	14?	Sisters of Mercy	Galway		
MAGOHP/19/ANON	Pearl	15/02/2013	Survivor	12		Baggott Street?		
MAGOHP/22	Celine Roberts	27/03/2013	Survivor					
MAGOHP/23/ANON	Theresa	27/03/2013	Survivor					
MAGOHP/38	Maureen Sullivan	31/07/2013	Survivor	12	Good Shepherds	New Ross	1964	1969?
MAGOHP/24	Maeve O'Rourke	04/05/2013	Activist					
MAGOHP/26	Ellen Ward	09/04/2013	Survivor	15?	Good Shepherds, Religious Sisters of Charity	Peacock Lane, Donnybrook		
MAGOHP/27	Phyllis Morgan	29/04/2013	Activist	20?	Religious Sisters of Charity	Donnybrook		
MAGOHP/30	Nancy Shannon	13/06/2013	Survivor	16/17	Good Shepherds	Sundays Well	1969	Unsure
MAGOHP/31	Mary Smith	05/03/2013	Survivor	17?	Sisters Of Our Lady of Charity	High Park	1964	1967/8
MAGOHP/34/ANON	Kathleen	03/07/2013	Survivor					

(Continued)

Interview Code	Name	Interview Date	Interview Type	Age on Entry	Religious Order	Institution	Date entered	Date left
MAGOHP/36/ANON	Sarah	19/07/2013	Survivor	16?	Sisters of Our Lady of Charity	Sean McDermott Street		
MAGOHP/37/ANON	Doris	13/07/2013	Survivor	16?	Sisters of Our Lady of Charity	High Park	1950	1951
MAGOHP/40	Mary Creighton	16/05/2013	Survivor	17	Sisters of Our Lady of Charity	High Park		
MAGOHP/43	Mary Merritt	16/03/2012	Survivor	17	Sisters of Our Lady of Charity	High Park	1947	1960
MAGOHP/44	Martina Keogh	15/03/2013	Survivor	16	Sisters of Our Lady of Charity	Sean McDermott Street		
MAGOHP/45/ANON	Bridget O'Donnell	28/06/2013	Survivor	11 1/2	Religious Sisters of Charity	Donnybrook	1959	Unsure
MAGOHP/46/ANON	Pippa Flanagan	07/08/2013	Survivor	16	Good Shepherds	Limerick	1966	1968/9
MAGOHP/48/ANON	Martha	28/02/2013	Survivor	11	Good Shepherds	Waterford	1967	1970/1
MAGOHP/49/ANON	Angelina Mayfield	15/02/2013	Survivor	13/14	Sisters of Our Lady of Charity, Good Shepherd Sisters	High Park (An Grianan); Good Shepherds, Limerick	1973	1976
MAGOHP/50/ANON	Kate O'Sullivan	17/07/2013	Survivor	12	Good Shepherds	Sundays Well	1957	1963
MAGOHP/61	Trevor Heaney	July 2010	Key informant					
MAGOHP/64	Mary O'Mara	June 2010	Key informant					
MAGOHP/72	Patricia Burke Brogan	10/02/2012	Key informant					
MAGOHP/73/ANON	Kathleen R	01/04/2012	Survivor	16	Good Shepherds	Sundays Well	1959	1963
MAGOHP/74	Samantha Long	07/05/2012	Relative					
MAGOHP/77/ANON	Johanna Barrett	06/08/2012	Relative					
MAGOHP/80/ANON	Sadie O'Meara	20/03/2012	Survivor	15	Religious Sisters of Charity	Donnybrook; Cork		

Notes

Chapter 1

1. Throughout this book, I use the spelling 'Magdalene', following the precedent set by *Justice for Magdalenes*. However, when speaking about or referencing work which chooses to use 'Magdalen', I keep the original spelling.
2. See Appendix A for a full list of the institutions, including the dates they were founded and the dates they stopped operating.
3. Much of what is known about the High Park exhumations, and particularly the discovery of the additional twenty-two bodies, is due to the work of the journalist Mary Raftery, who in August 2003 published the results of a significant investigation into exhumations. Her work was invaluable in bringing the issue to the attention of the wider media and general public. After her death, *Justice for Magdalenes Research* were given access to the Mary Raftery Archive by her collaborator Sheila Ahern, and an in-depth discussion of these findings can be found on the *Justice for Magdalenes Research* website: http://jfmresearch.com/home/preserving-magdalene-history/high-park/
4. More work is currently being done on recording the names of women who died in Magdalene institutions through the Magdalene Names Project. This is a *Justice for Magdalenes Research* initiative which examines various archives and records, including gravestones, digitized census records, electoral registers, exhumation orders and newspaper archives. By recording and analysing the data from these archives the project seeks to offer a narrative that honours the lives of those who lived and died behind Magdalene Laundry walls. More information can be found at: http://jfmresearch.com/home/magdalene-names-project/
5. A similar story has recently emerged surrounding the Bon Secours Mother and Baby Home in Tuam, following work done by historian Catherine Corless in 2012.
6. For a more thorough overview of this campaign and the outcomes, see McGettrick et al. (2021) and O'Rourke (2015).
7. In Chapter 3, I engage further with how I understand the issues surrounding the production of knowledge through oral histories, thinking through the complexities involved in conceptions of credibility and reliability in memory work.

Chapter 2

1. This was a movement led by a coalition of pro-choice groups with support from a number of legal academics and members of the medical profession, including the Institute of Obstetricians and Gynaecologists. Building on organizing done by the Anti-Amendment Campaign in 1983, this group called for a repeal of the Eighth Amendment to the Constitution, which restricted abortion to circumstances where the life of a pregnant woman was at risk. The campaign ran from 2012 to 25 May 2018, when the Irish people voted by 66.4 per cent to remove the Eighth Amendment. This represented a huge achievement for reproductive rights, but the campaign was met with significant opposition from groups such as the Pro Life Campaign, Abortion Never and the Irish Catholic Bishops, who said that removing the Eighth Amendment would be 'a shocking step' and 'a manifest injustice' to the unborn (McGarry 2018).

Chapter 3

1. JFM began the process of gathering testimony for this in March 2012. These testimonies were gathered using strict ethical protocols which had been devised by Dr Katherine O'Donnell for the Magdalene Oral History Project. This testimony-gathering process became a collaborative effort, and served as the pilot phase of the oral history project, so that survivors who wished to participate in both processes would not have to give their testimony twice. In total, JFM submitted 796 pages of survivor testimony as part of their principal submission to the IDC.

Chapter 4

1. In this context, the phrase 'walking the streets with a shawl around your shoulders' is an inference to selling sex.

Chapter 5

1. 'Culchie' is a pejorative word used in Irish English to mean someone from the Irish countryside (or a small town or village), to imply someone is unsophisticated or uncultured. Since the late twentieth century, the term has also been reclaimed by some who are proud of their origins.

Chapter 6

1 This history is available at: http://jfmresearch.com/home/jfm-political-campaign-2009-2013/
2 For example, in October 2010, Minister for Justice, Mr Dermot Ahern, T.D., told the Dáil that, '[t]he Magdalen Laundries were private, religious run institutions without any legislative or State mandate for their general operation. As I have previously informed the House, the vast majority of females who entered or were placed in Magdalen Laundries did so without any direct involvement of the State' (quoted in Smith 2011: 12).
3 I took the decision not to conduct any analysis of this report in this book, primarily because of the lack of data from survivors which mentioned it, as it was published after the majority of the interviews were conducted. However, in doing this, I do not wish to imply that it was not a significant document, and there is undoubtedly further work to be done which connects the findings of this report and the position of survivor voices in contemporary Irish culture.
4 At an online seminar hosted by Oxford University on Wednesday, 2 June, Professor Mary Daly, a member of the commission, confirmed that they had entirely disregarded all oral evidence given by survivors to the confidential committee in compiling its main report and in coming to its findings.

Bibliography

Abrams, L. (2010), *Oral History Theory*, Oxford: Routledge.
Ahmed, S. (2004), *The Cultural Politics of Emotion*, Edinburgh: Edinburgh University Press.
Ahmed, S. (2010), 'Foreword', in R. Gill and R. Ryan Flood (eds), *Secrecy and Silence in the Research Process: Feminist Reflections*, xvi–xxi, Oxford: Routledge.
Ahmed, S. (2014), 'Selfcare as Warfare' [online], *Feminist Killjoys*. Available online: https://feministkilljoys.com/2014/08/25/selfcare-as-warfare/ (accessed 7 November 2017).
Alcoff, L. and Gray, L. (1993), 'Survivor Discourse: Transgression or Recuperation?', *Signs*, 18 (2): 260–90.
Alcoff, L. and Gray-Rosendale, L. (2018), 'Speaking "as"', in L. Alcoff (ed.), *Rape and Resistance*, 176–202, Cambridge: Polity Press.
Anderson, E. (2012), 'Epistemic Justice as a Virtue of Social Institutions', *Social Epistemology*, 26 (2): 163–73.
Anderson, P. (2016), 'Silencing and Speaker Vulnerability: Undoing an Oppressive Form of Wilful Ignorance' [online], *Women in Parenthesis*. Available online: https://www.womeninparenthesis.co.uk/silencing-and-speaker-vulnerability-undoing-an-oppressive-form-of-wilful-ignorance/ (accessed 4 May 2018).
Anthias, F. and Yuval-Davis, N. (1989), 'Introduction', in N. Yuval-Davis and F. Anthias (eds), *Women – Nation – State*, 1–15, Basingstoke: Macmillan Press.
Armour, E. T. (2012), 'Beyond the God/Man Duo: Globalization, Feminist Theology, and Religious Subjectivity' in S. Briggs and M. McClintock Fulkerson (eds), *The Oxford Handbook of Feminist Theology*, 378–81, Oxford: Oxford University Press.
Austin, J. L. (1962), *How to Do Things with Words*, Oxford: Clarendon Press.
Aylward, S. (2011), 'Sean Answers Questions from UNCAT Committee Members on Human Rights Violations in the Magdalene Laundries' [Online]. Available online: https://www.youtube.com/watch?v=tSrDbeO5wYs (accessed 10 July 2017).
Barclay, Sarah and Miller, A., dirs. (1993), *Washing Away the Stain* [Film], Scotland: BBC Scotland.
Beaumont, C. (1999), 'Gender, Citizenship and the State in Ireland: 1922–1990', in D. Alderson, F. Becket, S. Brewster and V. Crossman (eds), *Ireland in Proximity: History, Gender, Space*, 94–121, London: Routledge.
Berenstain, N. (2016), 'Epistemic Exploitation', *Ergo: An Open Access Journal of Philosophy*, 3 (22): 569–90.
Bondi, L. (2005), 'Making Connections and Thinking Through Emotions: Between Geography and Psychotherapy', *Transactions of the Institute of British Geographers*, 30 (4): 433–48.

Bourdieu, P. (1977), *Outline of a Theory of Practice*, Cambridge: Cambridge University Press.

Bourdieu, P. (1986), 'The Forms of Capital', in J. G. Richardson (ed.), *Handbook of Theory and Research for the Sociology of Education*, 241–58, New York: Greenwood Press.

Brennan, C. (2018), 'Marie Collins: Pope was "not familiar" with Magdalen Laundries or Industrial Schools', *The Journal*, 27 August. Available online: https://www.the journal.ie/pope-mother-and-baby-homes-magdalens-4203407-Aug2018/ (accessed 19 May 2019).

Brown, T. (2004), *Ireland: A Social and Cultural History 1922–2002*, London: Harper Perennial.

Burke Brogan, P. (1988), *Eclipsed*, Galway: Salmon Drama.

Cameron, J., Nairn, K. and Higgins, J. (2009), 'Demystifying Academic Writing: Reflections on Emotions, Know-how, and Academic Identity', *Journal of Geography in Higher Education*, 33 (2): 269–84.

Campbell, R. (2002), *Emotionally Involved: The Impact of Researching Rape*, New York: Routledge.

Casey, N. (2018), *Please RT: A special band of heroes arriving Tuesday - would be lovely to give them a big welcome and make...* [Twitter], 2 June. Available online https:// twitter.com/norahcasey/status/1002847847451168768? (accessed 18 January 2019).

Castelli, E. (2001), 'Women, Gender, Religion: Troubling Categories and Transforming Knowledge', in E. Castelli and R. Rodman (eds), *Women, Gender, Religion: A Reader*, 3–25, New York: Palgrave.

Catholic News Service (2018), 'Irish President Apologises to Women Sent to Magdalene Laundries', *The Tablet*, 06 June. Available online: https://www.thetablet.co.uk/news /9201/irish-president-apologises-to-women-sent-to-magdalene-laundries (accessed 2 February 2019).

Clough, M. (2017), *Shame, the Church and the Regulation of Female Sexuality*, Oxford: Routledge.

Connerton, P. (2008), 'Seven Types of Forgetting', *Memory Studies*, 1 (1): 59–71.

Cooper, A. J. ([1892] 1988), *A Voice from the South by a Black Woman of the South*, New York: Oxford University Press.

Coyne, E. (2018), 'Plea for Magdalene Inquiry Is Rejected', *The Times*, 14 August. Available online: https://www.thetimes.co.uk/article/plea-for-magdalene-inquiry-is-rejected-3q9xnvt6v (accessed 22 April 2019).

Crowley, U. and Kitchin, R. (2008), 'Producing Decent Girls: Governmentality and the Moral Geographies of Sexual Conduct in Ireland, 1922–1937', *Gender, Place and Culture*, 15 (4): 355–72

Das, V. (2007), *Life and Words: Violence and the Descent into the Ordinary*, Berkeley: University of California Press.

Department of Children, Equality, Disability, Integration & Youth (2021), 'Mother and Baby Homes Commission of Investigation Final Report' [online]. Available online:

https://assets.gov.ie/118565/107bab7e-45aa-4124-95fd-1460893dbb43.pdf (accessed 10 March 2021).

Department of Justice and Equality (2011), 'Statement on the Magdalene Laundries' [online]. Available online: http://www.justice.ie/en/JELR/Pages/PR11000082 (accessed 10 April 2018).

Dickson-Swift, V., James, E., Kippne, S. and Liamputtong, P. (2008), 'Risk to Researchers in Qualitative Research on Sensitive Topics: Issues and Strategies', *Qualitative Health Research*, 18 (1): 133–44.

Dotson, K. (2011), 'Tracking Epistemic Violence, Tracking Practices of Silencing', *Hypatia: A Journal of Feminist Philosophy*, 26 (2): 236–57.

Dotson, K. (2012), 'A Cautionary Tale: On Limiting Epistemic Oppression', *Frontiers: A Journal of Women Studies*, 33 (1): 24–47.

Dotson, K. (2014), 'Conceptualizing Epistemic Oppression', *Social Epistemology*, 28 (2): 115–38.

Drozdzewski, D. and Dominey-Howes, D. (2015), 'Research and Trauma: Understanding the Impact of Traumatic Content and Places on the Researcher', *Emotion, Space and Society*, 17: 17–21.

Earner-Bryne, L. (2007), *Mother and Child: Maternity and Child Welfare in Dublin, 1922-60*, Manchester: Manchester University Press.

Enright, A. (2015), 'Antigone in Galway', *London Review of Books*, 37 (24): 11–14.

Enright, M. (2021a), 'Mother and Baby Home Aoptions May Have Been Legal But That Does Not Make Them Right', *The Irish Times*, 16 January. Available online: https://www.irishtimes.com/opinion/mother-and-baby-home-adoptions-may-have-been-legal-but-that-does-not-make-them-right-1.4459471 (accessed 16 June 2021).

Enright, M. (2021b), 'Mairead Enright: Flawed Mother and Baby Report Cannot Be Allowed to Stand', *Irish Examiner*, 04 June. Available online: https://www.irishexaminer.com/opinion/commentanalysis/arid-40305245.html (accessed 16 June 2021).

Fischer, C. (2016), Gender, Nation, and the Politics of Shame: Magdalen Laundries and the Institutionalization of Feminine Transgression in Modern Ireland', *Signs: Journal of Women in Culture and Society*, 41 (4): 821–43.

Fischer, C. (2017), 'Revealing Ireland's "Proper" Heart: Apology, Shame, Nation', *Hypatia*, 32 (4): 751–67.

Finnigan, F. (2001), *Do Penance or Perish: Magdalen Asylums in Ireland*, Oxford: Oxford University Press.

Fricker, M. (2007), *Epistemic Injustice*, Oxford: Oxford University Press.

Foster, R. J. (1989), *Modern Ireland, 1600-1972*, London: Penguin Books.

Foster, R. J. (2007), *Luck and the Irish: A Brief History of Change, 1970-2000*, London: Allen Lane.

Foucault, M. (1977), *Discipline and Punish: The Birth of Prison*, trans. A. Sheridan, London: Allen Lane.

Foucault, M. (1980), *The History of Sexuality: Volume I: An Introduction*, trans. R. Hurley, New York: Vintage.

Fuller, L. (2002), *Irish Catholicism Since 1950: The Undoing of a Culture*, Dublin: Gill and Macmillan.

Gardiner, F. (1993), 'Political Interest and Participation of Irish Women 1922–1992: The Unfinished Revolution', in A. Smyth (ed.), *Irish Women's Studies Reader*, 45–78, Dublin: Mount Press.

Gira-Grant, M. (2014), *Playing the Whore*, London: Verso.

Gill, R. (2010), 'Breaking the Silence: The Hidden Injuries of the Neoliberal University', in R. Gill and R. Ryan Flood (eds), *Secrecy and Silence in the Research Process: Feminist Reflections*, 228–44, Oxford: Routledge.

Gilmore, L. (2017), *Tainted Witness: Why We Doubt What Women Say About Their Lives*, New York: Columbia University Press.

Glynn, E. (2011), 'Breaking the Rule of Silence', *Limerick College of Art*, Available online: http://www.magdalenelaundrylimerick.com/ (accessed 16 March 2017).

Goffman, E. (1990), *Stigma: Notes on the Management of Spoiled Identity*, London: Penguin Books.

Goffman, E. (2009), *Relations in Public: Microstudies of the Public Order*, New Brunswick: Transaction Publishers.

Griffin, G. (2012), 'The Compromised Researcher: Issues in Feminist Research Methodologies', *Sociologisk Forskning*, 49 (4): 333–47.

Guenther, L. (2012), 'Resisting Agamben: The Biopolitics of Shame and Humiliation', *Philosophy and Social Criticism*, 38 (1): 59–79.

Hall, S. (2003 March), 'Spiritual Abuse', *Youth Work*, 32–5.

Hayes, A. and Urquhart, D., eds (2001), *The Irish Women's History Reader*, London: Routledge.

Herman, J. (1992), *Trauma and Recovery: The Aftermath of Violence – From Domestic Abuse to Political Terror*, New York: Basic Books.

Hilliard, B. (2004), 'Motherhood, Sexuality and the Catholic Church', in P. Kennedy (ed.), *Motherhood in Ireland*, 139–59, Cork: Mercier Press.

Hornsby, J. (1995), 'Disempowered Speech', *Philosophical Topics*, 23 (2): 127–47.

Hollway, W., and Jefferson, T. (2013), *Doing Qualitative Research Differently: A Psychosocial Approach*, London: Sage Publications.

Howell, P. (2003), 'Venereal Disease and the Politics of Prostitution in the Irish Free State', *Irish Historical Studies*, 33 (131): 320–41

Humphries, S., dir. (1998), *Sex in a Cold Climate* [Film]. Ireland: Testimony Films, Channel 4.

Irish Human Rights Commission (2010), 'Assessment of the Human Rights Issues Arising in Relation to the "Magdalen Laundries" November 2010', [online]. Available online: http://jfmresearch.com/wp-content/uploads/2017/03/ihrc_assessment_of_t he_human_rights_issues_arising_in_relation_to_the_magdalen_laundries_nov_20 10.pdf (accessed 2 May 2019).

Inglis, T. (1998), *Moral Monopoly: The Rise and Fall of the Catholic Church in Ireland*, Dublin: University College Dublin Press.

Inglis, T. (2005), 'Religion, Identity, State and Society', in J. Cleary and C. Connelly (eds), *The Cambridge Companion to Modern Irish Culture*, 59–77, Cambridge: Cambridge University Press.

Inglis, T. and McKeogh, C. (2012), 'The Double Bind: Women, Honour and Sexuality in Contemporary Ireland', *Media, Culture and Society*, 31 (1): 68–82.

Justice for Magdalenes (2008–2013), [online]. Available online: http://www.magdalenelaundries.com/index.htm (accessed 4 October 2015).

Justice for Magdalenes (2011), 'Submission to the United Nations Committee Against Torture, 46th Session, May 2011' [online]. Available online: http://jfmresearch.com/wp-content/uploads/2017/03/jfm_comm_on_torture_210411.pdf (accessed 4 April 2019).

Justice for Magdalenes Research (from 2014) [online]. Available online: http://jfmresearch.com/ (accessed 5 June 2017).

Justice for Magdalenes Research (2015), 'NGO Submission to the UN Committee on the Elimination of Discrimination Against Women in respect of Ireland' [online]. Available online: https://tbinternet.ohchr.org/Treaties/CEDAW/Shared%20Documents/IRL/INT_CEDAW_NGO_IRL_21860_E.pdf (accessed 2 March 2019).

Justice for Magdalenes Research (2017) 'Implementation of the Magdalene "Restorative Justice" Scheme: Where Are We Now?' [online]. Available online: http://jfmresearch.com/wp-content/uploads/2017/03/JFMR-briefing-note-on-Magdalene-scheme-12.3.17.pdf (accessed 3 May 2019).

Justice for Magdalenes Research (2018), 'GOVERNMENT CALLED ON TO HELP HONOUR HUNDREDS OF MAGDALENE SURVIVORS: Special Two-Day Event for Magdalene Survivors Announced for Dublin in June & Businesswoman Norah Casey as Ambassador' [online]. Available online: http://jfmresearch.com/wp-content/uploads/2018/03/Dublin-Honours-Magdalenes-Embargoed-Press-Release-6.3.18.pdf (accessed 15 March 2019).

Johnson, B. and Clarke, J. (2003), 'Collecting Sensitive Data: The Impact on Researchers', *Qualitative Health Research*, 13 (3): 421–34.

Kandiyoti, D. (1997), 'Identity and Its Discontents: Women and the Nation', *American Journal of Political Science*, 20 (3): 429–43.

Kenny, E. (2013), 'In full: Enda Kenny's State Apology to the Magdalene Women', *The Journal*, 19 February. Available online: https://www.thejournal.ie/full-text-enda-kenny-magdalene-apology-801132-Feb2013/ (accessed 17 April 2017).

King, U. (1989), *Women and Spirituality: Voices of Protest, Voices of Promise*, Basingstoke: Macmillan.

Kinmond, K. and Oakley, L. (2013), *Breaking the Silence on Spiritual Abuse*, London: Palgrave Macmillan

Kotzee, B. (2017), 'Education and Epistemic Injustice', in I. J. Kidd, J. Medina and G. Pohlhaus Jr. (eds), *The Routledge Handbook of Epistemic Injustice*, 324–35, Abingdon: Routledge.

Lewis, M. G. (1993), *Without a Word: Teaching Beyond Women's Silence*, New York: Routledge.

Leydesdorff, S., Dawson, G., Burchardt, N. and Ashplant, T. G. (2004), 'Introduction: Trauma and Life Stories', in K. Lacy Rodgers, S. Leydesdorff and G. Dawson (eds), *Trauma: Life Stories of Survivors*, 1–26, London: Transaction Publishers.

Limerick Institute of Technology (date unknown), 'About Clare St' [online]. Available online: http://www.lit.ie/Campus/clarest/default.aspx (accessed 28 May 2019)

Lind, J. (2008), *Sorry States: Apologies in International Politics*, New York: Cornell University Press.

Llewellyn, D. (2015), *Reading, Feminism, and Spirituality: Troubling the Waves*, London: Palgrave Macmillan.

Llewellyn, D. and Trzebiatowska, M. (2013), 'Secular and Religious Feminisms: A Future of Disconnection?' *Feminist Theology*, 21 (3): 244–58.

Lorimer, H. (2003), 'Telling Small Stories: Spaces of Knowledge and the Practice of Geography', *Transactions of the Institute of British Geographies*, 28 (2): 197–217.

Luddy, M. (1995), *Women and Philanthropy in Nineteenth-Century Ireland*, Cambridge: Cambridge University Press

Luddy, M. (1999), '"Angels of Mercy": Nuns as Workhouse Nurses, 1861–1898', in G. Jones and E. Malcolm (eds), *Medicine, Diseases and the State in Ireland, 1650–1940*, 102–17, , Cork: Cork University Press.

Luddy, M. (2005), 'Convent Archives as Sources for Irish History', in R. Raughter (ed.), *Religious Women and Their History*, 98–115, Dublin: Irish Academic Press.

Luddy, M. (2007), *Prostitution and Irish Society: 1800 to 1940*, Manchester: Manchester University Press.

Luddy, M. (2011), 'Unmarried Mothers in Ireland, 1880–1973', *Women's History Review*, 20 (1): 109–26.

Lummis, T. (1988), *Listening to History: The Authenticity of Oral Evidence*, New Jersey: Barnes and Noble Books.

Lynch, G. (2012), *The Sacred in the Modern World: A Cultural Sociological Approach*, Oxford: Oxford University Press.

Lynch, G. (2015), *Remembering Child Migration: Faith, Nation-Building and the Wounds of Charity*, London: Bloomsbury.

Mac, J. and Smith, M. (2018), *Revolting Prostitutes*, London: Verso.

Magray, M. (1998), *The Transforming Power of the Nuns: Women, Religion, and Cultural Change in Ireland, 1750–1900*, Oxford: Oxford University Press.

Mahmood, S. (2004), *The Politics of Piety*, Princeton: Princeton University Press.

May, V. M. (2013), 'Speaking into the Void? Intersectionality Critiques and Epistemic Backlash', *Hypatia*, 29 (1): 94–112.

McAleese, M. (2013), 'Report of the Inter-Departmental Committee to establish the facts of State involvement with the Magdalen Laundries' [online]. *Dublin: Dept of Justice and Equality*. Available online: http://www.justice.ie/en/JELR/Pages/MagdalenRpt2013 (accessed 2 October 2017).

McClintock, A. (1997), '"No Longer in a Future Heaven": Gender, Race and Nationalism', in A. McClintock, A. Mufti and E. Shohat (eds), *Dangerous Liaisons:*

Gender, Nation and Postcolonial Perspectives, 89–112, Minneapolis: University of Minnesota Press.

McGarry, P. (2011), 'Laundry Orders Run Sex Workers' Aid Group', *The Irish Times*, 25 June. Available online: https://www.irishtimes.com/news/laundry-orders-run-sex-workers-aid-group-1.606313 (accessed 13 August 2021).

McGarry, P. (2013) 'Magdalene Nuns Hit Back at Critics and Defend Their Role', *The Irish Times*, 08 March. Available online: https://www.irishtimes.com/news/magdalene-nuns-hit-back-at-critics-and-defend-their-role-1.1319508 (accessed 2 May 2019).

McGarry, P. (2018). 'Catholic Bishops: Repeal of Eighth Would Be "manifest injustice"', *The Irish Times*, 06 March. Available online: https://www.irishtimes.com/news/social-affairs/catholic-bishops-repeal-of-eighth-would-be-manifest-injustice-1.3417362 (accessed 16 April 2019).

McGettrick, C. (2021), *17/ In 2013, once the Magdalene apology came, nobody (apart from @ococonuts…* [Twitter], 12 January. Available online: https://twitter.com/cmcgettrick/status/1349095828028272640 (accessed 12 February 2021).

McGettrick, C. (2021), 12 January. Available online: https://twitter.com/cmcgettrick/status/1349095790581604352 (accessed 12 February 2021).

McGettrick, C. and Justice for Magdalenes Research (2015), 'Death, Institutionalisation & Duration of Stay: A critique of Chapter 16 of the Report of the Inter-Departmental Committee to establish the facts of State involvement with the Magdalen Laundries and Related Issues' [online]. Available online: http://clannproject.org/wp-content/uploads/Death-Institutionalisation-Duration-of-Stay_FINAL.pdf (accessed 22 May 2019).

McGettrick, C., O'Donnell, K., O'Rourke, M., Smith, J. and Steed, M. (2021), *Ireland and the Magdalene Laundries: A Campaign for Justice*, London: Bloomsbury.

McGrath, L. (2016), 'In Donnybrook, Future of Crumbling Magdalene Laundry Is Uncertain', *Dublin Inquirer*, 09 March. Available online: https://www.dublininquirer.com/2016/03/09/in-donnybrook-future-of-crumbling-magdalene-laundry-is-uncertain (accessed 22 May 2019).

McHugh, N. A. (2017), 'Epistemic Communities and Institutions', in I. J. Kidd, J. Medina and G. Pohlhaus Jr. (eds), *The Routledge Handbook of Epistemic Injustice*, 270–8, Abingdon: Routledge.

McMahan, E. M. (2015), *Elite Oral History Discourse: A Study of Cooperation and Coherence*, Tuscaloosa: The University of Alabama Press.

Medina, J. (2012), 'Hermeneutical Injustice and Polyphonic Contextualism: Social Silences and Shared Hermeneutical Responsibilities', *Social Epistemology*, 26 (2): 201–20.

Mills, C. (2007), 'White Ignorance', in S. Sullivan and N. Tuana (eds), *Race and Epistemologies of Ignorance*, 13–38, Albany: SUNY Press.

Mills, C. (2017), 'Ideology', in I. J. Kidd, J. Medina and G. Pohlhaus Jr. (eds), *The Routledge Handbook of Epistemic Injustice*, 100–11, Abingdon: Routledge.

Mullan, P., dir. (2003), *The Magdalene Sisters* [Film], England: Momentum Films.

Nash, C. (1997), 'Embodied Irishness: Gender, Sexuality and Irish Identities', in B. Graham, (ed.), *In Search of Ireland: A Cultural Geography*, 108–27, London: Routledge.

Niezen, R. (2017), *Truth and Indignation: Canada's Truth and Reconciliation Commission on Indian Residential Schools*, Ontario: University of Toronto Press.

O'Donnell, K. (2008), 'Introduction: Lesbian Lives and Studies in Ireland at the Fin de Siècle', in M. McAuliffe and S. Tiernan (eds.), *Tribades, Tommies and Transgressives: Histories of Sexualities, Volume I*, 1–26, Newcastle: Cambridge Scholars Publishing.

O'Donnell, K. (2018a) 'Academics Becoming Activists: Reflections on Some Ethical Issues of the Justice for Magdalenes Campaign', in P. Villar-Argáiz (ed.), *Irishness on the Margins: New Directions in Irish and Irish American Literature*, 77–100, Cham: Palgrave Macmillan.

O'Donnell, K. (2018b), 'Let's Listen Attentively to Survivors of Magdalene Laundries', *The Irish Times*, 05 June 2018. Available online: https://www.irishtimes.com/opinion/let-s-listen-attentively-to-survivors-of-magdalene-laundries-1.3519069 (accessed 5 May 2019).

O'Donnell, K., and McGettrick, C. (2018), 'MAGOHP/LE/5, Table 5: Elina Eriksson', Magdalene Institutions: Recording an Archival and Oral History, pp. 1–54.

O'Donnell, K., Pembroke, S. and McGettrick, C. (2013), 'Magdalene Institutions: Recording an Archival and Oral History', Government of Ireland Collaborative Research Project, Irish Research Council.

O'Donnell, K., Pembroke, S. and McGettrick, C. (2013), 'Topic Guide for Survivors', Magdalene Institutions: Recording an Archival and Oral History. Government of Ireland Collaborative Research Project, Irish Research Council. Available online: http://jfmresearch.com/wp-content/uploads/2017/04/Topic-Guide_Survivors.pdf (accessed 4 April 2016).

Ó Fátharta, C. (2013a), 'Order Refuses to Offer Explanation on Burials', *Irish Examiner*, 04 February. Available online: https://www.irishexaminer.com/ireland/order-refuses-to-offer-explanation-on-burials-221538.html (accessed 7 September 2018).

Ó Fátharta, C. (2013b), 'Just One Religious Order Apologises', *Irish Examiner*, 06 February. Available online: https://www.irishexaminer.com/ireland/just-one-religious-order-apologises-221782.html (accessed 9 December 2018).

Ó Fátharta, C. (2018), 'Historic Gathering for Magdalene Survivors', *Irish Examiner*, 29 May. Available online: https://www.irishexaminer.com/ireland/historic-gathering-for-magdalene-survivors-471218.html (accessed 4 July 2019).

O'Mahoney, J. (2015), 'Waterford Memories Project'. Available online: https://www.waterfordmemories.com/home (accessed 31 January 2019).

O'Mahoney, J. (2018), 'Advocacy and the Magdalene Laundries: Towards a Psychology of Social Change', *Qualitative Research in Psychology*, 15 (4): 456–71.

O'Mahoney-Yeager, J. and Culleton, J. (2016), 'Gendered Violence and Cultural Forgetting: The Case of the Irish Magdalenes', *Radical History Review*, 126: 134–46.

O'Rourke, M. (2015), 'The Justice for Magdalenes Campaign', in S. Egan (ed.), *International Human Rights: Perspectives from Ireland*, 145–68, London: Bloomsbury.

O'Rourke, M and Smith, J. (2016), 'Ireland's Magdalene Laundries: Confronting a History not yet in the Past', in A. Hayes and M. Meagher (eds), *A Century of Progress? Irish Women Reflect*, 107–33, Dublin: Arlen House.

O'Sullivan, E. and O'Donnell, I. (2012), *Coercive Confinement in Ireland: Patients, Prisoners and Penitents*, Manchester: Manchester University Press.

O'Sullivan, C. (2013), 'Interviews Lack Transparency Say Victims' Groups,' *Irish Examiner*, 7 February. Available online: https://www.irishexaminer.com/news/arid-20221877.html (accessed 19 January 2021).

Olick, J. (2007), *The Politics of Regret: On Collective Memory and Historical Responsibility*, New York: Routledge.

Orsi, R. (2002), *The Madonna of 115th Street: Faith and Community In Italian Harlem, 1880–1950*, New Haven: Yale University Press.

Orsi, R. (2005), *Between Heaven and Earth: The Religious Worlds People Make and the Scholars Who Study them*, Princeton: Princeton University Press.

Orsi, R. (2016), *History and Presence*, Cambridge: Harvard University Press.

Pargament, K., Murray-Swank, N. and Mahoney, A. (2008), 'Problem and Solution: The Spiritual Dimension of Clergy Sexual Abuse and its Impact on Survivors',. *Journal of Child Sexual Abuse*, 17 (3–4): 397–420.

Parpart, J. L. (2010), 'Choosing Silence: Rethinking Voice, Agency and Women's Empowerment', in R. Gill and R. Ryan Flood (eds), *Secrecy and Silence in the Research Process: Feminist Reflections*, 15–29, Oxford: Routledge.

Patterson, P. M. (2000), 'The Talking Cure and the Silent Treatment: Some Limits of "Discourse" as Speech', *Administrative Theory & Praxis*, 22 (4): 663–95.

Pheterson, G. (1996), *The Prostitution Prism*, Amsterdam: Amsterdam University Press.

Pine, E. (2011), *The Politics of Irish Memory*, London: Palgrave Macmillan.

Pine, E. (2019), 'We Have a Culture of Not Listening to Abuse Survivors', *The Irish Times*, 14 May. Available online: https://www.irishtimes.com/opinion/we-have-a-culture-of-not-listening-to-abuse-survivors-1.3891074 (accessed 15 May 2019).

Portelli, A. (1991), *The Death of Luigi Trastulli and Other Stories: Form and Meaning in Oral History*, New York: SUNY Press.

Quirke, J. (2013), 'Magdalen Commission Report' [online]. Dublin: Department of Justice and Equality. Available online: http://www.justice.ie/en/JELR/Pages/PB13 000255 (accessed 17 May 2018).

Raftery, M. (2003), 'Restoring Dignity to Magdalenes', Opinion, *The Irish Times*, 21 August. Available online: https://www.irishtimes.com/opinion/restoring-dignity-to-magdalens-1.370373 (accessed 5 May 2019).

Raftery, M. (2011), 'Ireland's Magdalene Laundries Scandal Must be Laid to Rest'. *The Guardian*, 8 June. Available online: https://www.theguardian.com/commentisfree/2011/jun/08/irealnd-magdalene-laundries-scandal-un (accessed 6 June 2019).

Raftery, M. and O'Sullivan, E. (1999), *Suffer the Little Children*, Dublin: New Island Books.

Rambo, S. (2010), *Spirit and Trauma: A Theology of Remaining*, Louisville: Westminster John Knox Press.

Redmond, J., Tiernan, S., McAvoy, S. and McAuliffe, M. (2015), 'Politicising Sexuality in Modern Ireland', in J. Redmond, S. Tiernan, S. McAvoy and M. McAuliffe (eds), *Sexual Politics in Modern Ireland*, 1–15, Sallins: Irish Academic Press.

Reidy, C. (2015), '"Loose and Immoral Lives": Prostitution and the Female Criminal Inebriate in Ireland, 1900-18', in J. Redmond, S. Tiernan, S. McAvoy and M. McAuliffe (eds), *Sexual Politics in Modern Ireland*, 53–72, Sallins: Irish Academic Press.

Religious Sisters of Charity (2013), 'Statement regarding The McAleese Report' [online]. Available online: https://www.rsccaritas.com/rscnews/458-response (accessed 28 May 2019).

Riessman, C. K. (1993), *Narrative Analysis*, Sage: London.

Robinson, M. (1993), 'Women and the Law in Ireland', in A. Smyth (ed.), *Irish Women's Studies Reader*, 100–6, Dublin: Mount Press.

Ruhama (2018), 'About Ruhama' [online]. Available online: https://www.ruhama.ie/about-ruhama/ (accessed 2 August 2019).

Ryan-Flood, R. and Gill, R. (2010), 'Introduction', in R. Gill and R. Ryan Flood (eds), *Secrecy and Silence in the Research Process: Feminist Reflections*, 1–11, Oxford: Routledge.

Scharff, C. (2010), 'Silencing Differences: The "unspoken" Dimensions of "speaking for others"', in R. Gill and R. Ryan Flood (eds), *Secrecy and Silence in the Research Process: Feminist Reflections*, 83–95, Oxford: Routledge.

Scrutton, A. P. (2017), 'Epistemic Injustice and Mental Illness', in I. J. Kidd, J. Medina and G. Pohlhaus Jr. (eds), *The Routledge Handbook of Epistemic Injustice*, 347–55, Abingdon: Routledge.

Seal, L. and O'Neill, M. (2019), *Imaginative Criminology: Of Spaces Past, Present and Future*, Bristol: Bristol University Press.

Sedgwick, E. K. (2003), *Touching Feeling: Affect, Pedagogy, Performativity*, Durham: Duke University Press.

Serisier, T. (2018), *Speaking Out: Feminism, Rape and Narrative Politics*, London: Palgrave Macmillan.

Shklar, J. (1960), *The Faces of Injustice*, New Haven and London: Yale University Press.

Skeggs, B. (1997), *Formations of Gender and Class: Becoming Respectable*, London: SAGE Publications.

Skeggs, B. (2004), *Class, Self, Culture*, London: Routledge.

Smith, J. (2007), *Ireland's Magdalen Laundries and the Nation's Architecture of Containment*, Manchester: Manchester University Press.

Smith, J. (2011a), 'The Justice for Magdalenes Campaign', in C. Holohan (ed.), *In Plain Sight: Responding to the Ferns, Ryan, Murphy and Cloyne Reports*, 272–7, Dublin: Amnesty International Ireland.

Smith, J. (2011b), 'A Narrative of State Interaction with the Magdalene Laundries' [online]. Available online: http://jfmresearch.com/wp-content/uploads/2017/03/JFM_Narrative_State_Interaction.pdf (accessed 4 December 2018).

Smith, R. C. (2002), 'Analytic Strategies for Oral History Interviews', in J .F. Gubrium and J. A. Holstein (eds), *Handbook of Interview Research: Context and Method*, 711–31, London: Sage Publications.

Social Democrats (2019), 'The Dublin Agreement 2019–2024' [online]. Available online: https://www.socialdemocrats.ie/wp-content/uploads/2018/06/Dublin-City-Agreement-Final.pdf (accessed 10 September 2019).

Spivak, G. C. (1988), 'Can the Subaltern Speak?', in C. Nelson and L. Grossberg (eds.), *Marxism and the Interpretation of Culture*, 271–313, Chicago: University of Illinois Press.

Sullivan, M. (2017), 'Epistemic Injustice and the Law', in I .J. Kidd, J. Medina and G. Pohlhaus Jr. (eds), *The Routledge Handbook of Epistemic Injustice*, 293–302, Abingdon: Routledge.

Summerfield, P. (2004), 'Culture and Composure: Creating a Narrative of the Gendered Self in Oral History Interviews', *Culture and Social History*, 1 (1): 65–93.

Taylor, C. (1991), *The Ethics of Authenticity*, Cambridge: Harvard University Press.

Thompson, P. (1988), *The Voice of the Past*, Oxford: Oxford University Press.

Thor, J. (2019), 'Religious and Industrial Education in the Nineteenth-Century Magdalene Asylums in Scotland', *Studies in Church History*, 55: 347–62.

Truth, S. ([1867] 1995) 'When Woman Gets Her Rights Man Will Be Right', in B. Guy-Sheftall (ed.), *Words of Fire: An Anthology of African-American Feminist Thought*, 37–42, New York: New Press.

Tyndall, P. (2017), 'Opportunity Lost: An investigation by the Ombudsman into the administration of the Magdalen Restorative Justice Scheme' [online]. Available online: https://www.ombudsman.ie/publications/reports/opportunity-lost/Magdalen-Scheme.pdf (accessed 25 January 2019).

United Nations Committee Against Torture (2011), 'Consideration of Reports Submitted by States Parties under Article 19 of the Convention. Concluding Observations of the Committee Against Torture, Ireland'. CAT/C/IRL/CO/1. Geneva. Available online: https://tbinternet.ohchr.org/_layouts/15/treatybodyexternal/Download.aspx?symbolno=CAT%2fC%2fIRL%2fCO%2f1&Lang=en (a ccessed 23 May 2019).

United Nations Committee Against Torture (2011), 'Summary Record of the 1005th Meeting Held at the Palais Wilson', Geneva. Available at http://www.bayefsky.com/s ummary/ireland_cat_c_sr1005_2011.pdf (accessed 9 July 2019).

United Nations Committee Against Torture (2017), 'Concluding Observations on the Second Periodic Report of Ireland', CAT/C/SR.1565 and CAT/C/SR.1566. Geneva. Available online: http://docstore.ohchr.org/SelfServices/FilesHandler.ashx?enc=6QkG1d%2FPPRiCAqhKb7yhstySI%2BO7WcYaiEOWzYSqa3PQ0QCZkEUtkhuvK2j5JR6zJ0sj%2Fv5Y7B2BlmFEF0D2ekQfhz0rGuBb%2BYho%2F%2B8OAj7sfaMPbWsjdk5oS2YwSzcI (a ccessed 3 January 2019).

Valiulis, M. (1995), 'Power, Gender and Identity in the Irish Free State', *Journal of Women's History*, 6 (5): 117–36.
Weber, C., dir. (1998), *Les Blanchisseuses de Magdalen* [Film]. France: France 3.
Winter, S. (2011), 'Legitimacy, Citizenship and State Redress', *Citizenship Studies*, 15 (6–7): 799–814.
Winter, S. (2014), *Transitional Justice in Established Democracies: A Political Theory*, London: Palgrave Macmillan.
Winter, S. (2015), 'Theorising the Political Apology', *Journal of Political Philosophy*, 23 (3): 261–81.
Waterford Institute of Technology (date unknown), 'Campus Development' [online]. Available online: https://www.wit.ie/about_wit/at_a_glance/campus_development#tab=panel-3 (accessed 2 February 2019).
Yuval-Davis, N. (1997), *Gender and Nation*, London: Sage Publications.
Zur, J. (2004), 'Remembering and Forgetting: Guatemalan War Widows' Forbidden Memories', in K. Lacy Rodgers, S. Leydesdorff and G. Dawson (eds), *Trauma: Life Stories of Survivors*, 45–59, London: Transaction Publishers.

Index

Abrams, L. 48, 49
abuse. *See also* institutional abuse; physical abuse
   child 11–12, 34
   clerical sexual abuse 1, 34, 125–6
   by family 74–6, 117
   IDC's position on 87, 88, 154, 157
   psychological 96–8
   State complicity 57–8
accountability
   lack of 199
   religious congregations' eliding 170–1, 173
   of State 5, 149–50, 159, 199–201
activism
   speaking out as 45, 46–7
adoption 201
Ahern, D. 209 n.2
Ahmed, S.
   on coping with injustice 140, 142
   on distinction between choosing to be silent and being silenced 47–8
   on emotions and women 61–2
   on national shame and public apology 162–3, 167
Alcoff, L. and Gray-Rosendale, L.
   on conditions of speech 50
   on speech 45–6
   on survivor testimony 45
Anderson, E. 197–8
Anderson, P. 49
anger
   of researcher 54–9
anti-nostalgia 163–5
apology
   concept of 160, 170
   and epistemic injustice 18, 147, 148–9, 159–62, 182–4
   lack of religious congregations' apology 159, 170, 172
   Magdalene survivors' desire for apology from religious congregations 159, 168
   nuns' refusal 193
   State (*see* State apology)
archives and records
   denial of access to IDC's 171–2
   denial of access to religious congregations' 10, 12, 13, 81, 171, 172
   IDC's access to religious congregations' 150–1, 171
   Mary Raftery Archive 207 n.3
   Retention of Records Bill (2019) 200
Armour, E. T. 27
atheism 128
attentive listening 183, 201–2
Aylward, S. 4

bodily discipline 17, 66, 67, 83–4, 187
   impact on religious subjectivity 20, 24, 128–9, 132–3
   resistance to 90–6
   work as 88–90
Bondi, L. 62
Bourdieu, P. 136
Brown, T.
   Ireland: A Social and Cultural History 1922-2002 3
burial/graves
   identity issues and discrepancies 3–4, 198–9
Burke Brogan, P. 69
   Eclipsed 7

Casey, Eamonn, Bishop 33–4
Casey, N. 181
Castelli, E. 26
Catholic Church/Catholicism. *See also* religious congregations/orders
   acceptable womanhood 21, 31–2, 34, 105, 118, 136
   changing attitudes towards 33–4
   clerical abuse 1, 34, 125–6
   collusion in shaming of women 11

control of Magdalene institutions   2–3
lack of accountability for abuse in
    mother and baby homes   200–1
and Magdalene institutions'
    legitimacy   18, 190, 191
Magdalene survivors' disengagement
    from   126, 129–33
Magdalene survivors' engagement
    with   124, 133–5
role in national education   125
scandals   33–4
significance to Irish identity   20,
    31–2, 33, 126, 135, 144,
    189–90
Catholic identity   126, 133–5
child abuse/child sexual abuse   11–12, 34
children of Magdalene women
    Samantha Long   51–2
    as source of pride   138–9
Christian Brothers   11
citizenship   15, 160–1
class
    and credibility of subject   39–40
clerical sexual abuse   1, 34
    impact on religious subjectivity   125–6
clothes
    uniforms as visible markers   91,
        92, 93
Clough, Miryam
    Shame, the Church and the
    Regulation of Female
    Sexuality   11
Commission to Inquire into Child
    Abuse   200
communion   131–2, 133
communities of epistemic
    resistance   195–8
Congregation of the Sisters of
    Mercy   7
    statement of regret   169, 171
Connerton, P.   1
Constitution of Ireland
    Article 41   29–30, 31
    Eighth Amendment   208 n.1
containment
    'architecture of containment'   6–7,
        11–12, 171
Coogan, PJ   55–9
Cooper, A. J.   22
Corless, C.   207 n.5

credibility
    denial of   67, 77–8, 104–5, 144
    and DHM Event   178–9, 181
    and knowledge production   13, 15,
        16, 20, 37, 39–40, 44, 63–4, 147,
        148, 152–5, 198, 201–2
    and perception by social
        audiences   48–50
    and religious congregations'
        statements of regret   172, 173
    routes to   104, 135–6
    and State apology   167, 173
credibility deficit   21, 23–4, 27, 173, 188
    McAleese/IDC meetings   153,
        154–5
    and silent subject   67, 73–8
    and social identity   52–3, 104–5, 144,
        182–4

Daly, M.   209 n.4
Das, V.   136, 141, 142, 144
death certificates
    absence of   3–4
dehumanization   96–103
Department of (the) Environment   3–4
Department of Justice   174
depersonalization   96–8, 189
disciplinary institutions   2, 18, 67, 83–4,
    104–5, 132–3, 187, 188–90
docility   66, 83, 111, 187
documentary films   7–8, 11
Donnybrook Magdalene Laundry
    (Dublin)   169, 186
Drozdzewski, Danielle and Dominey-
    Howes, Dale   60, 62
Dublin City Council   186
Dublin Honours Magdalenes (DHM)
    Event (2018)   174–5
    and epistemic injustice   18, 148
    Garda escort   175–6
    Listening Exercise   43, 175,
        178–9, 192
    media coverage   179–81
    Presidential booklet   177–8
    public reception at Dawson
        Street   181
    as source of information   42–3
    and value of community   196
duration of stay in Magdalene Laundries
    lack of information on   79–81

Earner-Byrne, L. 32
education
    State-funded/Church-run 125
emotionality
    at departure from Magdalene
        Laundries 108–15, 143
    in research 53–4
        anger 54–9
        tears and shame 59–63
enforced silence 68
    gendered experiences 68–9
    resistance to 82–3
    through denial of credibility 67,
        77–8, 104–5, 144
    through denial of information
        67, 72
Ènright, M. 201
entry to Magdalene Laundries
    routes of 2, 74–8
    'voluntarily' 74
epistemic injustice 14–16, 19–22, 49–50,
        66–7, 182–3, 195–6
    concept of 20–1
    forms of 21–2
    and IDC inquiry 149–50, 155,
        158–9
    and identity formation 23–4, 34–5
    impact of public voice on 183
    resistance to 195–8
    trauma caused by 18, 187, 194–5
equality
    and epistemic justice 198
escapes/escapees 56–7, 90–4, 176
    as resistance 90, 94–5
ethics in research
    of representation 17, 37, 50–3
    of self-care 17, 37, 53–63
everyday life
    mundane acts of 136, 140–3
exhumations at High Park Magdalene
        Laundry 3–4, 6–7, 207 n.3
exit from Magdalene Laundries
    abrupt departures 108–10
    abrupt departures and conflicted
        feelings 109–15, 143

family
    abuse by 74–6, 117
    Constitutional 30–1
    inability to share Magdalene Laundry
        experiences with 116–17,
        121–2
    patriarchal 31–2
    as source of pride 137–9
    testimonies of (see oral history/
        testimony: of family and
        relatives)
female deviant sexuality
    association between Magdalene
        institutions and 10–11, 17, 27,
        69, 116–17, 191–3
    and Irish State 2, 27–32, 34, 35,
        68, 105
feminism 33
    and Irish Constitution 30
    and religious subjectivity 26–7
    and subordination of emotions 62
    and women's voices 22, 46, 49
Finnegan, F.
    Do Penance or Perish 10
Fischer, C. 11
Flanagan, C. 174
forced and unpaid labour 5, 57, 78, 88,
        95, 130, 177
Fortune, Seán, Father 34
Foster, R. J. 33
    Modern Ireland, 1600-1972 3
Foucault, M.
    on disciplinary institutions 188
    on docile bodies 66, 83
    on enforced silence 68
Francis, Pope 1
Fricker, M. 14, 16, 19–23, 27, 34–5, 53,
        69, 182–3, 195–6
friends/friendship
    disallowed to say goodbye to 109,
        110, 111
    as a problem 70–2

Gaer, F. 200
Gannon, G. 186
Garda Síochána (Police)
    capture and return of escapees 56–7,
        90–3, 176
    escort for Magdalene survivors to
        DHM event 175–6
Gardiner, F. 30
gender 18, 188–9

Church/State impact on 2, 20, 21, 27–32, 34, 35, 105
and credibility of subject 39–40
and emotional labour of research 61–2
and experiences of silence 68–9
and labour norms 89–90
and national identity 11, 15, 27–32, 68, 117
and religious subjectivity 26–7, 66–77, 187
Gill, R. 61
Gilmore, L. 39
Glasnevin Cemetery (Dublin)
inaccuracies on headstones 4, 198–9
memorial gravestones 4
Glynn, E. 9
Goffman, E. 118, 160
greed (material) 129–31
Griffin, G. 59
Guenther, L. 118

Hayes, A. and Urquhart, D.
The Irish Women's History Reader 33
heathen 127
Herman, J. 47
hermeneutical injustice 14, 16
after leaving Magdalene Laundries 115–16, 144–5, 182–3, 188
challenging 178–9, 196
concept of 21–2
impact on subjectivity 20, 23
Higgins, M. D. 175, 177
High Park Magdalene Laundry (Drumcondra, Dublin) 75, 92
exhumations at 3–4, 6–7, 207 n.3
Hilliard, B. 33
Hirschman, L. 47
Hollway, W. and Jefferson, T. 52–3
Hornsby, J. 49

IDC. *See* Inter-Departmental Committee to establish the facts of State Involvement with the Magdalen Laundries
identity
coercive formation of 14, 15, 103–4, 105, 191
being a nobody 96–8, 107, 118–19, 142
Magdalene names 99–103
as penitents 24, 66, 73, 83–4, 89, 100, 116–17, 143, 179–80, 199
and epistemic injustice 23–4, 34–5, 66–7
fear of visibility of spoiled/shamed identity 115, 118, 121, 192
and lack of knowledge/information 81
renegotiation of 17, 108, 135–43
stigmatized 17, 69, 81, 108, 115–23, 143–4, 179–81, 191–3
identity prejudice 21, 23–4, 27
incarceration 15, 18
duration of 79–81
justification for 15, 18, 29, 102, 105, 115, 188–94
physical and temporal nature of 84–6
and religious subjectivity 24–7
shame around 107–8, 115–23
sound as marker of 86
of unmarried mothers 29
industrial and reformatory schools 11–12
lives and experiences in 96
(key) informants 6, 40–1
affective response from 58
anger towards 55–7
testimonies of (*see* oral history/testimony: of key informants)
informed consent 50–1
Inglis, T. 31–2, 33, 136
institutional abuse 1, 7, 25
children 11–12
public inquiries into 197
religious subjectivity of survivors of 125–6
State's disinclination to address 199–201
survivors' resistance to 27
institutionalisation
ongoing/lingering effects of 17, 107–8, 115–23
terror of 122–3
institutional silence
of religious congregations 168, 172, 200–1

and the state of 'not knowing' 78–81, 172
Inter-Departmental Committee to establish the facts of State Involvement with the Magdalen Laundries (IDC) 41
　access to religious congregations' archives and records 150–1
　archives and records of 171–2
　and epistemic injustice 149–50, 155, 158–9
　establishment of 5
　fact-finding aim of 150–2
　JFM's 2012 'Principal Submission' to 5, 151, 157, 208 n.1
　religious congregations' cooperation with 169, 171
　survivors' meetings with 152–5
Inter-Departmental Committee to establish the facts of State Involvement with the Magdalen Laundries (IDC) Report 18, 147–8
　Chapter Nineteen 'Living and Working Conditions' in Laundries 156, 157
　critique on 151–2, 158–9, 191
　as 'document of truth' 152, 157–8
　on Gardaí's role in returning escapees 176
　on lack of physical abuse in Magdalene Laundries 87, 88, 154, 157
　omission of survivors' testimonies submitted by JFM 151, 157
　physical space given to survivor testimony 44
　on routes of entry 74
　as source 42, 44
　on State involvement 5, 149–50, 159
　survivors' accessibility to 155–6, 158
　survivors' views on 149–50, 154–5
　survivors' voices and narratives in 149, 156–7
Irish Free State/Ireland
　anti-nostalgia 163–5
　conception of womanhood 2, 15, 20, 21, 27–32, 34, 35, 105
　family as a 'moral institution' 29–30
　'Irish mother' role in 21, 27–8, 30, 31–2, 136, 137, 140
　Magdalene survivors' wider disconnect 134–5
　moral purity and social stability 12, 20, 28, 108, 117, 123
　significance of Catholicism 31–2, 33, 125–6, 135–6, 144, 189
Irish Human Rights Commission (IHRC) 149
　Assessment of the Human Rights Issues Arising in relation to the 'Magdalen Laundries' 5
Irish Research Council 6, 40

Justice for Magdalenes (JFM) 7, 41, 207 n.1
　2011 submission of inquiry application to IHRC 5
　2011 submission to UNCAT 5
　2012 'Principal Submission' to IDC 5, 151, 157, 208 n.1
　gathering of testimony 208 n.1
　objectives of 4
　political campaign 4–6
Justice for Magdalenes Research (JFMR)
　access to Raftery's archive 207 n.3
　establishment and objectives of 6
　visit to Glasnevin cemetery 198–9
　website of 149, 207 n.3

Kandiyoti, D. 15
Kelly, M. 4
Kenny, E.
　apology to Magdalene survivors 5–6, 18, 42, 127, 148, 159, 162–6, 174, 200
　on IDC 152, 157, 164
knowledge/information
　denial of 66–7, 187
　about exit from Magdalene Laundries 108–15
　silence enforced through 67, 72
　and the state of 'not knowing' 78–81, 172
　and voluntary entry into Magdalene Laundry 74
　Magdalene survivors as producers of 13, 15, 16, 19, 20, 37, 39–40, 44, 63–4, 147, 148, 152–5, 198, 201–2

Leydesdorff, S.   45
Limerick School of Art and Design (LSAD)
  'Breaking the Rule of Silence'   9
Lind, J.   182
Listening Exercise at Dublin Honours Magdalenes Event (2018)   43, 175, 178-9, 192, 196
literature on Magdalene Laundries   3, 10-12
  contemporary   12-13
lives and experiences
  after departure from Magdalene Laundries   17, 22, 107-8, 123-4, 140-5, 187
  in Magdalene Laundries   17, 65-6, 104-5
    abrupt departures from Magdalene Laundries   108-15
    IDC Report on   156, 157
    perception of age impact on   85-6
    testimonies on   41-2 (*see also* oral history/testimony)
Luddy, M.   3, 28
  Prostitution and Irish Society   10
Lynch, G.   171, 189

McAleese, M.   149, 153-4, 169
McAleese Report. *See* Inter-Departmental Committee to establish the facts of State Involvement with the Magdalen Laundries Report
McClintock, A.   15
McCormack, C.   193
McDonald, P.   4
McGarry, P.   193
McGettrick, C.   4
  critique on IDC Report   151
  on IDC's meetings with Magdalene survivors   153
  on inconsistencies in names on gravestones   199
  on mother and baby homes investigation   201
McHugh, J.   200
McHugh, N. A.   195
McMahan, E.   38
Magdalene institutions
  as historical spaces of confinement   12
  ignorance/lack of visibility of   1
  Irish context   2-3
  list of   203
  as sites for 'fallen women'   10-11
'Magdalene Institutions: Recording an Archival and Oral History' project   6, 40-2. *See also* Magdalene Oral History Project
Magdalene Laundries
  as care institutions   32, 76-7, 169, 170, 171, 188-9, 193-4
  Irish context   2-3
  and Irish social life   95-6
  justification and necessity for   15, 18, 67, 83-4, 104-5, 132-3, 187, 188-9, 193-4
  mundane and repetitive nature of   66
  as 'private' establishments   209 n.2
  public awareness of   57-8
  as religious carceral institutions   16, 18, 25, 35, 124, 132, 147, 188, 189-90
  and 'wrong' kind of women   10-11, 17, 27, 69, 116-17, 191-3
Magdalene Memorial Committee   4, 7, 70
Magdalene Names Project   207 n.4
Magdalene Oral History Project   13-15, 148
  significance of   186-7
The Magdalene Sisters (film: Mullan)   8
Magdalen Restorative Justice Ex-Gratia Scheme   174, 178
Magray, M.   31
Mahmood, S.   27
Mass (liturgy)   131-2, 133
media
  America   193
  BBC Scotland
    Washing Away the Stain (documentary)   8
  CBS *60 Minutes*
    The Magdalen Laundries (documentary)   8
  Channel Four (Britain)
    Sex in a Cold Climate (documentary)   8
  DHM event   179-81
  France 3
    Les Blanchisseuses de Magdalen (documentary)   8

High Park exhumations 4
The Irish Times 193, 200
RTÉ Radio 1
  The God Slot 193
RTÉ Television
  Sex in a Cold Climate
    (documentary) 8
  States of Fear (documentary) 11
memorials and memorialisation 178
  bench in St Stephen's Green 4, 6–7
  Kenny on 164
memory
  about day of exit from Magdalene
    Laundry 109–10, 113–14
  and anti-nostalgia 163–5
  bodily religious memory 131–3
  of noises of enclosure 86
  and oral history 38, 39
  public 1, 57–8, 147–8
morality 10–11
  Church/State role in 12, 20, 28–32,
    108, 117, 123
  gendered notion of 34
  women as signifiers of 28–32, 117,
    136–7
  and women's speech 68–9, 71
  and work 89–90, 97
mother and baby homes 1, 11, 207 n.5
Mother and Baby Homes Commission of
  Investigation (MBHCOI) 184,
  200–1
motherhood
  Church/State conception of 21,
    27–8, 30–2, 136–7, 140
  respectability through 108, 136–40
  as source of pride 137–9
  'wrong' kind of mother 27
mothers, unmarried
  changing attitudes towards 33
  incarceration of 29
  'a problem' 32
  stigma 116
  as vulnerable and threatening 28–9
Mullan, P. 8
Murphy, A. 4

names
  'house names' 99–103
  new/religious 3, 191
  reclamation of 103–4
national identity 16, 20
  and gender 11, 15, 27–32, 68, 117
  and State apology 160–1
New Ross Magdalene Laundry
  (Wexford) 94
Ní Chinnéide, B. 4
noise
  disruptive potential of 70–1
  as method of resistance 82
  and traumatic memory 86

Oakley, L. and Kinmond, K. 124–5
O'Donnell, K. 6, 40, 41, 208 n.1
  on attentive listening 183
  on DHM Event 174
  on religious congregations'
    treatment of Magdalene
    women 6
  on reparative reading 62–3
  on social role of women 33
  on vicarious trauma 60, 62, 64
Olick, J. 147
O'Mahoney, J. 1, 9, 48
Ombudsman
  critique on Magdalen Restorative
    Justice Scheme 174
oral history/testimony 9–10, 12–15,
  205–6
  of activists/journalists 41
    Maeve O'Rourke 151–2
    Phyllis Morgan 80, 97, 119–21, 123
    PJ Coogan 55–7
  and construction of self 16–17, 37,
    44, 48–50
  cultural approach to 38–9
  ethical implications 51–2
  of family and relatives 41
    Mari Steed 150
    Patricia Dervan 71, 73, 76, 88, 90,
      98, 122–3, 133, 161, 190
    Rose Brian Harrington 74
    Samantha Long 51–2
  of key informants 28, 41, 55, 58,
    76, 103
    'Bridget Flynn' 58
    Dr. M 118–19, 193–4
    in IDC Report 156
    Jane 97, 117, 127

John Kennedy   156
Mary O'Mara   87
a member of Dublin Lions
    Club   156
Patricia Burke Brogan   69
Trevor Heaney   87
as methodology   14–15, 37–44, 63
Mother and Baby Home Commission
    of Investigation   183
of survivors of Magdalene
    Laundries   41
    Angelina Mayfield   142, 143
    Bernadette   65, 66, 71, 79–80,
        84–5, 113, 125, 138–9
    Bernadette and Francis
        Murphy   97, 99, 111–12, 137,
        166–7
    Bridget O'Donnell   51, 133
    Celine Roberts   107, 131–2
    Doris   81, 121–2
    Ellen Ward   129, 142
    Esther   74
    Evelyn   70, 72–3, 75–7, 82,
        88, 113
    in IDC Report   44, 149, 156–7
    Julia Brown   77, 166
    Kate O'Sullivan   133–4, 153–4,
        155, 165–6
    Kathleen   92, 116–17, 131, 142–3
    Kathleen R   95
    Lucy   70–1, 74–5, 84, 88, 91–2,
        119, 122, 129–30, 137
    Margaret Burke   82, 84, 85,
        103–4, 147, 165
    Martha   97, 98, 154, 168
    Martina Keogh   83, 154
    Mary   71–2, 82, 91, 95, 97, 101,
        114, 137, 176
    Mary Creighton   70
    Mary Currington   93–4, 101–2,
        107, 109–10, 112, 113–14,
        130–1, 166, 167
    Mary Merritt   92
    Mary Smith   80, 85–6, 96, 98, 105,
        127–8
    Maureen Sullivan   94–5, 153, 155
    meetings with McAleese/
        IDC   153–5
    Molly McCarthy   166, 167

Nancy Shannon   101, 104, 116
Nuala   161
omission of JFM's submission in
    IDC Report   151, 157
Pippa Flanagan   69, 72, 89, 96,
    102–3, 110–11, 112, 127, 138
projects on   9
Sadie O'Meara   77–8, 119
Sarah   85
self-introduction   75
as source   8
speech and silence in   44–8,
    63–4
Theresa   132
O'Rourke, M.   5
    critique on IDC Report   151–2
O'Rourke, M. and Smith, J.   199
Orsi, R.   24–6, 124, 125, 132
O'Toole, F.   7

Parpart, J. L.   47
Patterson, P. M.   73
Peacock Lane Magdalene Laundry (Cork
    city)   169
Pembroke Partnership Ltd.
    (Dublin)   186
penance   24, 66, 73, 83–4, 89, 100,
    116–17, 132, 143, 179–80, 199
personal God   126, 129–33
Pheterson, G.   192
physical abuse   57, 67, 88–90. See also
    abuse
    beatings   87–8, 129, 154
    concept of   88
    IDC Report on   87, 88, 154, 157
physical freedom
    loss/lack of   67, 84–6
Pine, E.   163, 201
power
    and agency   27
    and form of speech and
        context   45–6
    oppression, knowledge and   21–2
    and religious capital   31–2, 33, 136
    and research process   50–3
prayer   72–3, 132
primary sources   10, 16, 40–1. See also
    oral history/testimony
    for IDC   152–7

Magdalene survivors as   13, 15, 16,
    19, 20, 37, 39–40, 44, 63–4, 147,
    148, 152–5, 198, 201–2
pro-choice groups   208 n.1
productivity
    and docility   83
    and morality   89–90, 97
    and silence   70–1
prostitutes/prostitution   2, 10, 29, 69
    stigma of   116–17, 191–3
    threat of   97
public consciousness
    attitude towards Magdalene
        survivors   201
    impact of State apology on   167
    of Magdalene institutions   1, 57–8,
        147–8
public inquiries
    creation of new narratives   156–9,
        184, 187–8
    and epistemic injustice   18, 147,
        149–56, 182, 184, 197
public support   181–2, 184
public voice   14, 18, 42–3, 147–9, 182–4
    concept of   147
    lingering associations   179–80
    new narratives   183–4, 187
Punchbag Theatre (Galway)   7
punishment
    work as   88–90

Quirke, J., Justice   6, 127, 174, 178

Raftery, M.   207 n.3
    States of Fear (documentary)   11
Raftery, M. and O'Sullivan, E.
    Suffer the Little Children   11–12
redress   6, 150, 181
    and epistemic injustice   18, 147, 148,
        180, 182, 183, 196
    Quirke recommendations   174, 175
    religious congregations' refusal to
        engage in   168, 172
    and State apology   161
    UNCAT recommendations   5
reflexivity   64
Reidy, C.   29
religion. *See also* Catholic Church/
    Catholicism

Magdalene survivors' rejection
    of   126–9, 131, 134–5
religious congregations/orders
    cooperation with McAleese/
        IDC   169, 171
    denial of access to archives of   10, 12,
        13, 81, 171, 172
    eliding responsibility   170–1,
        173, 199
    IDC's access to archives of   150–1, 171
    and Kenny's apology   162
    lack of apology   159, 170, 172, 193
    Magdalene survivors' desire for
        apology from   159, 168
    Magdalene survivors' hatred
        of   129–31
    silence of   168, 172, 200–1
    State funding of   10, 190
    statements of regret from   44, 148,
        159, 168–73
Religious Sisters of Charity   186
    institutions run by   203
    statement of regret   169, 170
religious subjectivity   20
    altered   108, 123–4, 126–35,
        189–90
    within carceral institution   24–7
    and Church   31–2
    of clerical abuse survivors   125–6
    within Magdalene Laundries   66–7,
        72–3, 187, 189
reparative reading   62–3
research
    as epistemic practice   63–4
    ethics in (*see* ethics in research)
    sensitive (*see* sensitive and trauma
        research)
    sources of information   40–4
Residential Institutions Redress Board
    (RIRB)   200
resistance   17
    bodily   90–6
    communities of   195–6
    to disciplinary acts   66, 67
    to enforced silence   82–3
    everyday survival as   140–3
respectability   20, 196
    and physical restrictions   85
    routes to   17, 108, 135–6, 144, 145–6

through motherhood   136–40
Retention of Records Bill (2019)   200
Riessman, C. K.   52
Robinson, M.   30
Ruhama (NGO)   190

St Mary's, Pennywell Road Magdalene
    Laundry (Limerick)   9, 77, 87
Seal, L. and O'Neill, M.   12
Sean McDermott Street (formerly
    Gloucester St) Magdalene
    Laundry (Dublin)   3, 75, 156
  escape from/runaways   91–2, 176
  physical nature of confinement at   84
Sedgwick, E. K.   62, 63
the self
  disciplining selves   96–104
  ethical care of   17, 37, 53–63
  impact of coercive renaming
      on   99–100
  impact of constant state of 'not
      knowing' on   78–81
  impact of enforced silence on   69–70
  impact of epistemic injustice on   19–20,
      23–4, 104–5
  impact of institutionalization
      on   115–23
  and motherhood   137
  narrative construction of   16–17, 37,
      44, 48–50
sensitive and trauma research   17, 37
  emotionality in   53–63
Serisier, T.   47
sexual (im)morality   2, 10–11, 28–9, 31
  and public speech   69
shame/shaming   11, 17, 96–8
  around incarceration   107–8
  collective shame   162–3, 167
  intersubjective nature of   118
  as method of self-regulation   102–3
  ongoing/lingering shame   115–23,
      143–4
  researcher's   59–63
  and State apology   11, 160, 161–2, 166
Shklar, J.   23
silence
  distinction between choosing to be
      silent and being silenced   47–8
  of emotional expression in research   60

enforced. (*see* enforced silence)
  humiliated   1
  institutional   78–81, 168, 172, 200–2
  liberating potential of   46–7
  as resistance   83
  in survivor narratives/testimony   44–8,
      63–4
  of survivors   1, 13, 116
Sisters of Our Lady of Charity of Refuge
  institutions run by   203
  State funding   190
  statement of regret   169, 170
Sisters of the Good Shepherd   56, 87, 128
  institutions run by   2, 9, 10, 203
  State funding   190
  statement of regret   169, 171
  transfers of girls and women to   98
Skeggs, B.
  on morality of nation and women   28
  on oral history and subjectivity   48
  on reflexive approach   64
  on respectability   139
Smith, J.
  on architecture of containment   6–7
  on documentary films   7
  *Ireland's Magdalen Laundries and
      the Nation's Architecture of
      Containment*   11–12, 13
  on Irish media   8
Sojourner Truth   22
speech. *See also* voices of survivors
  authorized form of   72–3
  disregard and discredit of   73–8
  and morality   68–9, 71
spiritual abuse
  and avoidance of communion   132
  concept of   124–5
  of Magdalene survivors   125–6
spiritual discipline   72–3, 186
Spivak, G.   22
State apology   5–6, 18, 42, 127, 148, 159,
    160–1, 174, 200
  JFM's advocacy/call for   4
  and legitimation of subjectivity of
      'survivor'   161–2, 173, 180
  and removal of shame   11, 160,
      161–2, 166
  survivors' ambivalence and elation
      to   165–8

words and tone of   162–5
State complicity   5, 57–8, 149–50, 159
State funding   10, 190
State responsibility
   eliding   199–201
   IDC report on   5, 149–50, 159
Steed, M.   4, 150
stigma   17, 81
   and forcible renaming   102–3, 191
   ongoing   108, 115–23, 143–4
   removal of, and State apology   161
   whore stigma   69, 116–17, 191–3
strikes   95–6
subjectivity
   formation of   16–18
   impact of epistemic injustice
      on   19–20, 23–4, 104–5
   and oral history/testimony   16–17,
      37, 44, 48–50
   religious (see religious subjectivity)
   role of religious carceral
      institutions   14, 24–7, 35
Sundays Well Magdalene Laundry
   (Cork city)
   discrepancies in names on
      gravestones   4, 185
   life and experiences in   85–6
   proposal to demolish and
      redevelop   186
survivors of clerical abuse
   religious subjectivity of   25–6, 125–6
survivors of Magdalene Laundries   33
   desire for apology from religious
      congregations   159, 168
   effects of institutionalization   17,
      107–8, 115–23
   experiences of DHM event   43
   inaccessibility of IDC Report
      to   155–6, 158
   lingering associations   179–81
   meetings with McAleese/IDC   152–5
   testimonies of (see oral history/
      testimony: of survivors of
      Magdalene Laundries)
   victim status and State apology   161–2,
      173, 180
   views on IDC Report   149–50,
      154–5
   views on State apology   165–8

survivor testimony. See oral history/
   testimony

The Tablet (magazine)   179–80
testimonial injustice   14, 16, 172–3
   challenging   178–9
   concept of   21, 27, 53
   impact on subjectivity   20, 23, 50,
      104–5, 144
Thompson, P.   38
trauma
   and anti-nostalgia   163–5
   continual nature of   145, 182, 194–5
   impact on religious subjectivity
      of survivors of institutional
      abuse   125–6
   of institutionalization   107–8, 122
   vicarious   60–2, 64
trauma research. See sensitive and trauma
   research
Tyndall, P.   174

United Nations Committee Against
      Torture (UNCAT)   74
   JFM's 2011 submission to   5
   recommendations of   5, 172
unpaid labour. See forced and unpaid
   labour

Varadkar, L.   174
vicarious trauma   60–2, 64
vicious paternalism
   rationale of   15, 18, 29, 102, 115,
      188–94
virtues of epistemic justice   53, 182–3,
   197–8
visibility of spoiled/shamed identity
   terror and fear of   115, 118, 121, 192
voices of survivors   1, 13. See also oral
      history/testimony; public voice
   credibility of   15, 16, 19, 21, 23–4,
      37, 63–4
   disciplining   67–83
   and IDC Report   149
   power of speaking out   44–8
   risks of speaking out   119–21, 153

Waterford Institute of Technology   9–10
Waterford Memories Project (WMP)   9

welfare institutions   18, 76–7, 169, 170, 171, 188–9, 193–4
   Church's involvement in   32, 125, 190
widowhood   139
Winter, S.   160
women
   acceptable womanhood   21, 31–2, 34, 105, 118, 136
   constitutional status   29–30
   credibility as knowledge producer   39–40
   denial and restriction of knowledge to   17
   and emotions   61–2
   'good' and 'bad' women   27–32, 68, 118, 188–9
   power of speaking out   46–7
   'problem women'/'fallen women'   2, 10, 15, 21, 116–17, 195
   and religion   26–7, 31–2
   role as reproducers of the nation   15
   shaming of   11
   as vulnerable and threatening   15, 18, 21, 28–9, 35, 191

Yuval-Davis, N.   29

Zur, J.   45

www.ingramcontent.com/pod-product-compliance
Lightning Source LLC
Chambersburg PA
CBHW062142300426
44115CB00012BA/2006